W9-BZU-529

PROFESSIONAL MANAGEMENT SPECTRUM, INC.
PO Box 30330
Pensacola, Florida 32503
(800) 346-6114

PROFESSIONAL LIBRARY

Writing Guide for Air Force Efficiency Reports

The Definitive Performance Writing Guide

Successful Leadership Today

Other books:

Writing Guide for Army Efficiency Reports

Navy Eval & Fitrep Writing Guide

Navy & Marine Corps Performance Writing Guide

Fitness Report Writing Guide for Marines

Navy Officers Manual

Chief Petty Officers Manual

Navy Petty Officers Manual

More

Visit our web site for more information:

www.servicebooks.com

TABLE OF CONTENTS

THIS WRITING GUIDE IS IDEALLY SUITED FOR THE PERSON WHO:

- Is new to the art of writing (and understanding) Air Force Efficiency Reports.
- Wants his/her performers to have a competitive edge in "passing" selection boards at all levels.
- Doesn't like to continually start writing performance appraisal narratives from scratch.
- Doesn't quite know how to word or document performance and potential.
- Wants to submit good, effective write-ups to impress the "boss."

THIS GUIDE CAN BE USED BY: Anyone who evaluates the performance of others. It will be used by those who are serious about getting the "jump" on the competition.

HIGHLIGHTS OF THE BOOK

The book *Writing Guide for Air Force Efficiency Reports (Fourth Edition)* was developed to aid in the drafting of:

** INDIVIDUAL RECOGNITION WRITE-UPS

** PERSONAL AWARDS

** AIR FORCE EFFICIENCY REPORTS (SUPERIOR & SUBSTANDARD)

Plus, the book contains:

** 2,000 WORD DICTIONARY - Alphabetical listing of 2,000 of the most used ADJECTIVES, NOUNS, & VERBS on PERSONAL PERFORMANCE/PERSONALITY TRAITS in the English language (with definitions).

** 2,000 WORD THESAURUS - The dictionary words are grouped in unique, easy-to-use sections by SUPERIOR -TO-SUBSTANDARD performance, AND, by PERFORMANCE and PERSONALITY TRAIT sections.

** 2,500 BULLETS-PHRASES - Ready to use, FAVORABLE & UNFAVORABLE Sections

** SPECIAL "PHRASE, THOUGHT, OR IDEA" SECTION filled with example statements for use in any letter or documentation.

* THE PEOPLE WHO USE THIS GUIDE HAVE A DEFINITE AND DECIDED ADVANTAGE OVER NON-USERS.

* 30 DAY MONEY-BACK GUARANTEE if not completely satisfied

This *Writing Guide for Air Force Efficiency Reports (Fourth Edition)* is available for $28.95 plus shipping (price subject to change). Government Purchase Orders Accepted. Write or Call. IMPAC Accepted.

PROFESSIONAL MANAGEMENT SPECTRUM, INC.

P. O. BOX 30330

PENSACOLA, FL 32503

PH: (850) 432-7697   FAX: (850) 432-3908

Web Site: www.servicebooks.com

Order Online

ORDERS 1-800-346-6114

WRITING GUIDE FOR AIR FORCE EFFICIENCY REPORTS

Fourth Edition

ISBN 0-9623673-3-8

Web site: www.servicebooks.com

The words "he," "him," and "his" in this Guide are used to communicate ideas, and are not intended to discriminate against anyone.

PRINTED IN THE UNITED STATES OF AMERICA

PERSONAL

AWARDS

&

INDIVIDUAL

RECOGNITION

INDIVIDUAL RECOGNITION

Individual recognition includes Letters of Commendation and Letters of Appreciation.

Most organizations encourage maximum use of Letters of Appreciation (LOAs) to recognize deserving personnel. LOAs are relatively easy to write and they do not require excessive research or documentation. Remember, commanding officers are not the only ones who can issue LOAs. Almost any senior can give a subordinate due recognition through a LOA. However, the more noteworthy the performance or accomplishment, the higher the LOA should go for signature.

Most people appreciate being officially recognized for superior performance. Additionally, timely recognition for quality performance gives the person receiving the LOA and others around him/her additional incentive and motivation. LOAs are an effective tool for improving performance and morale throughout an organization. Commanding officers are fully aware of the relationship between positive, timely, and official recognition and improved overall performance. Therein lies a personal benefit to the superior who drafts LOAs for deserving subordinates. That superior has demonstrated to his/her superior that he/she knows effective leadership principles. So, in these terms, the superior drafting the LOAs receives personal recognition. Maximum use of LOAs should be a fundamental part of any organization.

Letters of Appreciation usually encompass three primary areas:

(1) The event/activity, and date involved;
(2) A listing or notation of personal accomplishments or achievements along with the personality traits displayed; and,
(3) Appropriate closing "thank you" remarks.

In general, a Letter of Appreciation (or Commendation) has three numbered paragraphs, one each covering the above areas. The examples on the following pages are provided to show the kind or type of material that might be used in each paragraph.

EXAMPLE #1

From:

To:

Subj: LETTER OF APPRECIATION

1.   I take great pleasure in expressing my appreciation for your outstanding performance while assigned as/to (job) during the period (date) to (date).

2.   While serving in these areas your duties included (list duties). Other duties included (list). Throughout this time frame you executed your duties in an exemplary manner. You were quick to offer suggestions and viable ideas for improvement.   Several of your ideas have been implemented and have enhanced (area). You are a very reliable individual who consistently produced superior results.   Your ever-present considerate attitude and congenial disposition were positive assets in your day-to-day dealings with others. Your military appearance and bearing continually reflected your obvious pride in your work and the service. You approached problem situations intelligently and methodically, always employing the best use of resources at hand.

3.   Your keen sense of responsibility in the performance of your duties reflect great credit upon yourself, and are in keeping with the highest traditions of the United States Air Force.

/ Signature /

EXAMPLE #2

From:

To:

Subj: LETTER OF APPRECIATION

1.   During the period (date) to (date) you were assigned to the (element) of (organization). You performed your duties as (job) in an outstanding manner and helped contribute directly to the overall mission accomplishments of the command. Your dedication to duty and constant

insistence on error free performance was instrumental in (organization) earning the following distinctions: (list). Your outstanding efforts, in all areas of responsibility, have resulted in an overall upgrade of (area).

2.   Your (number) years of Air Force service included assignments to (...), etc. Your devotion to duty and outstanding support to the Air Force mission have been evident throughout your career. I commend you for your outstanding professionalism, devotion, and pride that you have exhibited during your Air Force service.

3.   On the occasion of your discharge from active Air Force service, I express my sincere desire for your continued success and join with your many friends at (organization) in wishing you and your family the best possible future.

/ Signature /

EXAMPLE #3

From:

To:

Subj: LETTER OF APPRECIATION

1.   During the period (date) to (date) you were attached to (organization). You were assigned to the (organizational element) as (job).

2.   With a keen sense of responsibility, you attained a high degree of expertise in your assigned duties. You further enhanced your value by constantly applying yourself to learning the many techniques and procedures used throughout (organization) and became proficient in numerous jobs normally assigned to more senior personnel. Additionally, you performed your additional duties of (list duties) in a manner as to bring credit to (organization) and the United States Air Force. Your cheerful countenance and easy manner during periods of austere manning and demanding operational commitments were an additional asset to this command.

3.   As you depart (organization) for duty at (command) it is with sincere appreciation that I congratulate you on a job well done.

/ Signature /

EXAMPLE #4

From:

To:

Subj: LETTER OF APPRECIATION

1.   During the period of (date) through (date) you were assigned as (job), (organization).   Throughout this period you displayed excellent dedication and devotion to duty.

2.   Your knowledge of and experience with (...) helped maintain the high state of operational readiness within (organization). During the time your were assigned, you planned and carried out a wide variety of ... projects to bring this (organization) to a higher state of material readiness. The overall effect of your performance led to (accomplishments). This was a direct result of your personal leadership and I commend you for this performance.

3.   It is with regret that your tour of active duty with the Air Force is ending. I am sure that you will continue your interest in the Air Force in your future endeavors. On your departure you take with you best wishes for continued success from everyone at (organization).

/ Signature /

EXAMPLE #5

From:

To:

Subj: LETTER OF APPRECIATION

1.   It is with great pleasure that I convey my sincere appreciation for your efforts regarding the (event) on (date).

2.   Comments received from (...) were very complimentary and confirmed my own thoughts pertaining to the professional manner in which the (...) was planned and carried out. I know that it took long, hard hours of work and considerable personal sacrifice to correlate the myriad details necessary to ensure the success of (...). Your display of exceptional skill and resourcefulness in coordinating (...) are noteworthy. Your dependability, initiative, and talent to surmount difficulties in your path enliven those who come in contact with you. Your constant dedication and ability to complete tasks in a superior manner is a direct reflection of the respect and support you receive from subordinates and seniors alike.

3.   I applaud your accomplishments and extend to you my personal BEST WISHES.

/ Signature /

EXAMPLE #6

From:

To:

Subj: LETTER OF APPRECIATION

1.   During the period (dates) you were assigned to the (organization) for duty. As (position), a job normally assigned to (senior pay grade), your performance, across the board, was nothing less than OUTSTANDING.

2.   You were responsible for (job highlights). The tireless hours you devoted to this task were instrumental to the timely completion of (task). Your contributions enabled (organization) to (list accomplishments). You consistently demonstrated maturity, persistence, and a "can do" attitude rarely observed among your peers.

3.   My personal thanks for a job WELL DONE.

/ Signature /

EXAMPLE #7

From:

To:

Subj: LETTER OF APPRECIATION

1.   During the period (dates) you were assigned to (organization) for duty. Your various duty assignments included (list jobs).

2.   Your individual performance and contribution to mission accomplishment in each and every assignment were OUTSTANDING. You were selected over your peers for special recognition as (...). Your dedication and performance of duty throughout your tour at the (organization) have been most commendable.

3.   As you prepare for separation from active duty, it is with sincere appreciation that I congratulate you for honorable and faithful service. Having served with distinction in the most powerful Air Force the world has ever known, you have earned the right to say: "I served my country with pride." I am confident that the excellent traits you displayed at (command) will ensure your continued success in civilian life. Your many friends and I wish you continued success in all your future endeavors.

/ Signature /

EXAMPLE #8

LETTER OF COMMENDATION

From:

To:

Subj: LETTER OF COMMENDATION

1.   Upon your retirement from active military service, I extend my personal gratitude and appreciation for your continuing faithful service to our country. You can be justifiably proud of your rewarding and patriotic career.

2.   To aid you in reviewing your (distinguished/successful) career, the below is a listing of commands at which you honorably served. You entered the service at (location) on (date) and have since served with the following commands:

COMMAND   FROM   TO
                    (Add commands and dates)

3.   You earned a considerable amount of personal and professional recognition in your career, including the following official awards and decorations: (Add list of awards)

4.   You, as much as anyone who has ever served, have helped foster and preserve the strong and honorable traditions of a mighty United States Air Force that has helped defend and preserve the freedom that you, your fellow countrymen, and others throughout the free world continue to enjoy.

5.   Your professionalism and loyal personal dedication to duty and country reflect great credit upon yourself and the United States Air Force. In behalf of all of your friends, past and present, I wish you every success and happiness as you depart the Service.

/Signature/

SPECIAL INDIVIDUAL UNIT/ORGANIZATION RECOGNITION INFORMATION

The criteria for nominating individuals for special unit or organization recognition are as many and varied as there are organizations and individuals involved in the process. In general, a write-up on an individual being nominated for special recognition should include personal and professional performance traits.

The write-up required at an individual command/unit is normally short and brief for two reasons: First, to encourage seniors to take the time and initiative to recommend their top performers. Second, a local nominating or screening selection board usually has the time and desire to personally interview everyone nominated. At this local level of competition the results of the screening board's personal interview usually carries more weight than the write-up.

When local commands/units forward the names of their nominees to higher echelons the supporting write-up must become more and more competitive and comprehensive. Geographic separation of lower echelon commands/units from higher echelons may prevent a personal interview of each individual nominated. As this level of competition is reached a screening board "narrows the field" of nominees, or selects the best candidate, using only the write-up. At this stage, command employment and pride may also come into play.

At the very top levels of competition, public attention becomes a factor and semi-finalists may be individually screened/interviewed by top staff personnel.

When nominating someone for this special recognition, most of the justification should be in terms of what the individual accomplished during the period for which the nomination is submitted. It may be helpful to briefly note prior performance and accomplishment to show a continuing trend of superior effort and performance. Some screening board members may not be fully familiar with the particular workload, schedule, or environment of an individual's organization. If this is the case, be sure to briefly highlight pertinent facts and details. It is also a good idea to include a few well-chosen personal traits (dependable, professional attitude, etc.).

When considering what information to put in the write-up, review the following subjects:

JOB PERFORMANCE
LEADERSHIP
TECHNICAL EXPERTISE
MORALE/TEAMWORK BUILDER
COUNSELING OTHERS
EDUCATION (MILITARY/CIVILIAN)
HELPING OTHERS
SPECIAL RECOGNITION RECEIVED
COMMAND/CIVIC INVOLVEMENT
RESULTS OF INSPECTIONS
NOTEWORTHY OFF-DUTY ACTIVITIES
INNOVATIVE IMPROVEMENTS
SECONDARY/COLLATERAL DUTIES
TRAINING GIVEN/RECEIVED
VOLUNTEER FOR ADDITIONAL DUTIES
MILITARY PROFESSIONALISM
APPEARANCE BEHAVIOR
INDIVIDUAL INITIATIVE

Remember that there isn't much difference in the text of a performance appraisal and in the text of an individual award or recognition. It might be helpful to review other sections of this book before writing your first draft.

INTERVIEW BOARD

If an individual is going to appear before a selection or screening board, it is a good idea for that individual's organization to hold its own selection board screening process. First, this gives the individual some practice at answering questions in a professional but familiar atmosphere. Second, screening board members can critique the individual after the interview and offer ideas and suggestions for improving interview performance.

A person going before almost any interviewing board can be expected to be tense and apprehensive because of the "unknown" elements if for no other reason. If other members of an organization have gone before the same, or a similar, board, get them together with the person who is going to be interviewed. Explaining the routine and process of the interview board can have a very calming effect. Additionally, going over the types of questions that may be asked will increase self-assurance and personal confidence. Those are good qualities to present to a selection board.

The questions board members ask are as varied and diverse as the members who sit on the board. There is no standard question list. Each member is free to venture into any area he may choose. "If you saw a close friend of yours taking drugs, what would you do?" "What do you think about the United States' policy on (whatever)?" Different people might give different answers to questions such as these--and all could be correct. Local interview board members, for the most part, want a candidate's thoughts, ideas, and opinions on subjects. They are not looking for cut-and-dry "right" or "wrong" answers.

INTERVIEW BOARD HINTS

*Be straightforward, honest and sincere.

*Don't talk too fast (or too slow).

*Don't talk with your hands (do not wave them around).

*Sit still. Don't squirm around.

*Keep eye-to-eye contact. Use eye-to-eye contact when talking to board members. Do not look at only one individual. You are talking to the entire board, so share your eye contact (and answers) with all members.

*Appearance. Must be above reproach. An excellent appearance always gives a person the inside track to selection.

*World/Military events. Be prepared to discuss world events. Watch the news on TV and read the newspaper--know at least what's behind the headlines.

   With the above "ground rules" covered, the following pages are provided to give ideas and examples of how to draft individual recognition write-ups. The first example attempts to show the total range and scope of an individual who is competing for selection at high levels of competition. The remainder of the examples gives a variety of ranges at the local level.

INDIVIDUAL RECOGNITION WRITE-UPS

EXAMPLE #1

(Name) is preeminently an Air Force man. His personal involvement and commitment to the goals and ideals of the Air Force are without equal. In high school he voluntarily joined the Junior Reserve Officers Training Corps (JROTC), completed the three year program in two years, and attained the rank of (...). In Basic Training he was selected to lead his company as its (...).

During a recent decline in (organization) manning, (Name) accepted new challenges and volunteered for a workload that equaled or exceeded that of any other (...) at (command). He was initially assigned responsibilities of (...). He launched himself into his new and unaccustomed duties with uncommon zeal and vitality. Immediately evaluating the jobs at hand, he set short and long range goals, restructured his available work force, and originated an ingenious and comprehensive management and supervisory control system. The system was an unqualified success and his work package was completed in half the allotted time.

(Name) volunteered and was assigned more responsibilities. Each time he met the challenge and asked for an even larger share of the workload. Within a brief period of time he had assumed (number) additional jobs, including (...). In his (...) duties he managed with flawless execution and attention to detail an (...) operation with a budget that exceeded (...). His assignment to career counseling duties proved immensely successful, (...) of (...) eligible personnel reenlisted.

(Name) has a rich technical experience and professional insight. He identified and solved potential (...) operational discrepancies. His professional manner and organizational acumen allowed him to (...) with 100% efficiency and accuracy. Constructing a (...) from scrap and surveyed material, he saved the Air Force (...) dollars.

(Name) was assigned to (organization) training duties because of his positive attitude, energetic personality and ability to inspire others. He enrolled in (...) College taking night classes in active pursuit of a Bachelor of Science degree in (subject). His professionalism and sterling personal example again set the pace. One hundred percent of his subordinates became (...) qualified. All advancement eligibility requirements were met. (...%) of his personnel completed at least on off-duty college course. (Name) proved once again that there is not substitute for leadership by example.

(Name) qualified as (...) Specialist despite the difficulty encountered during this busy operational period. He was one of only (...) persons to become so qualified in the past year.

Working unusually long hours to complete his myriad responsibilities did not detract from (Name) civic pride or involvement. He volunteered two weekends a month at a local church assisting in neighborhood projects. When the City of (...) asked for military participation in the annual Armed Forces Day celebration, he was first in line. He generously donated off-duty time supervising the (...). And, he earned my personal "well done" for his off-duty assistance in (...) Other civic activities include (...).

(Name) was able to accomplish much more than his peers because of his exceptional organizational keenness and his ability to work with and lead others. With a natural frankness and sincerity, he displays concern for the feelings of individuals and equality of human treatment. These traits, his honesty, integrity and unparalleled professional competence generated immediate confidence in others. He is an extraordinary leader.

In summary, (Name) has displayed a sustained superior performance without equal. He is that one individual in an organization whom superiors routinely rely on to supervise or solve difficult problems or demanding situations. He consistently seeks ways to improve the quality and enjoyment of Air Force life with an uncommon perception to the morale and welfare needs of others. His charismatic and cheerful attitude is infectious and spreads throughout the ranks. His military presence and appearance are "recruit poster quality." (Name) deep personal pride and inspirational leadership identify him as an exceptional career (peer group). (Command) is proud to nominate (Name) for (...).

EXAMPLE #2

(Name) has been an invaluable asset to his immediate superior throughout this selection period by voluntarily assuming direct responsibility for (...). His masterful control of this entire evolution allowed his supervisor to concentrate his efforts on other areas of responsibility, thereby saving numerous supervisory hours that were desperately needed to support on-going operations. Throughout this period he performed flawlessly and sacrificed significant personal time. Through (Name) industrious efforts and self-sacrifice, he initiated and implemented a plan to (...). This operation has been a definite asset to the successful operation of (organization) and a valuable tool and aid to (...).

Due to (Name) maturity and diligence he was charged with supervising the (...) Team which had the responsibility for all major and minor (...). He performed these duties in an exceptional manner, keeping the (organization) ahead of schedule while maintaining excellent quality of workmanship. (Name) professional performance, industrious attitude, and devotion to duty are unsurpassed by anyone in his specialty. Additionally, he is successfully filling the position of (...), which historically has been assigned to someone two pay grades his senior.

It is with distinct pleasure that (organization) nominates (Name) for recognition as (...).

EXAMPLE #3

(Name) consistently performs his duties in an exemplary and highly professional manner, demonstrating superior performance and attention to duty. I believe an individual must perform with excellence while on duty, and in addition, benefit himself personally and the (organization) professionally outside normal work hours to be worthy of special individual recognition. (Name) has met and exceeded all of these requirements and has earned my strongest endorsement for selection.

(Name) specific accomplishments for this selection period include:

*Conceived, formulated, revised, and then implemented a comprehensive program. He dedicated more than (...) hours of normal off-duty time on this project.

*Originated (...).

*Initiated the concept of (...) that led directly to increased operational efficiency.

(Name) has been taking off-duty college courses when the operating schedules permit. In this selection period he has complete (number) courses with an average of (...).

(Name) epitomizes those rare qualities most sought in today's military professional. He realizes that personal involvement and individual commitment are the cornerstones to any successful organization. Working with and understanding people is another of his strong areas. He knows each subordinate's abilities, limitations, and desires and integrates this knowledge into their daily activities. His uncommon maturity and common sense, coupled with his ability to apply the correct amount of diplomacy and direct tact, allows him to obtain the best possible results from subordinates in any situation.

(Name) knowledge of his technical specialty, total dedication to duty, and willingness to assist anyone in any capacity have made him a valued member of (organization). No better representative for (...).

EXAMPLE #4

(Name) current assignment as (...) requires a high degree of leadership skill, tact, and responsibility, all of which he possesses in abundance. In his job he provides direct leadership and guidance to (number) personnel in different technical fields. This organization is well organized and managed, and enjoys an unusually high degree of morale and pride in workmanship.

Though busy with the administration of an enormous number of personnel and equipment, (Name) manages to find time to become personally involved in resolving difficult maintenance problems. Very few weekends pass without him being called in to help correct some of the more serious problems. (Name) is dedicated to providing the best possible service twenty-four hours a day, seven days a week.

(Name) ability to comprehend and master the maintenance requirements of the most advanced (...) equipment through self-study and on-the-job training is overwhelming evidence of his technical superiority. He is an expert repairman on the (...) equipment despite no formal schooling.

(Name) dynamic leadership, initiative, and overall professional performance sets him apart from his peer group. His day to day work and value to the (organization) is head and shoulders above his contemporaries. (Name) is most strongly recommended for serious consideration as (...).

EXAMPLE #5

(Name) is a dedicated professional who strives for perfection in all endeavors. In all assignments he has demonstrated sound, mature judgment and flexibility not normally noted in someone of his paygrade. In addition to his normal duties of (...), he volunteered for assignment to (...) that routinely requires off-duty time to complete. In this capacity he performed with the highest degree of professionalism and dedication. He enjoys a full, busy work schedule and thrives on the additional responsibility.

(Name) is interested in people and is continually involved in projects to promote the welfare of others. During this selection period he assisted in the preparation, operation, and maintenance of (...). He also participated in Project (...), an evolution designed to give the general public some insight into the importance of the functions and mission of (organization).

(Name) is a superb leader and manager. He uses tact and superior supervisory skills as a highly productive management tool in directing the activities of others. He displays a genuine concern for others and his "can do" attitude is a definite asset to (organization).

(Name) other military traits are on par with his outstanding supervisory and personnel relations' traits. He consistently receives OUTSTANDING grades at personnel inspections. His effective verbal communications is marked with sincerity and conviction.

(Name) highly deserves for consideration as (...).

EXAMPLE #6

(Name) has consistently demonstrated an exceptionally high degree of military and professional excellence. His knowledge of technical specialty, total dedication to duty, and willingness to assist in any capacity have made him a valuable member of (organization). His technical competence is unsurpassed. He has, on his own initiative, learned to operate and troubleshoot many (equipment/systems) for which he has received no formal training. First and foremost is his sound working knowledge and understanding of the complicated (...) system. By setting the example and making himself a technical source of information, he has helped influence others to higher professional achievement and development.

(Name) worth and value to (organization) extends beyond his outstanding technical competence. During a recent period when (organization) was severely undermanned, he was called upon to assume a position of greater responsibility as (...) Supervisor for more than (time period). Only his thorough understanding of (organization) operation and mission, his leadership skills, and his total willingness to help out in any capacity made this assignment both possible and successful.

(Name) spends his off duty time--when he is not working extra time at his job--going to night school at the University of (...). Additionally, he has served as (organization) (...) key person. In both instances, his efforts produced superior results.

(Name) is deserving of serious consideration for (...).

EXAMPLE #7

(Name) is extremely efficient and highly motivated. He displays superior talent and industry in completing all tasks. He is directly responsible for (...). Since he assumed these duties, two operational evaluations and three administrative inspections have been conducted by offices outside the organization. In each case his area of responsibility received an OUTSTANDING grade. The grades are directly attributable to (Name) personal initiative, dedication, and devotion to duty. At no time during his tenure as (job) has there been an operational outage or missed commitment due to the need for services in his area.

In addition to (Name) regular duties, he has also continued to maintain his qualification as a (...). By doing so, he has helped immeasurably during critical personnel shortages by filling in as the occasion demands.

(Name) thoughtfulness, concern and compassion for his subordinates are tempered by fairness and military bearing. In his position of supervisor and counselor he displays the compassion, awareness, and professionalism of a model leader.

(Name) is actively involved in the retention program. His off-duty hours are frequently filled with activities and events involving junior personnel, and he misses no opportunity to point out the advantages of a military career.

(Name) represents the excellence, spirit, and dedication of the ideal supervisor and leader. His concern, involvement, and consideration for others contribute directly to sustained high morale. (Name) is most qualified and deserving to earn the distinction of (...).

EXAMPLE #8

(Name) has served as (...) since his arrival. He has kept himself cognizant of all matters pertaining to the management and operation of the organization. Additionally, during this time he willingly accepted the added responsibility of (...). Supervisor and has displayed consistently outstanding performance in that capacity.

Possessing exceptional organizational and planning abilities, (Name) has continually endeavored to improve the effectiveness of the organization. He has met with considerable success. He was quick to identify weak

17

areas in (...) and took immediate and positive steps to improve these areas. Through his efforts and initiative, a more efficient method of maintaining accountability of (...) was instituted. To fully perform his job, many hours of off time were often required, yet (Name) was uncomplaining and gave willingly and freely of his personal time and energy. His unselfish devotion to duty has contributed much to the successful completion of (...) and was a contributing factor that led to a grade of "OUTSTANDING" during a recent (...) Inspection.

Specifically, (Name) accomplishments include: *Revised and put in motion a new (...). *Revised and instituted new (...). *Drafted a comprehensive (...). *Conducted a comprehensive review of the (...), which resulted in a revision of existing policies.

(Name) is highly deserving of recognition as (...) and is so recommended. He is, and will continue to be, a model for others to follow.

EXAMPLE #9

(Name) military service has been highlighted by individual accomplishment and team contribution. He has a thirst for knowledge and an untiring desire for challenge. In addition to earning a (...) Degree, he has completed (...) military schools and (...) military correspondence courses. This education and knowledge, and his ability to apply that which he has learned, have been invaluable in helping this organization meet all operational commitments during the last (time period). He performed admirably in a listing of jobs that would have overwhelmed his contemporaries. Many of these jobs are routinely assigned to more senior people. Some of his major assignments and achievements include:

*Organized (...)

*Completed (...)

*Qualified (...)

A person of lessor initiative and drive would have been overcome by these assignments. Not only did (Name) thrive on this work, his leadership and personal contribution in these key responsibilities helped produce the following significant accomplishments (...).

(Name) individual effort and performance did not go unnoticed in these various evolutions and he earned the following special recognition during this period:

* ...

* ...

That he was able to successfully execute all of his additional duties with such continuing outstanding results while simultaneously standing extended watch hours throughout this period is testimony to the exceptional drive, motivation, and caliber of (name).

(Name) is particularly adept with working with others, both superiors and subordinates, with a natural sincerity and frankness which displays his concern and feelings of individuals and in equality of humane treatment. He represents the excellence, spirit, and dedication of a model career person. Taking his guide on sound judgment and Air Force tradition, he maintains an unwavering course through the many challenges of leadership. His concern, involvement, and consideration are not limited by self-interest, or in only getting the job done. He consistently seeks to improve the quality and enjoyment of military service throughout the organization.

(Name) is in the finest sense of the meaning, a quality candidate for (...).

EXAMPLE #10

(Name) is an exceptional career person whose performance exceeds all requirements of his assigned duties. Intelligent and conscientious, he requires neither motivation nor guidance in order to attain superb results. His performance during this selection period has been superior to the performance of (number) others as judged by a panel of his superiors. He has completed the requirement for (...) Supervisor and functions superbly in that capacity when called upon. He has submitted recommendations to streamline operational procedures that have been incorporated into organizational policy and have since proven highly beneficial. On several occasions during a recent high tempo operational period he remained on duty long after the rest of his team was relieved to assist in the operation.

(Name) is a highly competent individual who has virtually mastered every aspect of (...) operations. He is a qualified (...) Operator and (...)

Supervisor. He is an extremely flexible leader whose maturity allows him to confidently make correct and spontaneous decisions related to ever changing operational demands. He is one of only a few persons to ever earn distinction as (...), a noteworthy achievement that some more senior personnel have not been able to accomplish. While on duty he is continually busy; however, he is never too busy to take the time to explain operational procedures and equipment operation to new or less qualified personnel. He is a patient and tactful individual, well liked by everyone who knows him. He is a pacesetter, the person others look to for leadership and guidance in professional and personal matters.

(Name) has volunteered on numerous occasions to spend on and off duty time learning the duties of (...) to help minimize downtime on the (...) equipment. He is presently learning all of the qualifications for (...) in order to assist that understaffed unit. At his request, these additional repair duties will be in addition to his normal, already full workload.

(Name) is an outstanding candidate for this special recognition.

EXAMPLE #11

(Name) possesses the human qualities of leadership and the professional technical expertise of a "top notch" supervisor. Proficient at anticipating technical and personnel problems, he is able to head them off before they become acute and damaging to his organization. His adeptness in administering the proper combination of direction, encouragement, and discipline in supervising and leading subordinates elicits their most positive and productive response.

(Name) has been the key individual in the command responsible for placing the (...) system into fully operational status. Spending many off-duty hours in training and study, he has attained an in-depth working expertise of this highly intricate and sophisticated system.

(Name) is friendly and has an active, outgoing personality. He is frequently called upon by subordinates and peers alike for advice in professional and personal matters. He is an active member of three civic organizations, including (...). He is well versed in the challenges and opportunities offered in a military career and his opinions and knowledge are highly respected throughout the command.

(Name) is not only an outstanding leader, but also a most dependable manager and administrator. He leads by example; is always ahead of the

20

game in managing his financial budget, and he, prepares timely and correct staff work.

(Name) is currently attending night classes with the University of (...) where he has already completed (...) courses and expects to earn his Associates Degree within the next (...) months.

(Name) noteworthy achievements as a military man and an involved citizen of his community reflect great credit upon this command and the United States Air Force.

EXAMPLE #12

(Name) performs his assigned duties in a truly efficient, reliable, and professional manner. His resourcefulness and strong sense of professionalism are reflected in his every action. (Name) fully supports the necessary stringent training requirements inherent to his job. Since reporting aboard he has spent many hours of rigorous training to become fully qualified in (...) systems. Additionally, he has successfully completed an extensive locally administered written examination on the (...) system. (Name) actions and efforts were instrumental to (organization) receiving a grade of "OUTSTANDING" during a recent technical evaluation conducted by (...).

(Name) is a highly motivated individual who possesses a positive attitude toward the military and continually displays an intense desire to serve in any capacity. He has shown great personal interest in his co-workers' welfare by submitting suggestions and assisting in making improvements in the habitability of his workspaces. He presents an extremely sharp and well-groomed appearance both in uniform and civilian attire, setting an outstanding example for peers and juniors.

(Name) outside accomplishments include giving total support to command sporting activities. He is a member of the (...) and (...) sports teams. He is a member of the (...) Organization and actively participates in all organized activities and functions of (organization).

(Name) confidence in himself and pride in the Air Force are readily apparent by the enthusiasm and zeal displayed in any assignment, designated or assumed. (Name) is an excellent candidate for (...).

EXAMPLE #13

(Name) performance of duty has been absolutely outstanding. The technical skill and sound management practices he has displayed in planning, coordinating, and implementing the diverse requirements of (...) far exceed that normally expected of someone of his pay grade and experience. (Name) was the first (...) to qualify under a new and rigorous (...) training program. He presently is one of only two persons in (organization) to hold those qualifications. He has, without question, gained the respect and confidence of his superiors for his depth of knowledge, sound judgment, and initiative.

In his additional duty as (...), (Name) initiative and strong support for the Air Force as a career directly contributed to the impressive retention rates enjoyed by this command. He personally writes a letter to all new personnel before their arrival, introducing himself and explaining briefly his career (counseling/planning) duties, and asks if there is any way he may be of assistance. This personal touch is indicative of his thoroughness and dedication to this important duty. The net result of his effort has been enhanced career awareness throughout (organization), and a positive, career-oriented climate.

(Name) is a leader and a positive force in initiating the planning for (organization) parties, social, and recreational functions. He established (organization) intramural sports teams and fully supports command sponsored activities.

(Name) is a dedicated professional whose military conduct and bearing are outstanding. I have personally commended him for his sharp appearance at each formal personnel inspection I have conducted. He is a "military professional" in the fullest sense of the term and meaning. I most strongly recommend (Name) for selection as (...).

EXAMPLE #14

(Name) is an outstanding performer with a wealth of knowledge and experience in his technical specialty. He is an exceptional leader and is routinely selected to train new personnel, especially those without previous formal (...) training. The results have been impressive, producing effective (position) that makes ready contributions to mission accomplishment. The enthusiasm, sense of pride, and professionalism developed by trainees by

(Name) are intangible benefits that are difficult to measure but which contribute directly to operational readiness and mission accomplishment.

(Name) honesty and integrity, coupled with his sterling professional competence and leadership ability, generate immediate confidence in his superiors and subordinates. His sound knowledge of career programs, and his desire to put these programs into action are considered prime assets to (organization) reenlistment efforts. Because of his enthusiasm toward a successful career, he was recently appointed (...). He launched himself into his new duties with missionary zeal and vitality. On his own initiative, and because of his profound concern for others, he has made himself available twenty-four hours a day, seven days a week to any individual desiring information on career programs and patterns.

(Name) outside accomplishments are many and varied. As an exceptionally gifted sportsman, he represented the (organization) in (sport) competition. As busy as he is in on and off duty work and community involvement, he finds time to take night classes with the University of (...). In the past year he has completed (...) semester hours of undergraduate study.

(Name) Is an individual who is always on the move, always busy at his professional job or assisting others. In this exceptional example of a military professional, there is seen an individual who is deeply moved to demonstrate great concern for others. Confidence in self and pride in the Air Force is readily apparent by the enthusiasm and zeal displayed in undertaking each new task or assignment. (Name) would well represent (organization) as (...).

EXAMPLE #15

(Name) demonstrates daily extraordinary professional ability, in-depth technical knowledge and uncommon perceptiveness to the morale and welfare needs of his subordinates. Since his assignment to (job), he has brought about significant improvement to all aspects of (...) equipment, work output, and uncommon professionalism in subordinates.

Perhaps even more important than (Name) outstanding professional performance is his thoughtfulness, concern, and compassion for his personnel. In his position he displays the concern, awareness, and professionalism of a model leader. (Name) is an enthusiastic leader who believes that each individual should actively participate in all (organization) activities and events. Subordinates willingly follow his lead in these important morale-building areas.

In military and civilian attire, (Name) is a paragon of excellent appearance and bearing. His even tempered administration of assigned personnel and the superb example he demonstrates by his performance, appearance, and adherence to the spirit of Air Force traditions and regulations have earned him the respect of all.

In summary, (Name) represents the excellence, spirit, and professional dedication of a model career person. His concern, involvement, and consideration for others are not limited by self-interest, or in only getting the job done. He refuses to be content with merely accepting the "status quo," and always finds ways and means of improving morale, team spirit, and pride. (Name) is most worthy of sincere consideration, and selection, as (...).

GENERAL USE PARAGRAPHS

(Name) is an industrious and versatile individual who approaches any task enthusiastically and with dispatch. He is a skillful manager with the proven ability to attain a high standard of performance in any endeavor. He directs his unit with a firm but fair hand, and provides a unified purpose and sense of direction without dulling their initiative. Readily adaptable to changes in policy, procedure, or assigned workload, he always gives a personal contribution as a special effort to ensure cohesiveness and uniformity. He has established a good rapport with subordinates and does not hesitate to provide personal or professional assistance, when needed, and to encourage their trust through his genuine interest in their problems.

A proponent of physical fitness, (Name) actively participates in various sporting events and maintains a trim physique. His conduct and appearance, on and off duty, are models worthy of emulation. Well read, he has a good working knowledge of the English language; his written reports are clear and concise, and his oral presentations command the complete attention of a listening audience.

(Name) rare and successful blend of leadership coupled with his superior management and administrative abilities assure success in virtually any assignment. He stays with a job until it is completed, regardless of the time of day or night. During the past three months he worked over 100 off-duty hours refitting and organizing (...). (Name) has unlimited ability and potential.

Superior leader, manager, and organizer. Virtually unlimited potential. Continually supports and enforces command goals and policy. Mature, articulate, and dedicated, meets or exceeds all deadlines.

(Name) is a self-starter and inspirational leader. Seasoned counselor. Demanding yet fair, impressive leader and organizer. Strong moral fiber. Respected by subordinates and superiors. Top achiever of boundless potential and ability.

Unequaled ability to obtain maximum results of available material and manpower resources. Unyielding dedication and loyalty. Analytical in thought, reasoned in mind. Humane and compassionate. Works full day on operational situations and then dedicates off-duty hours to catch up on administrative matters. "Head and shoulders" above contemporaries.

Industrious, meticulous, and accurate, (Name) aggressively tackles any job. Intolerant of mediocre performance, yet aware of personal limitations. Unhesitatingly offers constructive criticism when warranted. Subordinates are tactfully led to desired level of performance. (Name) is a proven leader, manager and organizer. Unlimited potential.

(Name) optimizes available manpower and material resources. Firm and fair, an advocate of equal treatment and opportunity. Flawless planning and execution efforts virtually guarantee success of any job. Highly respected throughout chain of command for professional knowledge and personal professionalism.

(Name) most productive and versatile (...) at this command. Proven top quality organizer, administrator and manager. Unlimited potential for increased responsibility and authority. Possesses great deal of energy, highly industrious, doesn't believe in idle time. Friendly personality and quick wit establish and maintain atmosphere of pride and professionalism.

(Name) fully enjoys Air Force life, is quick to point out career benefits, and will not tolerate open dissent toward command policies or procedures. "Recruit Poster Quality" image. Poised and mature with a thirst for knowledge and a desire for challenge. Positive motivator, intelligent, and articulate.

(Name) is a self-starter whose great personal initiative and leadership skills identify him as being "head and shoulders" above contemporaries. He runs an orderly and highly productive organization in any environment. Commanding presence, decisive, and determined.

(Name) sets the standards by which excellence is measured. A proven manager and leader of unbounded ability. His superb working knowledge of systems and equipment has increased the operational excellence and capability of (organization). He displays the character, initiative, and resourcefulness to accept and accomplish the most demanding tasks. The energetic and conscientious dedication he displayed in transforming his work group to viable operating element within (time) of assuming charge set the example--and pace--for the entire (organization).

(Name) is a self-starter. He took it upon himself to take charge of an inexperienced maintenance crew, identify numerous material and wiring deficiencies, and then executed a highly successful repair and upgrade program. That he has been capable and able to accomplish these and more tasks, individually and collectively successful, attests to his bold and imaginative leadership and management style.

(Name) is especially adept in dealing with people. He understands the worth and dignity of each individual and successfully pursues a "follow me" leadership role. His demeanor, confidence, and spirit of cooperation have been highly commendable in many "crisis management" situations.

(Name) is a dedicated, cheerful, and hard-working individual who performs all duties in an accurate and enthusiastic manner. Boundless potential. His ability to adapt to change and perform in a superior manner became quite evident during periods when he was called upon to assume several different functions. Never wavering, he accepted all responsibilities and challenges in stride, demonstrating versatility and exceptional managerial skills. Displaying a positive attitude, he has generated enthusiasm at all levels within the (organization).

(Name) is a dedicated professional who strives on new challenges. A dynamic leader and a superb manager, he is ideally suited for top Air Force positions.

(Name) dress and grooming are impeccable. He always presents a neat and dignified appearance, reflecting obvious pride in self and service. Athletically inclined, he has been an active participant in a variety of command sponsored sporting events. (Name) calm and affable manner is a prime asset in his daily coordination of activities.

(Name) always contributes full measure to any task and his willingness to accept added responsibility enhances his potential for positions of higher authority. He is quick to take the lead in coordinating activities and providing necessary guidance and supervision. Completely self-reliant, he

26

strives for perfection and sees all projects through to their successful conclusion. Whatever the task or situation, he fully exploits the information and tools available to produce the most effective response. He gives fair and equitable treatment to all while ensuring the job at hand is done correctly.

(Name) is motivated toward a career in the Air Force, and his devotion to duty and willingness to perform above and beyond what is normally expected mark him as an excellent candidate for increased and more demanding duties. (Recommendation for advancement/duty assignment.)

(Name) is a consistent top performer, constantly seeking new and more effective methods in performing (organization) duties. He is knowledgeable of all methods and procedures within his area of responsibility and uses these skills as effective tools and guidelines in meeting all command tasks. (Name) individual drive is motivating and refreshing. He believes in the Air Force and its purpose, always upholding the highest tradition of the service.

He is an exceptional manager and organizer whose demonstrated expertise as a leader has measurably improved the overall performance and readiness of this command. An individual who commands the fullest respect and support of those with whom he works, he is willing to accept any assignment regardless of scope. He is an original thinker who has demonstrated the ability to devise and organize operational and administrative procedures that weigh time, personnel, and money while ensuring the most efficient and economic methods are applied to any task.

(Name) is a self-starter whose work is marked by integrity and initiative. He is meticulously accurate with a great sense of responsibility for the quality of his work. A tireless worker, he cheerfully devotes numerous extra hours to ensure that all projects and problems are being taken care of and are followed through to a successful conclusion.

He is a true professional in every sense of the word. The courage of conviction and strong moral character he exhibits foster high morale, esprit de corps, and a total winning attitude.

(Name) sterling performance has continued throughout this reporting period. He has consistently executed the weighty responsibilities of (...) with fervor, determination, and overall superb success. Very talented with a good sense of organization. A spontaneous propensity to leadership. A reputation for dependable and timely work. Strong and able in all areas, his most significant quality is his ability to impart his extensive operational experience and knowledge in subordinates.

(Name) has infused (organization) with his enthusiasm and dedication. His astute management of personnel and equipment assets and his close attention to the material condition of his workspaces has markedly improved the operation, working conditions, and physical appearance of (organization). (Name) has proven that he is a tactful, yet strong leader by instilling in each subordinate the same desire to excel as he displays. (Name) is truly an exceptional (...).

(Name) is an outstanding (...). Unlimited potential for future growth and increased value to the Air Force. Discharges all responsibilities with complete professionalism and tireless dedication. Ready, willing and able are his bywords. Conscientious, tireless and persevering.

(Name) is a top performer. Totally professional, poised, mature and dedicated. Enjoys loyalty, cooperation, and support of subordinates. Intelligent and dedicated always volunteers for additional work to help others and increase own potential, skill, and worth. A rising star of unlimited potential.

(Name) does not believe in idle time or unfinished projects. Manages own time and that of others to best possible advantage. Possesses managerial and organizational expertise rarely observed in contemporaries. Completes large volume of work each day, frequently working extra hours.

(Name) performance, both militarily and professionally, is nothing short of outstanding. Displaying a keen interest in his work, he sets and maintains a high standard of performance for himself and subordinates. He continually maintains a high state of operational and material readiness despite antiquated equipment and non-availability of spare parts and material support.

Methodical and extremely conscientious, (Name) actions are well planned, smoothly executed, and in the best interest of a job well done. In addition to his primary duties, he is a qualified (...) and is called upon to act in that capacity during personnel shortages. As expected of a man of his caliber, his unit consistently produces quality results and is sensitive to the needs of command.

Regardless of complexity or magnitude of the task at hand, (Name) can be relied upon to see that it is completed expeditiously and efficiently. An accomplished counselor, (Name) readily shares his experience with his personnel in both military and personal matters and they seek out his advice with regularity. He personally encourages all subordinates to set the highest possible goals for themselves and then counsels them on means available to realize those goals, both professional and personal.

(Name) is one of the finest (...) in the United States Air Force. His potential is unlimited. In his two years of dedicated service to this command he played a vital role in the achievement of this command's mission and is a cornerstone of technical knowledge, management skill and military tradition.

(Name) vast experience is enhanced by his intelligence, sincerity and ability to communicate effectively with all levels of command. Many of the improvements he either initiated or carried out have made their lasting mark on operations and administration within the (...). His intense dedication to duty, personal sacrifices, and uncompromising standards of conduct have provided the impetus for the organizational growth and development of the (organization).

(Name) is the most highly respected (...) assigned within this command. His total commitment to the Air Force, support of his seniors, and leadership of those who serve under him have significantly enhanced readiness, retention, and morale.

(Name) sets an exceptional example as a leader and manager. He works a full day in his assigned job and consistently puts in many extra hours assisting in areas outside his normal area of responsibility. As a result, he has attained professional and technical knowledge and competence rarely observed within his specialty. The ability to obtain quality results in any environment and to relate to all age groups are the cornerstones of (Name) success as a leader.

(Name) displays a genuine concern for his fellow man, and he always finds time to help those in need on counseling and personal assistance. The emphatic demeanor and timely responsiveness he is known for has inspired and maintained high morale and team spirit throughout the (organization).

(Name) ability to communicate his thoughts and commands, both verbally and in writing, is excellent. He is an exceptional orator, and his staff work is always timely and correct. Neat, trim and physically fit, he is a model of military bearing and Air Force tradition.

Throughout (Name) tenure as (...), the innovative approach he displayed in day-to-day operations, as well as special programs, were consistently above the expected norm. He has consistently performed all duties in an outstanding manner and has exhibited those traits that are highly desirous.

Strong leadership abilities; an excellent manager of material and equipment; tact and compassion; and, an innovative and intelligent view of the future.

(Name) is an intelligent, energetic manager and organizer. Enjoys fast-paced work environment. "Head-and-shoulders" above contemporaries with virtually unlimited potential. A quick thinker who makes positive decisions that are easily supported. Completely dependable, performs all tasks with accuracy and dispatch. Professional attitude radiates to subordinates, causing them to respond in kind with full effort and cooperation.

(Name) has a knack for getting job done where others fail. Informed on current Air Force career programs. Information is quickly passed on to supervisors who become highly responsive to needs of subordinates. Established routines that strengthened chain of command, facilitated smoother flow of correspondence, and created highly professional working atmosphere. Always a contributor to group effort. Works easily with seniors and subordinates. Sobriety, punctuality and strong sense of duty highlight daily performance. Trim, physically fit, always "inspection ready."

(Name) tact, coordination, and his ability to get to the heart of any problem have increased the operational and administrative efficiency and effectiveness of the unit. The impossibility of any situation does not occur to him. In addition to his other superb traits, he is an excellent counselor. His unique ability to reach a troubled person and give fair, honest guidance is without equal among his peers.

(Name) is a dedicated Air Force professional of unlimited potential. He looks out for his men, yet requires each to give a full measure of productive work each day. The imagination, intelligence and business-like manner he takes into each assignment virtually assure success.

(Name) is a dedicated professional who thrives on new challenge and responsibility. A continuing source of new ideas, he invariably submits well thought out and thoroughly evaluated plans to improve the efficiency of his organization. When implementing a new idea, he never fails to plan for the best, yet have a contingency to self-correct a shortcoming. Thus, he has been able to accomplish much more than any of his recent predecessors while using the same quantitative number of resources. Remarkably poised and confident, he maintains his composure under the most trying conditions.

(Name) performance continues to be underscored by pride, self-improvement, and accomplishment. He gets the job done regardless of circumstances.   Favorable personal traits include: Organized, efficient, charismatic, bold, and a sense of purpose and vision not evidenced in his contemporaries.

Working with others in a unified and cohesive manner is a particularly strong asset of (name).   He has the ability to immediately establish and maintain excellent rapport with subordinates on all levels.   Much of this is due to the fair, open, and unbiased manner he has in dealing with them. Each person knows that he will be given an equal opportunity, commensurate with capabilities, to work in any job or assignment, and that all will be given the opportunity to learn.

Superior ability and performance.   Exceptionally skilled in all facets of technical specialty.   Totally professional and dedicated.   Performance underscored by pride, personal involvement and accomplishment.

(Name) has unbound initiative and is extremely conscientious.   Actions well planned, organized, and smoothly executed.   Team player, fosters cooperation and harmony throughout command.   A forceful, dynamic, and compassionate leader knows how to motivate subordinates.

(Name) sustained superior performance has been an inspiration to each member of this command.   The deep respect and sincere affection he receives from subordinates manifests his superlative qualities of leadership, integrity and professional knowledge.   His example has fostered unparalleled productivity and esprit de corps in the command.

He represents the embodiment of pride and professionalism.   These concepts are, and have always been, his benchmark as an advocate of tradition, loyalty, and a strong Air Force.   His outspoken support of the chain of command, firm enforcement of military standards, and equitable treatment of each subordinate has optimized morale and promoted effective mission accomplishment within the command.

(Name) is never too busy to listen to a personal problem and is never reluctant to respond with positive action.   His ability to anticipate potential problem areas or external factors which impact on current and future operations have resulted in timely compliance with all administrative and operational requirements.

(Name) unparalleled ability to manage money, material and personnel place him number one.   To highlight his abilities, he: -Builds on understanding and encourages feedback from subordinates. -Instills high-performance motivation and creativity. -Stimulates individual growth and responsibility.

31

Truly outstanding (...). Demonstrates unfailing diligence, job-aggressiveness, and total dedication to excellence. Thoroughly prepared for every assignment. Self-starter. Personal initiative and leadership skills guarantee exceptional results of all tasks assigned or assumed. Top shelf organizer, manager and administrator. Unique ability to assimilate myriad of diverse inputs and produce timely, accurate and detailed results.

Poised and mature (...) with matchless thirst for knowledge and increased responsibility. Always quick to point out career benefits.

Most capable of making independent judgments and decisions required to run highly effective unit. A strong performer during entire tour. A proven top achiever, demonstrates those specific talents and character traits required for ascent to positions of higher responsibility. Extremely knowledgeable, industrious, completely resourceful. Performance of all duties singularly outstanding. Exceptionally fine administrator. Superb ability to write clear, concise and accurate material. All administrative matters submitted on time in smooth, ready for signature form.

(Name) plans ahead, stays on top of every project or assignment until quality results achieved. Superb watch team leader, takes rapid, effective action without guidance from above. Excellent counselor, particularly adept in solving problems encountered by junior personnel. Unlimited potential for responsibility and challenge.

(Name) is an accomplished leader, manager, and organizer who has demonstrated the following personal traits and characteristics:

* Convincing speaker.
* Meticulous administrative skills.
* Informed and well read.
* Alert, farsighted manager.
* Backs superiors and command policy.
* Tactful leader of subordinates.

* Keen judgment.
* Tireless worker.
* Diplomatic personality.
* Active, physically fit.

* Inspiring leader.

(Name) is a self-starter who has implemented many programs within his organization, which have served to upgrade operational capability and increase morale. (Name) is an informed, concerned individual with a gift for getting along with others. Juniors and seniors actively seek his advice. Aware of need for effective communications, he successfully elicits continued high performance and morale. A bold, imaginative leader.

(Name) is an efficient and highly knowledgeable (specialty) whose performance, singularly and collectively, has been outstanding. Demonstrated unbound ability and capacity to successfully assume positions of greater authority and jurisdiction.

(Name) has provided outstanding operational support as well as continued superior administrative skills to various critical elements of this command. Adaptable, polished, and receptive, he is the man to see when a job needs completion with dispatch and efficiency.

(Name) is a self-starter, confident of abilities and work. He volunteers to tackle any assignment without doubt or hesitation. Works zealously to complete each task as perfectly as possible. Possessed of a sound management background, the strong moral fiber of this (...) combined with an analytical mind and adaptability to changing situations makes him highly effective in any situation.

(Name) is an absolute top performer in every respect. His outstanding leadership, superb management techniques and total dedication to duty place him head and shoulders above (...). Unlimited growth potential. Under his supervision and influence, every operational commitment was met or exceeded. His organization has received numerous expressions of appreciation from various commands for superior support.

(Name) is a model (...). He always adds more to the job than expected, putting it ahead of his own interests. He is inquisitive, creative, and foresighted. He consistently makes sound management decisions. An energetic personality, positive "can do" attitude, and deep pride in his country and the Air Force highlight his daily performance.

(Name) superior management and leadership abilities identify him as a head and shoulders performer. His work habits and "follow me" style of leadership have won the respect and admiration of others. A cheerful, creative and industrious individual, he is, in every sense of the word, an "achiever."

(Name) honesty and integrity, coupled with his outstanding operational and technical competence, generates immediate confidence in his abilities by all with whom he comes in contact. His thoughtfulness, concern and compassion for all Air Force members further enhance his strong supervisory abilities. He believes in the proper training and professional development of all subordinates is a matter of personal concern and prime importance, and he has adeptly integrated this feeling into daily operations.

(Name) consistently performs in an enthusiastic and outstanding manner. His outstanding military bearing is complimented by his no-nonsense approach to his duties, his constant awareness of his responsibilities, both to his organization and to his subordinates, and his personal appearance that is always impeccable.

(Name) is a "hard-charger" who is an exceptionally talented and well-qualified (...). He is a forceful, dynamic leader who knows how to motivate others and get outstanding results.

(Name) has a cheerful, sincere, and professional attitude. He is always polite and courteous to his seniors, and is demanding, considerate, and imaginative in his leadership of others. (Name) believes in the Air Force, is highly motivated toward an Air Force career, and is an outstanding example for junior personnel to look to for guidance and assistance.

(Name) performance is second to none. He can be depended upon to accomplish any task presented to him and on several occasions sacrificed his off-duty time to insure that a job was completed with utmost accuracy. As a supervisor and leader his professional and military competence is continually tested and has never been found lacking. His steady and uncompromising approach toward good leadership leaves no doubt in the minds of his men as to what is expected of them and makes following his lead an easy choice.

(Name) is a top-notch leader, using an excellent blend of tact and direct supervision to elicit the maximum effort of subordinates. His correct appearance, military bearing, and flawless conduct project obvious pride in the service of the Air Force and his country.

(Name) demonstrates extraordinary professional ability, in-depth technical knowledge, and uncommon perceptiveness in advancing the morale and welfare needs of his people while at the same time meeting all command goals and objectives.

(Name) ability to adapt to any assignment and his strong motivation toward self improvement indicate the potential for outstanding performance in diverse occupational fields within the officer corps. His self-assurance, professional approach, and confident attitude make him an outstanding candidate for (...).

(Name) enthusiastic approach toward setting and achieving mission goals, and his natural flair for counseling significantly enhanced the performance of the (organization). Through his leadership, patience, and uniquely personalized instructional technique, many less than receptive personnel have been successfully motivated and inspired to work to the highest level of their ability.

A concerned and humane individual, (Name) affable personality and willingness to assist others in any capacity instills high morale and a strong sense of esprit de corps in those around him. Through personal industry and the effective use of correct management techniques he has shown that he can judiciously utilize personnel and material resources.

(Name) professional knowledge and technical competence are truly outstanding. He has fully demonstrated strong leadership, exceptional management ability, and meticulous administrative skills.

(Name) qualities of self-confidence, excellent physical condition, and commanding presence give him an unusual talent for the control of personnel. He maintains an impeccable personal appearance and commands similarly high standards from his subordinates, creating a deep respect for Air Force tradition and regulations.

(Name) daily demonstrated extraordinary professional ability, in depth technical knowledge, and uncommon perceptiveness in advancing the morale and welfare needs of subordinates demonstrate unlimited growth potential.

(Name) sense of humor, mental alertness, and ability to express himself both orally and in writing is excellent. He is a sound manager with the proven ability to successfully supervise the functions and activities of others while maintaining, or surpassing, objectives.

PERFORMANCE APPRAISALS

The sample write-ups provided in this guide reflect several writing styles. They give the reader a variety of ideas on how subject material can be written. When drafting performance appraisals, remember you are writing to "sell" the evaluee to selection boards by covering that individual's performance, ability, and potential. All writing styles in this guide accomplish this objective.

There is enough material available in this guide to form a sound base in the construction of hundreds of individual write-ups, each with its own uniqueness and individuality.

The material in one chapter can be used with the subject matter of other chapters.

REMEMBER:

* If you do not know how to draft a performance appraisal, you don't know how to read one--your own included.

* If you cannot author a good narrative, you are hurting the careers of those individuals working for you who deserve to be promoted.

INTRODUCTION

Every large organization has some means to evaluate the performance of its members. Administrators call this evaluation process "performance appraisal."

PRIMARY OBJECTIVES OF GIVING PERFORMANCE APPRAISALS

1. To identify promotion, retention, and future duty potential.

2. To select, promote and retain the best qualified personnel.

3. To provide feedback to the evaluee.

PERFORMANCES MEASURED

1. **PERSONAL TRAITS** - How something is done (for example, the leadership, initiative, etc. used or applied to accomplish something).

2. **JOB PERFORMANCE** - What and how much is done.

3. **JOB BEHAVIOR** - Appearance, adaptability, behavior, etc.

OBJECTIVE AND SUBJECTIVE ANALYSIS.

OBJECTIVE ANALYSIS should be used whenever possible to document an individuals performance. Objective analysis means to quantify performance results. How much was done? What was done? Use hours, time, percent, dollars, etc.

SUBJECTIVE ANALYSIS is the evaluator's perceptions, beliefs, or thoughts on how something was accomplished. This is an analysis of a person's "inner" qualities (or personality) and must be based on observations over a period of time. Subjective analysis is used to describe what prompted or caused an individual to do something (personal traits such as leadership, imagination, etc.).

PREPARATION CHECK-LIST

The more knowledge and tools an evaluator has at his/her disposal the better. The following information should be reviewed PRIOR to committing a subordinate's performance to print.

1. All performance appraisals should be handled discretely. They should be worked on in private.

2. Rough copies of past performance appraisals might be retained on file for reference for the next reporting period.

3. Insofar as practicable, reporting seniors should grade all performance appraisals of the same competitive category at one time. This will facilitate comparative grading.

4. Endeavor to obtain a just and equitable spread in the marks assigned to a comparative group.

5. Do not gravitate toward either a gratuitously high or rigidly severe policy of grading. The military is plagued by general over-assessment of average performers and occasional under assessment of "top performers." This serves to reduce the promotional opportunities of the "best qualified."

6. Exercise care to mark objectively, avoiding any tendency which might allow general impressions, a single incident or a particular trait, characteristic, or quality to influence other marks unduly.

7. When uncertain, due to limited observation, as to the appropriate evaluation of any rating area, mark the "Not Observed" block rather than assign a "middle-of-the-road" mark.

8. Avoid marking a new person somewhat lower than he/she deserves in order to reflect improved performance in subsequent performance appraisals. This malpractice can result in unjust advancement or assignment actions.

9. Before beginning to write, check over available performance data and determine which category you are going to place an individual being reported on:
    a. Head and shoulders above his contemporaries--promote early/now.
    b. Above many contemporaries--promote above most.
    c. Good performer--promote with majority of contemporaries.
    d. Behind peer group performance--do not promote.

When a decision has been reached, write a performance appraisal that will support and justify your position.

10. The "head and shoulders" performers should be immediately identified at the start of the narrative. The remaining write-up must justify and reinforce your position.

11. Ensure realistic marks are assigned to individuals whose performance of duty has been manifestly unsatisfactory. Impersonal grading and concise statements of fact best serve overall interests under such circumstances.

12. Conversely, ensure that due consideration is accorded when an individual demonstrates truly outstanding or exceptional professional competence and potential. In such cases accentuate the positive. State major accomplishments that have been achieved. More importantly,

comment constructively on capacity or potential for future increased responsibility or promotion.

13. If the command has made an outstanding performance during the reporting period, an individual's personal contribution to this effect should be included. Of course, the converse is true.

14. After completion of a performance appraisal, review previous worksheets on the same person, if available, to ensure that any changes in the marks on the current report are intended. Any significant shift of marks in reports signed by the same reporting senior should be substantiated in the narrative.

15. When making subsequent reports on the same person, guard against repetitive phraseology, as this will reflect lack of thought on your part and it will not help an individual's promotion chances.

16. Before submitting a smooth performance appraisal, analyze the narrative to make sure that what is meant to be said is, in fact, actually being said. Give careful thought not only to what the chosen words mean to the evaluator, but also how they may be construed by a selection board.

17. When the performance appraisal is finished, review it to ensure that:
    a. All parts are consistent (marks & narrative agree).
    b. The trend in performance (increase or decrease) is correctly conveyed.
    c. All spelling and grammatical errors are corrected.

18. Bear in mind that performance appraisal narratives reflect the degree and extent in which evaluators measure up to their moral obligation. And, an evaluator's write-up may be used to judge his/her performance.

19. Words are both valuable and dangerous tools. Choose them carefully.

20. Words mean what they say. Review the following:

POTENTIAL CAPACITY ABILITY

To indicate that an individual has these qualities without supporting evidence will register to a selection board as "insufficient data." A person can have POTENTIAL, CAPACITY, or ABILITY and yet accomplish nothing. Write how these qualities were demonstrated.

TRIES   STRIVES

Someone can TRY or STRIVE without accomplishing anything. As above, note how these qualities were positively demonstrated.

ACCEPTS   ASSIGNED   NORMALLY   GENERALLY

Simply ACCEPTING assignments does not show initiative. Performing ASSIGNMENTS does not show initiative. NORMALLY and GENERALLY mean less than always.

AVERAGE ABOVE AVERAGE EXCELLENT OUTSTANDING

These words have "canned" meanings and understandings. ABOVE AVERAGE is generally assumed to mean less than EXCELLENT or OUTSTANDING. AVERAGE means less than ABOVE AVERAGE, etc.. If you are going to place someone's performance in one of these categories, be sure to choose the correct word(s).

"DO" Check List:

-**DO** submit performance appraisals on time and in correct format.

-**DO** write performance appraisals directed **TO** selection boards.

-**DO** write on how someone contributed above or below what is normally expected.

-**DO** write to express, not impress.

-**DO** be fair, honest, and objective.

-**DO** comment of growth potential and qualifications for advancement and future duty assignments.

-**DO** write on hard, pertinent facts, not "faint praises" without substance.

-**DO** use short, concise phrases or complete sentences with proper grammar.

-**DO** use underline to highlight key areas only.

"DON'T" Check List:

-DON'T assign marks that are inconsistent with the narrative.

-DON'T write performance appraisals directed TO the individual.

-DON'T assign exceptionally high/low marks without comments in the narrative that clearly distinguish the performance.

-DON'T include minor, isolated, or insignificant imperfections which do not affect performance.

-DON'T use glittering generalities which go on and on without saying anything useful.

-DON'T use long words when shorter words will do.

-DON'T be verbose or redundant.

-DON'T restate the job description in the narrative. That space is too valuable.

-DON'T write "during the period of this report" or words to that effect. It is understood, unless otherwise stated, that all actions and events in a performance appraisal occurred during the reporting period being covered. Again, narrative space is too valuable.

-DON'T start too many sentences with the same: He... He... His... etc.... Reading becomes sluggish and boring and shows lack of attention or ability on the part of the drafter.

-DON'T use a person's name without associated rank. For example, do not write "Jones is..."; instead, it should be "LT Jones is..."; A performance appraisal is an official document and an individual's rank should always accompany his/her name.

-DON'T use the term "ratee." It is too impersonal and impresses no one.

PERFORMANCE APPRAISALS

DRAFTING THE NARRATIVE

1. **OBJECTIVE**. Performance appraisals should be drafted with two objectives in mind. These objectives are:

    a. To document, in SPECIFIC terms, what an individual contributed to command, and department/division effectiveness and accomplishment; and,

    b. To document the subjective "inner" qualities demonstrated by an individual on how performance was accomplished.

2. **GUIDANCE.**

    a. **BE POSITIVE**: Any shortcoming or deficiency mentioned in the narrative should be significant, either in terms of performance or potential. At any level in an organization some occasional, routine guidance is necessary. If the comment is made that someone requires occasional instruction or guidance, that means he/she requires more instruction or guidance than would normally be expected. In effect, comments on minor deficiencies are automatically magnified when they are included in the narrative.

    b. **BE CORRECT**: A direct, hard-hitting write-up is better than an elegant one--concentrate more on content and specific accomplishments.

    c. **BE FACTUAL**: Quantify individual achievements and accomplishments when possible.

    d. **BE SPECIFIC**: A few well worded phrases or sentences on individual accomplishment and achievement mean much more than pages on billet description, command employment, etc...

    e. **BE OBJECTIVE**: To the maximum extent possible, comment on quantifiable "objective" accomplishments, not on "subjective" personal notions.

OPENING FORMAT

The most closely read sentences in a performance appraisal are the opening sentences. The opening should be a powerful and persuasive statement--an "attention getter" to immediately capture the attention of the reader. The opening format can be limited to four themes:

(1) Overview of best attributes/performance (or the converse for substandard performers);

(2) Organizational ranking (for top performers);

(3) Potential (for top performers); and,

(4) Awards or other forms of recognition received. The opening format sets the "theme" for the remaining narrative.

OPENING FORMAT SAMPLES

...(Name) is an exceptionally well qualified (...). Extremely well organized, mission-oriented and empathic with his subordinates and work environment. Infused (organization) with enthusiasm and dedication. Unlimited potential. Awarded (...) Medal for (...).

...(Name) professional talents, dedication, and aggressive work habits are an asset to the (organization). Virtually unlimited potential. Awarded Letter of Commendation for (...).

...(Name) is an outstanding manager and organizer. Willing to accept any assignment regardless of scope. Boundless potential. Selected as (...) of the Year.

...(Name) is an energetic, industrious, and conscientious individual who has proven himself time after time to be a top performer. (Potential...Awards)

...(Name) has continually proven himself to be a (peer group) of exemplary character and outstanding ability. (Potential...Awards)

...(Name) professional knowledge, self-motivation, and determined, tireless efforts have made excellent contributions to the efficient functioning of (organization). (Potential...Awards)

43

CLOSING FORMAT

The CLOSING FORMAT is another good place for a drafter to "sell" an individual to a selection board. : Top-notch performers' performance appraisals might close with one of the following:

...Virtually unlimited potential

...Limitless potential

...Unbounded potential

...Extraordinary growth potential

SUMMARY

Performance appraisal systems are relatively easy to understand. To properly draft one of these performance appraisals, simply refer to and follow the appropriate instruction for administrative and procedural guidance. However, today there is keen competition for the limited number of available promotion slots. Writing a performance appraisal that just meets the instructional requirements by no means assures success or promotion. Proper use of the material available in this book should enhance promotion competitiveness.

NARRATIVE STRUCTURE SAMPLES

(Name) is well read, with good working knowledge of the English language. Written reports clear and concise. Oral presentations command complete attention of a listening audience.

(Name) is ready for positions of increased responsibility and trust now. Recommended for (...) duty and for a billet as (...). (Name) is most strongly recommended for immediate selection to (...).

(Name) rare and successful blend of leadership coupled with superior management and administrative abilities assure success in virtually any assignment. Stays with a job until it is completed, regardless of the time of day or night. During the past three months worked over 100 off-duty hours re-outfitting and organizing (...). Unlimited ability and potential. Highly recommended for (...).

(Name) career continues to be underscored by pride, self-improvement and accomplishment. Initially assigned the primary duties of (…), he found time to assume other, equally demanding tasks. Filling in as the (…), organized the monumental task of (…). In the area of training, personally planned and scheduled (…). Volunteered to assume increased and diverse duties of … In this capacity managed successful efforts to (…).

(Name) most outstanding (peer group). Top notch leader. Well versed in all facets of professional specialty. Energetic and resourceful. Always plans ahead. Self-starter with great desire for professional challenge. Firm, fair, unbiased leader. Demands high standards of performance from self and subordinates. Effectively capitalizes on subordinate strengths and improves weaknesses. A highly talented front-runner in peer group. Promote early.

The wide and varied technical background (Name) brought to this job were instrumental in starting the successful operation of (…). Being undermanned, the job was particularly demanding and time consuming. Working with others in a unified and cohesive manner is a particularly strong asset of (Name). Ability to immediately establish and maintain excellent rapport with subordinates on all levels. Much of this is due to the fair, open, and unbiased manner of leadership style. Each person knows that they will be given an equal opportunity commensurate with capabilities in all assignments, and that all will be given the opportunity to learn. He personally counsels each newly reporting person, setting forth organizational requirements and what the individual can expect in return. Communicates thoughts and ideas with ease and clarity. Written reports are brief, concise, and to the point. Conduct and appearance beyond reproach. Demonstrating a continuing great personal pride in self with uniform proudly worn. Instills this same pride in others.

(Name) is an industrious and versatile individual who approaches any task enthusiastically and with dispatch. A skillful manager with the proven ability to attain a high standard of performance in any endeavor. Directs watch team with firm but fair hand, and provides a unified purpose and sense of direction without dulling initiative. Readily adaptable to changes in policy, procedure, or assigned workload. Always gives a personal contribution as a special effort to ensure cohesiveness and uniformity. Established good rapport with subordinates and does not hesitate to provide personal or professional assistance, encouraging their trust through genuine interest in their problems. Accomplishments include: (…).

(Name) watch team operational effectiveness graded at (…) during (…)--highest grade in (organization). Received verbal and written praise from (name/title/billet) for the outstanding work and effort put into job as (job name). A proponent of physical fitness, (Name) actively participates in various sporting events and maintains a trim physique. Conduct and appearance, on and off duty, are model worthy of emulation by the entire (…) community.

(Name) fully enjoys military life, is quick to point out career benefits. Will not tolerate open dissent toward command policies or procedures. Personally responsible for convincing others to take initial or additional off-duty educational courses.

(Name) is the most productive and versatile (peer group) at (organization). Proven top quality organizer, administrator, and manager whose potential for increased responsibility and authority is boundless. Supplying much of the early leadership and planning proved to be a major force in the successful (…). Has a great deal of energy, is highly industrious, and doesn't believe in idle time. These rare qualities, coupled with his friendly personality and quick wit, allow him to establish and maintain an atmosphere of pride and professionalism in any organizational environment. A partial listing of personal accomplishments include (…).

(Name) is eager to stay abreast of the latest changes in management, technology, and operations. Currently enrolled in (…). To accomplish these and other varied tasks (Name) routinely reports to duty early and remains later than contemporaries. (Name) is a steadying and guiding influence to subordinates and peer group. (Name) is ready now to meet increasingly more responsibility and challenge. Most strongly recommended for promotion ahead of peer group.

A poised and mature (peer group) with a thirst for knowledge and a desire for challenge. Soft spoken with an authoritative manner and commanding presence. A positive motivator who displays compassion, decisiveness, and determination. Intelligent and articulate, runs an orderly and highly productive organization.

(Name) is a self-starter whose great personal initiative and leadership skills identify him as being "head and shoulders" above contemporaries.

(Name) is a top performer. Unlimited potential. Totally professional, poised, mature, and dedicated. A self-starter. Intelligent. Always volunteers for additional responsibility. Rising superstar of boundless ability. Does not believe in idle time or unfinished projects. Manages own time and that of others to best possible advantage. Possesses managerial and organizational expertise rarely observed in contemporaries. Completes large volume of work each day, frequently working extra hours.

Neat, trim, and fit. Immaculate "recruit poster" quality appearance. Articulate in speech, polite in manner. Submits timely, accurate staff work. Enjoys loyalty, cooperation, and total support of subordinates.

(Name) ready for promotion now. Possesses superior management and leadership abilities. Extremely knowledgeable, industrious, totally resourceful. Performance of all duties singularly and collectively outstanding. Head and shoulders above contemporaries. Original thinker, thrives on challenge and responsibility. Articulate self-expression. Proven competence and unparalleled ability. Particularly adept at gaining immediate support and loyalty of others. Compassionate, demanding leader.

(Name) absolute quality performer. A high achiever with unlimited growth potential. Concerned counselor, tactful leader. Reliable, responsive, and articulate. Adds more to job than expected. Places duty ahead of personal interests. Continually alert for ways to increase personal and professional knowledge. Personable and outgoing. A real morale booster.

(Name) is work-aggressive and highly productive. Unlimited potential for professional growth. Volunteers for additional tasking. Has a knack for administrative detail. Provides strong, positive leadership. Enthusiastic, "take charge" attitude. Cheerful and personable, promotes high morale and works well with superiors.

Excellent all-around (peer group). Conscientious and totally dependable. Professional, "can-do" attitude. Unbound personal initiative. Enthusiastic leadership. In tense or trying situations can always be counted on to provide appropriate spark of leadership, humor, or energy.

(Name) proven ace performer with endless potential and ability. Energetic, industrious, and conscientious. Outstanding performance contributed significantly to high level of readiness and efficiency. Has knack for getting the job done where others fail. Punctuality and strong sense of duty highlight daily performance. Exceptional military attitude and bearing. Commanding presence. Infectious, cheerful personality elicits maximum support and cooperation. Promote now.

(Name) is my number one (peer group). Promote ahead of all others. Dedication to duty and attention to detail without equal. Energetic self-starter. Demands and receives only top quality performance. Deep sense of personal responsibility and pride of duty. Special talent for organizational detail. Ready sense of humor and a pleasant personality. Fosters high morale throughout the ranks.

(Name) an exceptional leader, manager, and organizer. Demonstrated performance as a leader significantly improved overall performance and readiness. Pride, personal involvement, and job accomplishment underscore daily performance. Industrious and creative, enjoys finding viable solutions to complex situations. Possesses unbounded initiative and potential. Actions well planned, organized, and executed. Dynamic, compassionate leader knows how to motivate subordinates.

WORD PICTURE PERSONALITY

Documenting exactly what a person accomplishes in a performance appraisal is both useful and necessary. Work accomplishment alone, however, does not give a complete description or "picture" of an individual. The careful use of a few well chosen "word picture" Adjectives can describe a person's inner qualities--what possesses a person to do something--what a person "IS."

By combining what a person accomplishes and putting to print along with those accomplishments a person's personality characteristics, a complete "picture" of an individual is possible. Take, for example, the following:

"(Name) is energetic, resourceful, and self-reliant. He (go on to list exactly what he accomplished)."In the above example, a selection board will know what was accomplished. More importantly, the board will gain valuable insight to the individual's "inner" qualities, capabilities, and potential-- "energetic, resourceful, and self-reliant."

Selection boards do not promote people simply because they do a good job in their present pay grade. The potential to successfully discharge the greater duties of higher pay grades must be clearly in evidence. Potential must be documented in performance appraisals.

By using the appropriate "word picture personality" characteristics listed on the following pages, selection boards can "see" and evaluate the full worth and potential (or lack thereof) of an individual.

FAVORABLE APPRAISALS
PERSONALITY

The following list of words express, define, state, or describe FAVORABLE personality characteristics, traits, performance, or results.

ADJECTIVES

ACE	ADEPT	ADMIRABLE
ADROIT	AFFABLE	AGILE
ALERT	ALL-AROUND	AMIABLE
AMICABLE	APPEALING	ARTISTIC
ASSERTIVE	AUSPICIOUS	BENIGN
BLITHE	BRISK	CANDID
CHARISMATIC	CHARMING	CHEERFUL
COMPOSED	CONGENIAL	CONSONANT
CORDIAL	COURAGEOUS	COURTEOUS
DAUNTLESS	DETERMINED	DEVOTED
DEXTEROUS	DIPLOMATIC	DISCREET
DISCRIMINATING	DISTINGUISHED	DYNAMIC
EAGER	EFFERVESCENT	ELEGANT
ENERGETIC	ENGAGING	ENTERPRISING
ENTHUSIASTIC	ETHICAL	EXCEPTIONAL
EXPERIENCED	EXPERT	EXUBERANT
FAIR-MINDED	FEARLESS	FESTIVE
FIRST-STRING	FORTHRIGHT	FORWARD-LOOKING
FRANK	FRIENDLY	GALLANT
GENEROUS	GENTEEL	GLAD
GOOD-HUMORED	GOOD-NATURED	GRACIOUS
GREGARIOUS	GUNG HO	HIGH-MINDED
HONEST	HONORABLE	HUMOROUS
IMPOSING	INDUSTRIOUS	INFLUENTIAL
INNOVATIVE	INQUISITIVE	INSPIRED
INTREPID	INSPIRING	INTREPID
JOCOSE	JOCULAR	JOLLY

JOVIAL	JOYFUL	JUDICIOUS
LARGE-MINDED	LEADING	LEVELHEADED
LIGHTHEARTED	LIMPID	LIVELY
LOYAL	MANNERLY	MASTERFUL
MASTERLY	MATURE	MERRY
METICULOUS	MORALISTIC	NOBLE
OPEN-EYED	OPENHANDED	OUTGOING
PEERLESS	PERSONABLE	PERSUASIVE
PLEASANT	PLEASING	PLEASURABLE
POLISHED	POLITE	PREDOMINANT
PREEMINENT	PRESTIGIOUS	PROFICIENT
PROGRESSIVE	PROMINENT	PROUD
PROVIDENT	PRUDENT	PRUDENTIAL
RADIANT	REFINED	RELIABLE
RELIANT	RENOWNED	REPUTABLE
RESERVED	RESOLUTE	RESOURCEFUL
RESPECTABLE	RESPONSIBLE	RIGHTEOUS
SAPID	SCRUPULOUS	SELF-COMPOSED
SINCERE	SKILLED	SKILLFUL
SNAPPY	SOCIABLE	SOCIAL
SOLITARY	SPIRITED	STALWART
STELLAR	STERLING	STUDIOUS
SUAVE	TACTFUL	TEMPERATE
THANKFUL	TIDY	TRUSTWORTHY
TRUTHFUL	UNASSUMING	UNFLAPPABLE
UNINHIBITED	UP-AND-COMING	UPRIGHT
VERACIOUS	VERSATILE	VERSED
VIGOROUS	VIRTUOUS	VIVACIOUS
WELL-ADVISED	WELL-BRED	WELL-CONDITIONED
WELL-DISPOSED	WELL-GROOMED	WHOLESOME
WILY	ZEALOUS ZESTY	
ZIPPY		

PERSONALITY - NOUNS

ACCLAIM	ACCOLADE	ACHIEVER
AGILITY	AMITY	ANIMATOR
A1	APLOMB	ADEPT
BENEVOLENCE	CHARISMA	CHARMER
COMPETITOR	COURAGE	DETERMINATION
DEXTERITY	DIGNITY	DIPLOMACY
DIPLOMAT	EAGER BEAVER	EAGERNESS
EARNEST	ELEGANCE	ENTHUSIASM
ENTHUSIAST	EPITOME	ESPRIT DE CORPS
ESTEEM	ETIQUETTE	EUPHORIA
EXCITER	EXPERTISE	FELICITY
FERVOR	FINESSE	FLAIR
FORTE	FORTITUDE	FRIENDLY
GIFT	GLORY	GOOD FAITH
GOODWILL	GRIT	GUSTO
HERO	HONESTY	HONOR
HUMOR	INDUSTRY	INFLUENTIAL
INITIATIVE	INSPIRATION	INTEGRITY
INTESTINAL FORTITUDE		JACK-OF-ALL-TRADES
JOURNEYMAN		JOY
KINDLINESS		KINDNESS
LAUREL	LIVELINESS	LOYALTY
MASTERMIND	MATURITY	MOTIVATION
PARAGON	PATHFINDER	PATRIOT
PATRIOTISM	PEP	PILLAR
PINNACLE	POISE	PRESTIGE
PRIDE	PROFESSIONAL	PROFESSIONALISM
PROMINENCE	PROPRIETY	PROWESS
PRUDENCE	RENOWN	REPERTOIRE
RESOURCE	RESPECT	SANITY
SELF-ASSURANCE		SELF-CONFIDENCE
SELF-CONTROL		SELF-DETERMINATION
SELF-DISCIPLINE		SELF-ESTEEM

SELF-IMPROVEMENT		SELF-RELIANCE
SELF-RESPECT	SELF-RESTRAINT	SELF-SACRIFICE
SELF-STARTER	SELF-WILL	SINCERITY
SPECIALIST	SPARTAN	SPIRIT
STALWART	STANDARD-BEARER	
STANDOUT	STAR	STIMULATOR
TACT	TEMPERANCE	TROUBLE-SHOOTER
VERACITY	VERVE	VIGOR
VIM	VIRTUE	VITALITY
WHIZ	WINNER	WORKHORSE
WELL-BEING	ZEAL	ZEALOT
ZEALOTORY	ZEST	ZESTFULNESS

PERSONALITY VERBS

ACCLAIM	ADMIRE	CHAMPION
CHARM	CORUSCATE	EFFERVESCE
ENCHANT	ENCOURAGE	ENGENDER
ENHANCE	ENTRUST	EPITOMIZE
EXALT	EXCEL	EXEMPLIFY
FLOURISH	GRATIFY	INSPIRE
MOTIVATE	OUTCLASS	OUTDO
OUTMATCH	OUTSHINE	OVERSHADOW
PERSONIFY	POLISH	PRAISE
PREDOMINATE	PREVAIL	RADIATE
RESPECT	SOCIALIZE	SPARKLE
SPIRIT	ZIP	

OF OR WITHIN THE MIND

The following list of words express, define, state, or describe **FAVORABLY** individual intellect. intelligence, knowledge, wisdom, or reasoning.

ADJECTIVES

ABLE	ACCOMPLISHED	ACUTE
AGILE-MINDED	ALERT	ANALYTIC
ANALYTICAL	APT	ARTFUL
ASTUTE	AWARE	BRIGHT
BRILLIANT	CALCULATING	CAREFUL
CLAIRVOYANT	CLEAR-HEADED	CLEAR-SIGHTED
CLEAR-WITTED	CLEVER	COGENT
COGNIZANT	COMMON SENSE	COMPREHENSIBLE
CONCEIVABLE	CONCENTRATING	CONCEPTIVE
CONCEPTUAL	CONSCIOUS	CRAFTY
CREATIVE	CULTIVATED	CULTURED
CUNNING	CURIOUS	DEDUCTIVE POWER
DEEP-THINKING	DELIBERATING	DEXTEROUS
DISCERNIBLE	DISCERNING	DISCREET
EDUCABLE	EDUCATED	ENLIGHTENED
ERUDITE	FARSEEING	FARSIGHTED
FORESIGHTED	FECUND	FERTILE
FREE-SPOKEN	GIFTED	IDEAL
IDEALISTIC	IDEALIZE	IMAGINABLE
IMAGINARY	IMAGINATION	IMAGINATIVE
INCISIVE	INNATE	INFORMED
INGENIOUS	INSIGHTFUL	INSPIRATION
INTELLECTUAL	INTELLIGENT	INVENTIVE
JUDICIAL	JUDICIOUS	KEEN
KEEN-WITTED	KNOWING	KNOWLEDGEABLE
LEARNED	LEGERITY	LETTERED
LEVELHEADED	LITERARY	LITERATE
LOGICAL	MATURE	MENTAL
MENTOR	METHODICAL	MINDFUL
NIMBLE	OMNISCIENT	PENETRATING

PERCEPTIVE	PERSPICACIOUS	POLITIC
PONDERABLE	POWERFUL	PRAGMATIC
PRESENCE OF MIND	PROFICIENT	PROFOUND
PRUDENT	PUNGENT	QUICK
QUICK-THINKING	QUICK-WITTED	RATIONAL
REASONABLE	RECEPTIVE	RETENTIVE
SAGACIOUS	SAGE	SANE
SAPIENT	SCHOLARLY	SELF-TAUGHT
SENSIBLE	SHARP	SHARP-WITTED
SHREWD	SKILLFUL	SLY
SMART	SPECULATIVE	STUDIOUS
TALENTED	THINKABLE	THINKING
THOUGHTFUL	VIVID	WELL-GROUNDED
WELL-INFORMED	WELL-READ	WELL-VERSED
WIDELY-READ	WISE	WITTED
WITTY	WORLDLY-WISE	

OF OR WITHIN THE MIND - NOUNS

ABSTRACT	THOUGHT	ACUITY
ACUMEN	ACUTENESS	APTITUDE
APTNESS	ARTISTIC IMAGINATION	
AWARENESS	BOLD IMAGINATION	
BRAINCHILD	BRAIN TRUST	BRILLIANCE
CLAIRVOYANCE		CLEVERNESS
COGITATION	COGNIZANCE	COHERENCE
COMMON SENSE		COMPREHENSION
CONCEPTION		CONSCIOUSNESS
CONSTRUCTIVE-IMAGINATION		CRAFTINESS
CREATIVE ABILITY	CREATIVE IMAGINATION	
CREATIVENESS		CREATIVE POWER
CREATIVE THOUGHT		CREATIVITY
CUNNING	CURIOSITY	DEDUCTION
DEDUCTIVE POWER	DEXTERITY	EDUCATOR

ENLIGHTENMENT   ERUDITION   EXPERIENCE
EXPERTISE   FACILITY   FACULTIES
FACULTY   FERTILE MIND   FORESIGHT

FORESIGHTEDNESS   FREETHINKER
GENIUS   GUMPTION   HEADWORK
HIGHER EDUCATION   HIGHER LEARNING

HINDSIGHT   IDEA   IMAGINATION
INGENUITY   INSIGHT   INSPIRATION
INTEGRATIVE POWER   INTELLECT

INTELLECTION   INTELLECTUAL
INTELLECTUAL FACULTY   INTELLECTUAL GRASP
INTELLECTUAL POWER INTELLIGENCE   INVENTION

INVENTIVENESS   INVENTOR   JUDGMENT
KEENNESS   KEEN-WITTEDNESS   KNOW-HOW
KNOWLEDGE   LEARNING   LEVELHEADEDNESS

LITERACY   LITERATE   LIVELY IMAGINATION
LOGIC   LOGICAL THOUGHT   MASTERY
MENTAL ALERTNESS   MENTAL CAPACITY

MENTAL FACULTY   MENTALITY   MENTAL PROCESS
ORIGINALITY   OUTLOOK   PENETRATION
PERCEPTION   POSTULATOR   POWER OF MIND

POWER OF REASON   POWER OF THOUGHT
PRACTICAL KNOWLEDGE   PRACTICAL WISDOM
PRODUCTIVE IMAGINATION   PROFICIENCY

PROFOUND KNOWLEDGE   PRUDENCE
QUICKNESS   QUICK THINKING   QUICK WIT
RATIONALE   RATIONAL FACULTY

RATIONALISM   RATIONALITY   READY WIT
REASON   REASONING   REASONING FACILITY
RECALL   RESOLUTION   RESOLVE

RETENTIVITY   RICH IMAGINATION
SAGE   SCHOLAR
SEASONED UNDERSTANDING   SENSIBILITY

SHARPNESS
SHREWDNESS   SMARTNESS
SOUND UNDERSTANDING

SHARP-WITTEDNESS
SOUNDNESS
SPECULATION

STRAIGHT THINKING TALENT
THINKER   THOUGHT
UNDERSTUDY   VISION

TECHNIQUE
UNDERSTANDING
VISUALIZATION

VIVID IMAGINATION
WISDOM   WISENESS
WITS   WITTICISM

VOCABULARY
WIT

OF OR WITHIN THE MIND - VERBS

COGITATE   COMPREHEND   CONCEIVE
CONCENTRATE   CONCEPTUALIZE   CONTEMPLATE
CREATE   DIFFERENTIATE   DISCERN

ENLIGHTEN   ENTERTAIN IDEAS   ENVISION
FABRICATE   FORESEE   IMAGE
IMAGINE   INVENT   IRRADIATE

KNOW   LEARN   MEDITATE
ORIGINATE   OUTTHINK   OUTWIT
PENETRATE   PERCEIVE   PICTURED

PONDER   POSTULATE   PRODUCE
RATIONALIZE   REASON   RE-EXAMINE
RESOLVE   RETHINK   REEVALUATE

SAVVY   SPECULATE   TEACH
THINK   THINK-UP   UNDERSTAND
VISUALIZE   VISION

SPEAKING AND WRITING

The following list of words express, define, state, or describe FAVORABLY an individual's ability or capacity to convey information and thoughts to others through the mastery of the English language.

ADJECTIVES

ARTICULATE	CLEAR-CUT	CONCISE
CONVERSANT	ELABORATE	ELOQUENT
EMPHATIC	EXPLICIT	FAIR-SPOKEN

FLUENT	IMPLICIT	INFORMATIVE
LUCID	PERSPICUOUS	POLYGLOT
SILVER-TONGUED		SMOOTH-SPOKEN

SMOOTH-TONGUED		SUCCINCT
TACIT	TACITURN	TALKATIVE
TERSE	VOLUBLE	WELL-SPOKEN

SPEAKING & WRITING - NOUNS

CLARITY	DICTION	DISCOURSE
ELOQUENCE	FORUM	LUCIDITY
ORATOR	QUIP	SAVOIR-FAIRE

VERBALISM	VERBALIST	WORDING
WORDPLAY	WORDSMITH	

SPEAKING & WRITING - VERBS

CONFUTE	EDIT	EDITORIALIZE
EDUCATE	ELUCIDATE	EMPHASIZE
ENUNCIATE	EXPOUND	INSINUATE

HUMANE QUALITIES

The following list of words express, define. or describe how an individual inter-relates with others.

ADJECTIVES

BENEVOLENT	BIG-HEARTED	COMPASSIONATE
CONGRUOUS	EMPATHETIC	EMPATHIC
FEELING	FERVENT	FORGIVING

GENIAL	GENTLE	GOOD-HEARTED
GREATHEARTED	HARMONIOUS	HEARTFELT
HEARTY	HOSPITABLE	HUMANE
KIND	KINDLY	MERCIFUL
NICE	OPENHEARTED	PENSIVE
POIGNANT	REGRETFUL	RESPECTFUL
SELFLESS	SENSITIVE	SENTIMENTAL
SYMPATHETIC	TENDER	TENDERHEARTED
THOUGHTFUL	TRUSTFUL	TRUSTING
UNSELFISH	WARM	WARMHEARTED

HUMANE QUALITIES - NOUNS

AMENITY	COMPASSION	CONSONANCE
COURTESY	EMPATHY	FAIR PLAY
FORGIVENESS	HARMONY	HUMANITARIAN
MERCY	NICETY	PITY
SENSITIVITY	SOLACE	SOLICITUDE

HUMANE QUALITIES - VERBS

| EMPATHIZE | FORGIVE | SYMPATHIZE |

POSITIVE - ACTIVE

The following express FAVORABLE, positive, active words.

ADJECTIVES

ABSOLUTE	ACCOMPLISHED	AGGRESSIVE
AGOG	ANXIOUS	ARDENT
ARDUOUS	AUDACIOUS	AVID
BANNER	BOLD	CHALLENGING
COMPELLING	COMPETITIVE	COMPLEX
COMPLICATED	COMPREHENSIVE	COMPULSIVE

CONSUMMATE	CONTAGIOUS	CONVINCING
CRISP	CRITICAL	CRUCIAL
DECISIVE	DIVERSE	DOMINANT
DOMINEERING	DRAMATIC	DRASTIC
EFFICIENT	ELATED	ELEVATED
EMINENT	EMOTIONAL	ENGROSSING
ENVIABLE	ENVIOUS	ESSENTIAL
EXACT	EXACTING	EXCEEDING
EXCELLENT	EXCITABLE	EXCITING
EXCLUSIVE	EXEMPLARY	EXPEDIENT
EXPEDITIOUS	EXPLOSIVE	EXTENSIVE
EXTRA	EXTRANEOUS	EXTRAORDINARY
EXTREME	EXULTANT	FABULOUS
FANTASTIC	FAR-REACHING	FASCINATING
FAULTLESS	FEISTY	FEVERISH
FIDUCIARY	FIERCE	FIERY
FINE	FIRST-RATE	FIVE-STAR
FLASHY	FLUID	FOOLPROOF
FORCEFUL	FORCIBLE	FOREMOST
FORMATIVE	FORTHWITH	FOUR-STAR
FRANTIC	FREQUENT	FRESH
FRUITFUL	FULL-FLEDGED	GLORIOUS
GRANDIOSE	GRATIFYING	GRUELING
HANDS-ON	HASTILY	HASTY
HEADLONG	HECTIC	HIDDEN
HIGH-FLYING	HIGH-POWERED	HIGH-PRESSURE
HIGH-SPIRITED	HURRIED	HYPER
IDEAL	ILLUSTRIOUS	IMAGINABLE
IMMACULATE	IMPASSIONED	IMPECCABLE
IMPORTANT	IMPRESSIBLE	IMPULSIVE
INCISIVE	INCREDIBLE	IN-DEPTH
INERRANT	INEXHAUSTIBLE	INEXTINGUISHABLE
INFALLIBLE	INFECTIOUS	INSATIABLE

INSTANTANEOUS   INSTINCTIVE   INSTRUMENTAL
INTEGRAL   INTENSE   INTERESTED
INTRICATE   IRREPRESSIBLE   JUBILANT

LAUDABLE   LAUDATORY   LETTER-PERFECT
LONG-RANGE   MARVELOUS   NOTABLE
OUTSTANDING   PARAMOUNT   PARLOUS

PERFECT   PERPETUAL   PERSISTENT
POSITIVE   POSSESSIVE   POTENT
POWERFUL   PRECISE   PREVAILING

PREVALENT   PRIME   PROLIFIC
PROMPT   PROSPEROUS   PROVOCATIVE
PROVOKING   PUNCTILIOUS   PURPOSEFUL

QUICK   QUIZZICAL   REFRESHING
REGENERATE   RELENTLESS   REMARKABLE
RENASCENT   RESILIENT   RESOUNDING

RESURGENT   ROBUST   ROSY
SERIOUS   SEVERE   SHIPSHAPE
SHREWD   SIMPLISTIC   SINGLE-HANDED

SPONTANEOUS   SPEEDY   SPLENDID
SPOTLESS   STAGGERING   STIMULANT
STRENUOUS   STRICT   STRINGENT

STRONG   STRONG-MINDED   STRONG-WILLED
STUPENDOUS   SUBSTANTIAL   SUCCESSFUL
SUPERB   SUPERFINE   SUPERIOR

SUPERLATIVE   SUPPORTIVE   SUPREME
SURPASSING   SWIFT   TENACIOUS
TERRIFIC   THRIFTY   TOUGH

TOUGH-MINDED   TRENCHANT   ULTIMATE
UNBEATABLE   UNBOUNDED   UNEQUIVOCAL
UNERRING   UNFAILING   UNPARALLELED

UNQUESTIONABLE   UNRIVALED   UNYIELDING
UNSTOPPABLE   VALUABLE   VIGILANT
WELL-DEFINED   WELL-DONE   WELL-FOUNDED

WELL-HANDLED   WELL-MEANING   WELL-KNOWN
WELL-OFF   WELL-ROUNDED   WELL-TIMED
WIDE-RANGING   WONDROUS   WORTHFUL

WORTHWHILE   WORTHY   YOUTHFUL

POSITIVE, ACTIVE - NOUNS

ACHIEVEMENT   ACME   ACTIVATION
AGITATOR   ALACRITY   ANXIOUSNESS
APEX   AROUSAL   ASPIRATION

ASSET   AVERSION   BRAINSTORM
CAMARADERIE   CATALYST   COMMENDATION
COMPLEXITY   COMPLIMENT   CONTRIBUTION

CONTROVERSY   CRISIS   DIEHARD
DRIVE   EMBODIMENT   EMULATION
ENCHANTMENT   ENCOURAGEMENT   ENDEAVOR

ENERGY   ENJOYMENT   ENTERPRISE
EXCELLENCE   EXCITEMENT   EXPECTATION
EXPEDIENCE   EXPERIENCE   EXPEDIENCY

EXUBERANCE   FASCINATION   FEAT
FIRST   FIRST CLASS   FOCUS
FORCE   FRENZY   GIMMICK

GRANDEUR   GRAVITY   HEADWAY
IDEAL   IMMEDIACY   IMPETUS
IMPORTANCE   INCITEMENT   IMPROVEMENT

IMPROVISATION   INCENTIVE   INDUCEMENT
INFLUENCE   INNOVATION   JEST
JESTER   KEYNOTE   KILTER

KINK   KUDO   LANDMARK
LIFE BLOOD   MANIPULATION   MASTERY
MAXIM   MERIT   MIGHT

MOTIVE   NURTURE   ORDEAL
PARADOX   PASSION   PASSIONATE
PECULIARITY   PERFECTION   PERSEVERANCE

PERSONIFICATION PERSUASION PLAUDIT
PLEASURE POTENCY POWER
POWERHOUSE PRECISION PREMIUM

PREPAREDNESS PREPOTENCY PROGRESS
PROMOTER PROMPTITUDE PROPONENT
PROPOSAL PROSPERITY PROTOTYPE

PUNDIT QUALITY QUERY
QUEST QUIRK RADIANCE
REDRESS RESILIENCE RIVAL

SACRIFICE SCRUTINY SELF-ASSERTION
SELF-EXAMINATION SELF-IMAGE SEVERITY
SIMPLICITY SPARK SPEARHEAD

SPECTACLE STIMULUS STRENGTH
SUCCESS SUPERLATIVE SUPPORTER
SUPREMACY SWIFTNESS TASKMASTER

TENACITY THRIFT VITALIZATION
WONDERWORK

ACTIVE, POSITIVE - VERBS

ABET ACHIEVE ADVOCATE
ANIMATE AGITATE ANALYZE
ANTICIPATE APPLAUD AROUSE

ASPIRE ASSERT AVOID
BOLSTER CAPITALIZE CIRCUMVENT
COMMEND COMPEL COMPLICATE

CONCEIVE CONFRONT CONTRIBUTE
CONTRIVE CREATE CULTIVATE
DELVE DETER DEVISE

DOMINATE ELICIT EMERGE
EMBODY EMULATE ENDEAVOR
ENERGIZE ENFORCE ENRICH

ENTHUSE ENTICE ERADICATE
ERUPT ESCALATE ESTABLISH
EXCEED EXCITE EXHORT

EXPAND	EXPEDITE	EXPLOIT
EXPLORE	EXPOSTULATE	FABRICATE
FACILITATE	FINE-TUNE	FORMULATE
FORTIFY	FULFILL	GENERATE
GLORIFY	GRIND OUT	HASTEN
HONE	HURDLE	IGNITE
ILLUSTRATE	IMMERGE	IMMERSE
IMPEL	IMPOSE	IMPRESS
IMPROVE	IMPROVISE	INCITE
INDUCE	INFECT	INFUSE
INITIATE	INNOVATE	INSPIRIT
INSTIGATE	INSTILL	INTEGRATE
INTERFUSE	INTRIGUE	INVIGORATE
JOSH	JUGGLE	KINDLE
KNUCKLE DOWN	LAUNCH	MINGLE
MANIPULATE	NOURISH	ORGANIZE
ORIGINATE	OUTLAST	OVERCOME
OVERSEE	OVERWHELM	PERPETUATE
PERPLEX	PERSEVERE	PERSIST
PERSUADE	PREPARE	PROD
PROLIFERATE	PROMOTE	PROPAGATE
PROPEL	PROPONE	PROSPER
PROVOKE	PURGE	QUANTIFY
QUICKEN	RALLY	RECTIFY
REDRESS	REFINE	REFORM
REFUTE	REHABILITATE	REJUVENATE
RENEW	RENOVATE	REORGANIZE
RESURGE	REVIVE	SCRUTINIZE
SPARK	SPEARHEAD	SPURT
STIMULATE	STRENGTHEN	STRIVE
STOKE	SURPASS	THRIVE
TRANSFORM	ZENITH	

BULLETS & PHRASES

What is a "bullet phrase?" A bullet phrase is a statement that may or may not have a verb, object, or subject. Bullet phrases serve to reduce the amount of space required to make a statement. Thus, using bullet phrases allows more material to be covered in the same space, or the same amount of material in less space, than in formal sentence structure.

EXAMPLE OF FORMAL SENTENCE STRUCTURE:

"He is highly intelligent, possesses a stimulating imagination, and routinely provides sound advice and recommendations for anticipated problems."

EXAMPLE OF BULLET/PHRASE:

"Highly intelligent, stimulating imagination, provides sound advice and recommendations."

The samples in this chapter are in bullet phrase form. They can be combined or used independently. The samples can be either shortened more, or they can be turned into complete sentences.

The sample bullet phrases are broken down into three basic categories to allow for ease of use. Although categorized into specific trait areas, many have universal application.

BULLET PHRASES - FAVORABLE

PERSONAL, PERSONALITY TRAITS

...Perceptive and alert
...Courteous nature
...Composed and calm

...Energetic spirit
...Great mental grasp
...Optimistic outlook

...A quick thinker
...Exceptional orator
...Personal magnetism

...Sincere and uncommonly likable
...Always enthusiastic
...Friendly and cheerful

...Strong moral fiber
...Emotionally stable
...Impeccable character

...Sound judgment
...Thoughtful and caring by nature
...Mentally alert

...Quick to learn
...Mental sharpness
...Bold, forward thinker

...Amiable, good natured
...Agreeable, pleasant personality
...Creatively inclined

...Admired courage
...Firm and resolute
...Pleasing personality

...Never gives up
...Frank and forward
...Capable of independent decision

...Cheerful, helpful personality
...Interesting, convincing speaker
...Projects air of dignity

...Great raw ability and talent
...Talented and charismatic
...Stimulating intelligence

...Calm and affable manner
...Interesting conversationalist
...Thirst for knowledge

...Broad and varied intellect
...Powerful, influential figure
...Alert, energetic personality

...Humorous and witty personality
...Sound of mind and judgment
...Sensitive and understanding

...Open minded
...Quick to perceive and act
...Determined and dedicated

...Honest, respectful reputation
...Contributes innovative ideas
...Intrepid, resolute drive

...Great personal drive
...Keen sense of ethical conduct
...Sharp mental keenness

...Exercises sound judgment
...Clear, orderly self-expression
...Resilient, resolute personality

...Resourceful and dedicated
...Honest and faithful
...Innovative and imaginative

...Advanced knowledge
...Presence and poise
...Matchless ingenuity

...Highly motivated
...Good common sense
...Extensive knowledge

..."Can do" enthusiasm
...Analytical mind
...Boundless energy

...Intellectual courage
...Thinks and plans ahead
...Exceedingly articulate

...Sound, prudent judgment
...High ethical principles
...Endless zeal and courage

...Relentless drive and ambition
...Well-calculated actions
...High personal integrity

...Briskly alert and energetic
...Keen rational powers
...Retentive mind

...Persuasive talker
...Great self control
...Matchless desire

...Unflagging zeal
...Keen sense of humor
...Self-motivated

...Great personal courage
...Organized and industrious
...Exercises sound judgment

...Stimulating imagination
...Full of energy and vitality
...Warm, friendly personality

...Spirit of inquiry and drive
...Optimistic outlook and attitude
...Correct mental approach

...Personal vision and courage
...Unlimited learning capacity
...Quick, penetrating mind

...Dominating spiritual force
...Cleverness and guild
...Stands behind principles

...Proper personal behavior
...Clear in thought
...Strong will of mind

...Even tempered
...Industrious nature
...Firm, caring attitude

...Engenders trust
...Well organized
...Brilliant, lively wit

...Emotionally stable
...Mentally and physically able
...Has vision and foresight

...Shrewdly astute and alert
...Adapts with uncommon ease
...Relentless drive and desire

...Confident of abilities
...Strong spirit and character
...Discriminating mind

...A pillar of strength
...Emotionally mature
...Inquisitive mind

...Sparks excitement
...Strongly motivated
...Results oriented

...Unequaled personal demeanor
...Has pride and self-assurance
...Well-adjusted personally

...Grasps essentials quickly
...Unyielding fair-mindedness
...Great verbal dexterity

...Shows courage under pressure
...Resilient and energetic
...Composed under pressure

...Boundless analytical ability
...Personal devotion to duty
...Radiates energy and enthusiasm

...Genuine concern for others
...Unwavering self-reliance
...Impeccable moral character

...Competitive, winning spirit
...Elegant and cultivated manner
...Convincing, persuasive talker

...Confident of abilities
...Acute, thorough thinker
...Good-natured and friendly

...Creative writing ability
...Keenly analytical individual
...Firm, resolute character

...Versatile, multi-disciplined
...Loyal, devoted subordinate
...Dynamic, energetic personality

...Proper and correct manner
...Full of energy and ability
...Alert, energetic personality

...Mentally artful and skillful
...Effervescent personality
...Unselfish and trusting

...Probing personality
...Mental courage
...A winning spirit

...Great foresight
...Mentally alert
...Articulate speaker

...Thoughtful of others
...Kind in manner
...Energetic personality

...Inspiring imagination
...Cheerful readiness
...Ingenious nature

...Refined personality
...Vision for the future
...Eager and capable

...Forward-thinking
...Skilled innovator
...Positive attitude

...Engaging personality
...Intellectually gifted
...Highly motivated

...Commanding presence
...Never loses temper
...A self-starter

...Strong initiative
...Creatively inclined
...Sound character

...Cordial and affable
...Exudes optimism
...Clear discerning wit

...Exacting nature
...Vibrant personality
...Good academic aptitude

...Kind, amiable disposition
...Forthright, confident manner
...Erect, trim in carriage

...Develops logical priorities
...Friendly, cooperative attitude
...Meticulously well groomed

...Self-motivated and resourceful
...Commands large vocabulary
...Boundless enthusiasm and energy

...Has high ideals, morals, and ethics
...Acts responsibly in all situations
...Unshakable, unyielding character

...Strongly motivated to succeed
...Originates well thought ideas
...Confident, easy-going mannerism

...Fosters friendly goodwill
...Ability to succeed
...Strong desire and ability to learn

...Polished, persuasive speaker
...Kind, benign disposition
...Never in doubt or confused

...Highly perceptive intellect
...Amicable, friendly disposition
...Great intellectual awareness

...Keeps composure under pressure
...Courteous and respectful manner
...Curious and inquisitive nature

...Great mental agility and skill
...Has endless zeal and courage
...Influential, persuasive personality

...Fully developed sense of loyalty
...Extremely energetic & enthusiastic
...Cooperative, cheerful personality

...Friendly and sociable
...Fighting enthusiasm
...Strength of character

...Sense of propriety
...Dares to dream
...Eager willingness

...Powerful figure
...Fresh, new ideas
...Forward-thinking

...Clear and logical in thought
...Always ahead of the action
...Indestructible sense of humor

...At ease in any situation
...Highly motivated achiever
...Displays an air of dignity

...Articulate, well groomed
...Impressive ability & motivation
...Abundant energy & enthusiasm

...Intellectually active
...Mentally quick & resourceful
...Energetic, resilient personality

...Ethical, honest personality
...Original, imaginative thinker
...Cheerful and good-natured

...Innovative and productive
...Positive attitude is profound
...Stays calm and collective

...Always a willing volunteer
...Clear, analytical mind
...Friendly, radiant personality

...Imaginative and inventive mind
...Firm and fair
...Decisive and efficacious

...Has practical, prudent wisdom
...Refreshing, lively personality
...High morality and ethical principles

...Even, steadying temperament
...Thoughtful and caring by nature
...Stable, well-adjusted personality

...Affable, pleasant personality
...Studious, perceptive, active mind
...Mentally alert, physically ready

...Quick and decisive in action
...Mannerly, courteous & polite
...Has vision for the future

...Persuasive, convincing speaker
...Relentless drive & dedication
...Has emotional stability and strength

...Pleasant manner & personality
...Thorough professional knowledge
...Always proper in manner & behavior

...Excellent foresight ability
...Straightforward and above board
...Strong loyalty and sense of duty

...Full of courage and compassion
...An intelligent & inquisitive mind
...Well informed sense of judgment

...Mentally quick and resourceful
...Magnetic charm and appeal
...Great initiative and persistence

...Of impeccable character
...Quick in mind
...Alert and responsive

...High ambition and achiever
...Creative and artistic nature
...Graceful in manner

...Commanding in presence
...Dominant personality
...Prompt in response

...Cheerful in nature
...Plans ahead
...Great inter-discipline

...Intense, eager performer
...Logical and coherent mind
...Intellectually productive

...Genuine concern for others
...Unselfish dedication to duty
...A front runner

...Positive, cooperative spirit
...Proven capacity to lead
...Matchless ingenuity

...Will not accept status quo
...Full of vigor and ability
...Calm & controlled personality

...Strong personality & will
...Pleasing, sincere personality
...Seasoned arbitrator

...Performs with aggressiveness of a zealot
..."Can do" attitude and amicable personality booster morale
...Progressive outlook, resilient and resolute personality

...Discriminates between fact and fiction
...Never caught off guard or loses sight of important developments
...Analytical mind, adaptable to changing situations

Gives quality results in any endeavor or situation
...Good Samaritan, dedicated to helping others
...Few people work harder or have more innate talent

...Intellectually gifted, technically experienced, always highly motivated
...Articulate in self-expression and innate ability to think logically
...Probing personality, quick to pick up on things

...Extremely friendly and sociable nature
...Can view situation as a whole in terms of its component parts, sort out
      pertinent facts, and come to realistic conclusion
...Effective in relating point of view and in winning an unbiased listener

...Possesses mental courage to stand on principles
...Dedicated, results-oriented individual
...A relentless drive and dedication evidenced in all endeavors

...A superb speaker who can stoke teamwork & cooperation
...Good ability to learn and understand, and then put that information to
      good use
...Sound in thought, good in judgment

...Unlimited capacity for solving difficult problems
...A proper blend of personal candor and sound professional judgment
...Exercises mature judgment and meticulous precision to detail

...Skilled, eloquent speaker and writer
...Has courage of character to challenge and forge ahead into new areas
...Exceptional professional competence and intellectual capacity

...Possesses finest personal qualities and moral strength
...Intelligent, inquisitive, and confident
...Long-standing record of creditability, loyalty, and dedication

...Drives to success by self-motivation and strong sense of purpose
...Uses common sense to tackle problems
...Logical in decision making process

...Does not await direction or guidance to proceed with task at hand
...Noteworthy demeanor and presence
...Demonstrates understanding and genuine concern for health and
      welfare of others

...Presents succinctly and eloquently prepared briefs
...Has presence of mind to act correctly during critical and short-fused situations
...Exceptional personal drive and energy

...Analytical thought process knows no bounds
...Daily actions marked by efficiency and practical logic
...Remains flexible and cooperative under any conditions

...Earned wide reputation for warm personality
...Friendly disposition, and total professionalism
...Never shows despair or resignation in face of seemingly insurmountable odds or problems

...Without equal in personal demeanor
...A pillar of high moral purpose and strength
...Individual drive and motivation are refreshing

...Innate ability to get to crux of any problem and provide correct fix
...Fully capable of meeting new situations in resourceful manner
...Great intellectual energy and capacity

...Has practical knowledge and skill, and the ambition to put to good use
...Not restrained in ideas by conventional thought processes
...Strength of character to tackle any assignment

...Irrepressible curiosity and ability to fix things
...Exhibits highest standards of loyalty, integrity, and personal behavior
...Has the will and courage to succeed, despite the tasking

...Converts ideas into positive action
...Possesses good judgment and foresight
...Mental capacity to properly weigh and evaluate complex matters

...Unmatched capacity and appetite for learning
...Positive mental attitude and outlook
...Ability to see through problem areas and provide fruitful solutions

...Innate ability to grasp and understand perplexing matters
...Thorough in nature, exercises sound and logical judgment
...Inspires self-improvement in others through sterling personal example

...Possesses unrestrained enthusiasm
...Faces demanding challenges head-on
...Courage of conviction and high sense of professional pride

...Talented and charismatic with a terrific sense of humor
...Bubbling enthusiasm permeates entire organization
...Expressed thoughts and opinions routinely prevail

...Imaginative skill and mental dexterity always produce quality results
...Thoughts are well written and orally expressed
...High ethical principles, and sound, sensible judgment

...Abundant initiative and personal drive
...Rational, logical, and responsive to all tasking
...Discriminates between important and inconsequential matters

...Enthusiasm and demeanor noteworthy
...Clear and positive in self-expression
...Refined presence and dignified manner

...Demonstrates sound, mature judgment
...Articulate and precise in speech and the written word
...Learning ability and growth potential unlimited

...Pursues new ideas with great success
...Innovative, always coming up with something better or improved
...Enjoys mental challenge of resolving complex problems and situations

...Friendly, enchanting personality
...Originates highly accurate and professionally written reports
...Stimulating, persuasive conversationalist

...Unending drive and urge for success
...Boundless enthusiasm and capacity for work
...Not limited or restrained by conventional thought

...Explores all situations and possibilities and then makes best use of
        available resources
...Possesses great moral strength, personal drive, and energy
...Amicable personality spiced with good wit and humor

...Thrives on pressures of immediacy and responds resourcefully with
        innovative suggestions
...Interesting speaker, convincing conversationalist
...Continually exhibits highest standards of loyalty, integrity and personal
        behavior

...Displays exceptional energy and drive
...Stands above contemporaries in personal commitment to
	professionalism and excellence
...Resourceful, respected & inspired

...Boundless enthusiasm and energy
...Wide diversity of personal and professional talent
...Feeds on adverse conditions that others would shun if given the
	opportunity

...Engaging and engrossing personality
...Capable of independent decision and action
...Outstanding attitude and good humor are major morale builders

...Impeccable personal moral character and behavior
...Steadfast, loyal dedication to duty and superiors
...Polished, persuasive speaker with an agreeable manners

...A strong advocate of equal opportunity
...Creative thinking and innovative problem solving techniques
...Written products are clear and cogent

...Fair and without prejudice
...Readlly embraces precepts of equal opportunity
...Well mannered with pleasant personality

...Excellent ablIlty to enunciate new ideas verbally and in writing
...Keen intellectual perception
...Composed, not easily excited under stress or pressure

...Possesses highest personal integrity
...Eager and interested in all professional matters, with a deep sense of
	responsibility
...Mentally quick and active, capable of complex reasoning

...Unequaled academic abilities and accomplishments
...Strong, positive drive toward professional excellence
...A constant source of innovative, workable ideas

...Intelligent and mentally stable with an orderly mind
...Personable, professional, and highly respected for point of view
...Selects logical and correct courses of action

...Especially skilled at painting vivid word picture in written and oral form
...Unquenchable thirst for knowledge
...Capable of good spontaneous judgment and decision making

...Unbeatable character and personality
...Contributes many innovative, workable solutions to complex problems
...Mentally skillful, unhesitant in action

...Possesses the utmost degree of accuracy and attentiveness
...A take charge attitude with great personal industry
...Mind is quick, innovative, and decisive

...Ready wit and an outgoing personality
...Capable of orderly and rational reasoning
...Stable in character, resolute in action

...Calm and composed in stressful situations
...Has high moral principles and personal values
...Continually seeks personal growth and development

...Methodical and highly conscientious
...An innovative and creative mind and manner
...Readily takes initiative for additional responsibilities

...Work is marked by initiative, integrity and excellence
...Dependable and reliable with uncompromising principles
...A pillar of moral strength and courage

...Possesses an impressive breadth of experience and knowledge, and
        knows how to use both to best advantage
...Dignified in presence and appearance
...Completely self-reliant with vast intellectual capacity

...Demonstrates ability to cope with stress-filled circumstances
...Possesses high personal moral standards
...Endless energy, initiative, and positive spirit

...Continually strives for, and achieves, self-improvement and professional
        development
...Tremendous personal courage and self-discipline
...Endless constructive mental energy

...Fair, open-minded, and unbiased in reason and action
...Has a friendly personality and a quick wit
...Displays compassion, decisiveness, and determination

...Highly developed sense of responsibility
...Keen sense of fair play, and intense advocacy of individual and human
      rights
...Communicates ideas and thoughts with ease and clarity

...Great personal initiative and drive for success
...Capable of independent thought and action
...Possessed of fine sense of moral prudence

...Makes independent decisions that have merit and substance
...Unafraid of rendering decisions despite some personal risks
...Special talent for areas requiring intellectual challenge

...Positive attitude, good common sense
...Fully developed purpose and sense of pride
...Well rounded individual with a diversity of talents and interests

...Exercises sound judgment in practical matters
...Has the mental faculty and attitude to lead others with great success
...Exhibits confident composure under stress

...Firmness of mind in face of difficulty
...Will, determination, and sense of purpose for job accomplishment
...Decisive in mind, determined in action

...Has strength of mind and character to accept and meet challenges
      beyond the scope and range of contemporaries
...Shows courage and determination in the face of adversity
...Possesses intellectual courage

...Has strong will, desire, and ability to succeed
...Extremely self-confident of abilities without being cock- sure
...Personal integrity is unassailable

...Actions and plans are calculated and well thought out in advance
...Strong will of mind and commanding presence
...Demonstrates considerable finesse and diplomacy

...Immensely rational, logical, and responsive to tasking
...Sensitive to needs and desires of others
...Amicable personality with social grace

...Has great moral strength and courage
...Uses own initiative to get things going in positive direction
...Sincere manner and caring nature

...Possesses requisite competence and aptitude to accomplish the most
    demanding tasks
...Always presents the proper mental attitude
...Ingrained strong pursuit of excellence

...Affects others with own enduring enthusiasm, pride and professionalism
...Has inquisitive mind and exacting nature
...Keen, enthusiastic desire for success

...Possesses abundance of zeal, enthusiasm, and exuberance
...Discriminates between important and unimportant
...Gets the job done correctly and timely

...Poised, adept, and well adjusted mentally
...Friendly and good-fellowship highlight personal traits
...Energetic with no wasted motions or actions

...Never lacking in spirit or exuberance
...Ideas and suggestions well organized and thought out and have
    considerable substance
...Ceaseless personal devotion to duty always in evidence

...Blessed with good sense of humor and compassion
...Can bring disagreeing parties into agreement and
    harmony
...Willing to stand up for principles and beliefs

...Spoken and written word punctuated by correctness and exactness
...Takes minor setbacks in full stride, keeps a clear mental picture of what
    is ahead
...Completely without bias or prejudice

...Polite, elegant, and graceful in manner
...Impressive posture and appearance
...Does not panic when faced with temporary or minor obstacles

...Effervescent and enchanting personality
...Judicious, sound decision-making facilities

FAVORABLE
LEADERSHIP, MANAGEMENT, & ADMINISTRATION

...Sound management procedures
...Inspires others
...Stirs the imagination

...Spreads infectious enthusiasm
...Creative management initiatives
...Exemplifies ideal leader

...Firm, resolute leader
...Bolsters spirits
...Always an inspiration

...Prompt, diligent administrator
...Inspires performance
...Astute money manager

...Skillful, direct leadership
...Promotes harmonious atmosphere
...Positive motivator

...Firm, yet fair leader
...Real morale booster
...Accomplished leader

...Respected by others
...Leads by example
...Uncommon leadership

...Inspires greatness
...Morally fair and just
...Uncommon leader perceptiveness

...Encourages professional pride
...No-nonsense leader
...Agile leadership

...Watchful, discerning manager
...Interested in others
...Impressive leader

...A real motivator
...Arouses and excites interest
...Molds character and courage

...Composed leader
...Fosters goodwill
...Good organizer

...Promotes sound leadership
...Accomplished counselor
...Takes charge, a real leader

...Exciting leader
...Firm, sympathetic leader
...Natural team leader

...Astute, experienced leader
...Adroit administrator
...Spirited, determined leader

...Inspires and encourages
...Unparalleled leadership
...Motivates and leads others

...Instills pride and purpose
...Well-rounded leadership skills
...Recognizes top performer

...Meticulous administrator
...Actively promotes human rights
...Stirs up enthusiasm

...Charismatic leader
...Knows success is team effort
...Concerned, caring leader

...Inquisitive leader
...Has personal leadership magic
...Sensitive to needs of others

...Inspires confidence
...Unifying presence
...An accomplished counselor

...Has "follow me" confidence
...Propagates goodwill and trust
...Aggressive management acumen

...Motivates others
...Stirs the imagination
...Inspires subordinates

...Impressive leadership record
...Engenders trust and confidence
...Instills loyalty and pride

...Tactful leader and motivator
...Enforces subordinate development
...Supports self-dignity and worth

...Capacity to successfully lead others
...Varied background and experience
...Invigorating supervisor and leader

...Promotes harmony & teamwork
...Equitable and impartial leadership
...Exhibits high trust level in subordinates

...An extremely perceptive individual
...Dedicated to betterment of others
...Has inspiring enthusiasm & spirit

...Invigorating, successful leader
...Extremely perceptive & hard working
...Instills pride and dignity in others

...Artful management of resources
...Compassionate, caring leader
...Superb material management

...Reputation for dependable results
...A forceful leadership figure
...Serious minded leadership

...Frank, direct leader
...Solid material manager
...Selfless leader

...Imposing presence
...Positive influence
...Team leader

...Vigorous leadership style
...Promotes esprit de corps
...Innate managerial skills

...Runs cohesive organization
...Fully taxes subordinates
...Inspires the imagination

...Generates self-confidence
...Engenders self-development
...Exuberant, enthusiastic leader

...Inspires zeal and obedience
...Manager extraordinary
...Keen managerial abilities

...Strict yet firm disciplinarian
...Possesses sound listening skills
...Charismatic leader

...Exceptionally fine administrator
...Epitome of tactful leadership
...Intense, compassionate leader

...Potent, productive leader
...Brings out best in others
...Concerned, caring leader

...Able leader, adept counselor
...Vigorous leadership
...Extremely versatile leader

...A good sense of organization
...Strong, decisive leader
...Astute manager of assets

...Fosters unparalleled productivity
...Persuasive and tactful leader
...Responsive to needs of others

...Own enthusiasm infiltrates the ranks
...Intolerant of mediocre performance
...Creates team spirit and unity

...Unflagging zeal and dedication
...Self-motivated & enthusiastic
...Unlimited capacity for challenge

...A master of positive leadership
...Truly cares about people
...Concerned and caring leader

...Solid leader and manager
...Tactful leader
...Exercises sound leadership principles

...A radiant, confident leader
...Friendly, congenial & cheerful
...Popular among peers

...A real morale booster
...Well liked and respected
...Unfailing devotion to duty

...Impressive manager & leader
...Frank & fair leadership
...Dedicated leader

...A real leader
...Quality leader
...A real motivator

...Action oriented

...Polished, mature leader, thinks and acts rationally
...Outstanding rapport with subordinates
...Able to extract the most from each individual

...Tailors leadership to the person and task at hand
...Careful, exact planner who gets positive results
...An exceptional leader, manager and organizer

...Has strong leadership attributes, strong desire to excel
...Displays genuine sincerity and concern for others
...Works on subordinate career planning and work development

...Inspire others to act decisively under stressful situations
...Establishes and enforces firm, sound management practices
...Generates positive attitude and spirit throughout the ranks

...Ability to make correct decisions in stressful situations
...Extremely accurate and careful about administrative detail
...Top candidate for increased positions of leadership

...Alert, perceptive, prompt-to-act manager
...Experienced, knowledgeable manager
...Energetic personality, stimulating leader

...Genuinely and warmly respected by all
...Takes charge and makes positive things happen
...Prudent, economical use of resources

...Skillful employment of personnel resources
...Wins support and maximum effort of others
...Has a special flair for expert management of assets

...Individual vitality and "can do" spirit has permeated entire organization
...A "leader by example" who obtains superior results
...Helps individuals recognize self-dignity and worth

...Strong, effective personal counseling and leadership abilities
...Displays uncommon leadership, enthusiasm, and initiative
...Molded efficient, smooth-running organization

...Organization enjoys high morale and unusually low discipline rate
...Always contributes 110% to team effort
...Able to assist others solve personal problems

...Excites and arouses others to action
...Leadership style elicits productive vigor
...Fosters complete harmony and teamwork

...A dynamic, motivating leader, achieves maximum success
...Always contributes maximum effort and energy
...Sets positive, realistic expectations and standards

...Unified and coherent management philosophy
...Consistently the leading element in implementing new procedures
...Animating leader, arouses enthusiasm and interest in others

...Gets others to come together for common purpose and action
...Breathed new life into a declining organization
...Demonstrates strong aptitude for administrative work

...Has firm grip on organizational management procedures
...Meticulous record keeping and timely submission of reports
...Encourages striving for excellence among subordinates

...Establishes an exciting and professional work environment
...A hard working individual who takes charge and gets the job done
...Consistently places mission first, personal interest second

...Reaches maximum efficiency without stretching assets too thinly
...Supervises and directs others with goal of improving professional skills
...Unqualified success as a leader and manager

...Can quickly identify and fix problem areas
...Provides calm, patient leadership to more junior personnel
...Met every diverse demand and challenge though exceptional ability to lead and motivate others

...Through personal effort heightened career awareness and self development
...A personal morale builder to every member of the organization
...A dynamic leader and vigorous worker

...Exhibits genuine concern for welfare of subordinates
...Encourages trust through genuine interest in others
...Dedicated to mission purpose, and displays firm and caring attitude

...Direct, hard-line leader with unyielding character
...Sets example anyone would do well to follow
...Does not hesitate to provide assistance to those in need

...Contributed directly to improving mission readiness and accomplishment
...Stimulates professional growth on others
...Provides training and counseling in weak areas

...Capitalizes on individual strengths
...Successfully researched various important projects and staff work
...Applies strict application of discipline and control

...Gives 100 percent loyalty and leadership support to chain of command
...Accomplished manager, attains all desired ends
...Alert, astute manager, can turn negative situations to advantage

...The personification of a dynamic and caring leader
...Ideally suited for top management and leadership positions
...Positive attitude generates enthusiasm at all levels

...Provides corrective counseling in positive, fruitful manner
...Achieves unusually high standards of performance from others
...Industrious manner and ability to get a job done correctly

... Inspires great trust and confidence in others
...Skillful manager with proven ability to get things done
...Unique ability to reach a troubled person and provide sound counseling

...Strong professional attitude radiates to others and causes them to
    respond with their full, best effort
...Calm, sincere and constructive counseling techniques
...Informed leader who genuinely cares about the well being of others

...Consistent outstanding professional and supervisory ability
...Sets stringent, achievable performance standards for subordinates
...Unwavering self-reliance in daily performance of duties

...Adapts leadership style to changing personnel and situations
...Earned personal trust and confidence of each individual
...Economically sound management practices

...Good leader, creates excitement and enthusiasm for the job at hand
...Establishes and pursues precise, clear-cut goals
...Performed multitude of administrative tasks with enviable punctuality and
    error free productivity

...Possesses unique ability to quickly and effectively train and direct
    inexperienced personnel
...Considerate for the feelings of others
...Treats others with dignity and self-respect

...Thoroughly proficient and efficient manager
...Fair, impartial, and honest treatment of others
...Continually provided calm and methodical leadership, creating a solid
    confidence that spread throughout the ranks

...Skillful direction and counseling ensure few problems
...Concerned for the welfare and interest of others
...Exceptionally adept at fine-tuning administrative matters

...Keeps organization on an even keel
...A catalyst of teamwork and high morale
...Earns the admiration and respect of subordinates

...Provides vital, life-giving leadership
...Artfully leads and controls subordinates
...Skillful in leading others to desired goals

...Leadership merits special praise and gratitude
...Provides inner drive to others that moves them to positive action
...Nurtures subordinate professional development

...Ability to create and maintain confidence and respect throughout
the ranks
...Always willing to share time and considerable talent with others
...Consistently demands and receives only the best from others

...Professional competence enhanced by adept ability to interact
harmoniously with others
...Gives others strong sense of direction without dulling their initiative
...Possesses unending ability to generate enthusiasm

...Actively enforces equal opportunity programs and goals
...Humane concern for others tempered by professional concern to fulfill
organizational commitments
...Quick to offer positive advice to others

...Embodies finest qualities of leadership

..Successfully couples strong professional drive for excellence with
sincere concern for welfare of others
...Displays aggressive and imaginative management acumen

...Admirable blend of tact and direct leadership
...Potent and productive supervisor, overcomes difficulties
...A demanding leader who gets impressive results

...Many personal accomplishments are impressive
...Fosters unity and spirit of pride throughout the ranks
...Possesses well developed, positive counseling techniques

...Provides valuable solutions to complex problems
...Highly respected leader and organizer
...Regularly worked long hours. Worked longer hours when necessary

...Inspires others to exhibit pride and dedication
...Personal contributions to morale have been a welcomed shot in the arm
...Calm and stable leader in crisis situations

...Arouses interest and maximum effort in team efforts
...Engenders trust and confidence throughout the ranks
...Demonstrates superb leadership and unbridled enthusiasm

...Contributed immeasurably to high morale
...Provides vigorous and work-aggressive leadership
...Perfect combination of direct leadership and compassion

...Superb leadership resulted in unequaled performance
...Ability to immediately establish and maintain excellent rapport
...A guiding and steadying influence on subordinates

...Master at providing direction and tactful leadership
...Management expertise and skilled leadership principles are personal
     trademarks
...A proven leader of unbounded ability

...Bold and imaginative leadership techniques
...Provided commendable results in many stressful leadership situations
...Instituted rigorous training program proved tremendously successful

...Establishes and maintains atmosphere of pride in accomplishment
...Poised, mature leader with an authoritative manner and presence
...Attains positive results regardless of tasking difficulty

...Detailed planning with positive results
...Provides positive guidance that improves skill level of others
...Superior knowledge of operations and administrative matters

...Provides energizing, stimulating leadership
...An assertive and considerate leader who gets results
...Dominating influence in any organization

...A proponent of strong, solid leadership
...Great faculty for exercising command and control
...Provides skillful direction to subordinates

...Impressive ability to motivate others
...Ignites the human spirit by providing assertive, positive leadership
...Concerned, caring leader, allows people to grow in new directions

...Ingrained aggressive pursuit of excellence
...Displays quality leadership and unstinting commitment to job
     accomplishment and excellence
...Possesses innate managerial skills

...Can quickly grasp management principles and concepts
...Leads with intensity, force, and energy
...High morale and exceptional enthusiasm demonstrated on a daily basis

...Highly motivated leader whose commitment to job accomplishment
        consistently results in highest quality
...Instituted rigid accountability in all areas
...Stands head and shoulders above peers

...Stimulates creative effort and work of others
...Compiled impressive record over a broad range of matters
...Astute and close scrutiny of assets ensured most effective use of scarce
        personnel and equipment resources.

...Doesn't get entangled in day-to-day individual problems
...Sets and achieves multiple long-range goals and objectives
...Made visible impact on intangible areas of pride & morale

...Great ability to plan and direct group operations and activities
...Actions produced immediate and lasting positive results
...Delegates responsibility wisely and successfully

...Spent extensive hours during high tempo operations assessing
        personnel capabilities and limitations
...Knows and understands worth and dignity of others and successfully
        integrates this human element in daily leadership
...Provides timely recognition for superior performance

...Rewards superior performance. Corrects substandard performance
...Develops subordinates at a rapid pace
...Makes optimum use of assigned personnel

...A personal and professional inspiration to each member of the command
...Firmly and fairly enforces rules and standards
...Equitable treatment of each individual optimized morale and increased
        command effectiveness

...Keen sense of fair play & intense advocacy of individual human rights
...Always active, but never too busy to listen to personal problems and
        provide sound advice
...Personal leadership has measurably improved overall organizational
        performance and readiness

...An individual who commands the fullest respect and support of others
...Encourages off-duty education and professional growth
...Fosters high morale and a total winning attitude and spirit

...Built a corps of supervisors who take pride in "taking charge" and
　　　　working together in cohesive, productive manner
...Instills constructive loyalty up and down the ranks
...Knows how to lead people, and more importantly, knows where to take
　　　　them

...Outstanding success as a negotiator, group leader, and arbitrator
...Extremely well liked and respected
...Displayed unique ability to grasp a broad scope of responsibilities

...Managed an incredible number of details associated with job
...Characteristic courage and coolness under pressure
...Provided steadying influence to others

...A quality leader with ability to lead others
...Led organization to an unparalleled high level of performance
...Inspires others to join in a common effort and team goal

...A natural instructor with exceptional ability
...Unique ability to coordinate group efforts
...Goals far exceed requirements of assigned duties and position

...Unwavering support and endless ability in meeting mission requirements
...Takes personal interest in welfare and well-being of others
...Creates favorable work environment for others

...Instills motivation in others by own willingness to listen and learn
...Provides valuable resolutions to wide range of problems
...Has positive leadership qualities that help mold any organization into
　　　　cohesive, productive unit

...Demands and receives positive results
...When in charge, successful conclusion never in doubt
...Serves as focus of loyalty to chain of command

...A take-charge individual
...Displays strong initiative and an infectious enthusiasm
...Strength of character and natural team leader traits mainstay of a well
　　　　rounded leadership style

...Leads unified and proud team of professionals
...Has the leadership spirit to lead people into action
...Personifies leadership by example

...Establishes and enforces clear-cut goals
...Organizational leadership contributes immeasurably to morale
...Enriches team spirit and pride in accomplishment

...Persistent and exceptional efforts were important factors in steadily
      improving organization quality and efficiency
...Repeatedly demonstrated exceptional leadership and initiative
...Professional expertise and personal involvement are cornerstones of
      individual leadership and management success

...Gives others helping hand and a pat on the back when most needed
...Diligent efforts and resourcefulness inspired others
...Greatly contributed to mission accomplishment

...Early identification of deficiencies led to incalculable savings in
      manpower and money
...A dynamic individual whose strong loyalty to others ensures their
      complete zeal, obedience and support
...Remains stable and calm during crisis situations

...Well known and thought of throughout organization
...Puts mission accomplishment ahead of personal interests
...Outstanding managerial talent in organizing watch team second to none

...Instills loyalty, drive and desire to excel in others
...Recognizes and rewards top performers
...Authoritative in action with commanding presence

...Unencumbered by superfluous matters
...Gets to the heart of problem areas and provides satisfactory solutions
...Aggressively reorganized and revitalized entire organization

...Established team "can do" spirit throughout
...All work is properly staffed and researched in a timely manner
...An expert at drafting smooth official correspondence and directives

...Leadership determination and experience leads peer group
...Ignites enthusiasm throughout the ranks
...Effective leadership qualities executed in exemplary manner

...The personification of the model leader
...Earned the trust and confidence of superiors and subordinates alike
...Has the willing support and cooperation of everyone

...Knows key to quality performance is people
...Receptive to and actively solicits constructive criticism
...All-around ability instrumental in establishing high state of morale and
    readiness

...Improves weaknesses and effectively capitalizes on strengths of others
...Personal leadership motivates others to a higher level of individual
    performance
...Understands leadership means getting a common vision and purpose to
    everyone

...Knows that you lead people and manage things
...Gained the respect and admiration of others
...Thorough management and staff work, leaves nothing to chance

...Truly representative of the highest caliber of talent and leadership
    available
...Demonstrates keen understanding of command objectives
...Establishes goals with exacting effort and coordination

...Ability to foresee and plan for problem areas before fully developed
...A leader in counseling people with personal and professional problems
...Deep concern and care for individual development

...Created and maintained excellent work environment
...Cultivates team work and a winning professional attitude
...Established new highs in team harmony and unity

...Applied managerial skills to good advantage and purpose
...Can apply knowledge and skill to any situation
...Does not have to wait for specific guidance before taking action

...Secures the energy and spirit of subordinates through innovative and
    imaginative leadership
...Makes things happen and is not content with anything less than
    maximum effort
...Arouses interest and excites competitive spirit of others

...Long-range strategy based on sound leadership principles
...Highly capable leader
...Always receives willing and spontaneous support of others

...A leader of dynamic character and stamina
...Met or exceeded all tasking with unique managerial skills
...Gives praise when most deserved or needed

...Radiant personality & confident manner quickly wins willing support
...Sparks a spirit of job excitement and self-sacrifice in each individual
...Propagates goodwill and an unmistakable drive and desire for
      excellence

...Unquestionable commitment to equality & equitable treatment of others
...Own radiant energy and zeal quickly picked up by others
...Potent, productive leader

...Ensures each individual's capabilities are fully taxed
...Highly effective in training others to assume more challenging and
      demanding positions of authority and responsibility
...Successfully faces the many challenges of leadership

...Pleasing, sincere personality blends well with everyone
...Eminent administrative abilities to produce a consistently uniform and
      quality of excellence
...Ideally suited to work with today's young professionals

...Takes personal interest in each individual
...Provides necessary guidance and direction to instill sense of belonging
      and individual worth
...Continually searches for ways to improve procedures and raise
      efficiency

...Many suggestions have been incorporated at management level
...Enlightened leadership technique arouses interest and participation
...Accomplished counselor

...Exudes spirit of well being, confidence and determination toward others
...Innovative and decisive style of leadership provided impetus in
      maintaining professional work environment
...Employs open and direct manner in supervising personnel

...Highly successful in obtaining maximum results regardless of situation
...Careful preparation and planning led to achieving outstanding level of
      performance in a broad operating spectrum
...Exercises sound leadership fundamentals

...Possessed of sound judgment and management acumen
...Keenly aware of personal side of leadership
...Projects indelible image of strong, steady leader

...Provides the electricity and spark of action that drives others in a
positive, constructive direction
...Provides balanced blend of strong leadership and personal compassion
...Exemplary management acumen and personal performance enhanced
organizational readiness and reputation

...Knows how to stir the imagination of others
...Exceptionally effective in personnel leadership and management
...Remarkable ability to plan and manage diverse operations

...Effective application of sound management practices and principles
...A unifying presence to any organization
...Leadership instilled new sense of pride and purpose in others

...Concerned for welfare and well being of all personnel
...Actively takes lead in backing new organizational programs
...Personalized style of leadership highly respected and effective

...Personally encourages each person to set high goals
...Standards of integrity and bearing are of highest quality
...Leads each subordinate to desired level of performance

...Organizational harmony and cohesiveness without equal
...Gives 100%, demands the same of others
...Contributes significantly to betterment of morale

...Exceptionally well organized and perceptive to the problems and needs
of others
...Demonstrates concern for the welfare and well being of others
...Personal achievements and ability to lead contributed immeasurably to
sustained superior performance

...Undertook exacting managerial duties with a keen sense of direction
...Accepts each task with positive and cooperative spirit
...Inspires high morale and esprit de corps among others

...Always contributes the maximum to group effort
...Quickly grasps the intricacies of new assignments
...Persuasive and tactful in conveying ideas

...Gives others responsibility and lets them grow professionally
...A leader of uncommon perceptiveness
...Helps individuals grow and develop skills through timely advice

...Solicits others for their thoughts and ideas
...Encourages maximum participation in a variety of matters
...Has special knack for bringing out the very best effort of each individual

...Eager and capable of doing superior leadership job across broad range
    of responsibilities
...Recognizes that success is a team effort
...Gets others involved so that they can learn and grow professionally

...Not content with anything less than maximum effort and results
...Steers straight and direct course of action
...Recognizes and rewards top performers

...Takes correct and decisive action on substandard performers
...Encourages professional development at every opportunity
...Individual productivity and personal desire for excellence significantly
    contributed to organization efficiency

...Personal time management concepts and leadership ability resulted in
    exceptional performance
...Optimistic outlook and "can do" enthusiasm radiates in all directions
...Unique ability to coordinate group efforts toward common goal

...Organization functions like a well-oiled machine
...Repeatedly demonstrated impressive ability to motivate others in any
    work environment
...Inspires others to put forth their best effort

...Projects positive leadership by own exciting and vibrant enthusiasm for
    any and all challenges
...Knows how to reach an objective
...Not diverted from task at hand by artificial barriers

...Considerate of others and uses restraint while obtaining desired results
...Infectious positive attitude and steadfast devotion to duty
...Has continuing willingness to lend a helping hand

...Routinely goes out of way to assist others

FAVORABLE

PERFORMANCE

...Totally committed to excellence
...Enterprising, intense performer
...Competitive spirit

...Stands above peers
...Reaches new heights
...Sound professional judgment

...True team player
...Takes wise courses of action
...Unparalleled success

...Stands above contemporaries
...Dramatic and exciting
...Highest standards of excellence

...Prompt and proper
...Exhibits professional accuracy
...Considerably advanced

...High achiever
...Unblemished record
...Seeks challenging assignments

...Acts decisively under pressure
...Smooth and flawless
...Delivers wholehearted support

...A top professional
...In-depth technical knowledge
...Ace technician

...Head and shoulders above peers
...Emerging as premier performer
...Decisive in action and deed

...Superior to others
...Highly respected by superiors
...Reliable and dependable

...Gives full effort
...Hard-working
...Finds and fixes problems

...Plans carefully and wisely
...Intense dedication to duty
...Always volunteers

...Work free from mistake
...Exceptional ability
...Maintains high standards

...Steadfast dedication
...Positive, fruitful future
...Constant vigil

...Great technical curiosity
...Adds extra dimension
...Strong professional pride

...Proficient and industrious
...A benchmark of excellence
...A role model

...Up and coming star
...Sets professional example
...Accustomed to success

...Overcomes all obstacles
...A standard bearer
...Impressive accomplishments

...Thrives on diversity
...Prompt in response
...Steady, faithful service

...Unblemished record
...Gives extra effort
...Clear cut goals

...Unrelenting work habits
...Always achieves desired ends
...Enjoys stressful situations

...Perceptive and hard working
...Capacity to meet challenges
...Proficient in all ventures

...Performs at peak intensity
...Prompt and proper action
...Meets diverse challenges

...Quick to take positive action
...Captures the imagination
...Keen technical abilities

...Reached full potential
...Technically capable
...Makes good things happen

...Decisive, action oriented
...Total, complete professional
...Comprehensive technical skill

...Impressive performer
...Springs into action
...Stellar performer

...Abundantly productive
...Uncommon excellence
...Quick to respond

...Promotes new ideas
...Strong desire to succeed
...Achieves desirable results

...Contributes maximum effort
...Diligent and persistent worker
...Enhances & improves morale

...Highly skilled in all phases of job
...Stimulates harmony & high spirit
...Unsurpassed devotion to duty

...Dominating force
...Action oriented
...Tireless worker

...Highest caliber work
...Mission oriented
...Makes things happen

...Gets results
...Bright, on the ball
...Work-aggressive

...Uses time wisely
...A driving force
...Without equal

...Multi-disciplined
...Hard charger
...Banner performer

...Durable and adaptable
...Promising newcomer
...Prolific performer

...Tough competitor
...Thoroughly proficient
...Extremely zealous

...Responsive to seniors
...Exerts total effort
...Skillful undertaking

...Resilient and energetic
...Intense, highly capable
...Always gives 100%

...A quality performer
...Always ahead of the action
...Always sets the example

...Totally reliable
...Initiates sound new ideas
...Exhibits technical excellence

...Dedicated to mission purpose
...Vast technical experience
...Intolerant of mediocre performance

...Keen technical abilities
...Always productively employed
...Puts forth unrelenting effort

...Accepts challenges with alacrity
...Achieves quality results
...Stimulates productive activity

...Unfailing performance to duty
...Prompt and responsive
...A real competitor

...Has well defined plans and goals
...Enterprising, intense performer
...Succeeds despite any adversity

...Extremely energetic and helpful
...Unswerving allegiance to duty
...A first-rate professional

...Self-sacrificing, a real team player
...Places a premium on punctuality
...Unrivaled professionalism

...Forward-thinking
...A model for all to emulate
...Steadfast in dedication

...Job-aggressive, a hard charger
...Decisive response to any tasking
...Rates first against any competition

...Unselfish devotion to duty
...Sets and achieves high goals
...Uses time wisely

...Intense dedication and enthusiasm
...Top performer in every respect
...Almost infinite growth potential

...At the forefront of peer group
...No wasted effort or energy
...Gives total support to seniors

...High technical ability and curiosity
...Dedicated, highly competent individual
...Vast and varied personal skills

...Promptly executes all orders

...Responsibilities discharged superbly and always consistent with policy
...Past performance, full-time dedication, and future ambitions all positive
        assets
...Ability to accomplish diverse tasking is without peer

...Provides unequivocal commitment and support to mission
        accomplishment
...Approaches each endeavor with positive attitude
...Works to learn the most from each situation

...Possesses the natural talent and acquired proficiency to accomplish the
        most demanding tasks
...Unafraid of setting and steering new course of action
...Enthusiastically tackles any project or tasking

...Contributed greatly to mission accomplishment
...Superlative contributions and achievements
...Provides timely advice and guidance

...Highly competent and dedicated
...Absolute quality performer in any tasking
...Consistently exhibits perfection in all technical aspects of job

...Long history of devotion to duty and self-sacrifice
...Ability to bring into focus the pertinent parts of any tasking
...Exemplary support of chain of command

...An extremely beneficial example for others
...Demands and receives quality performance
...Continues to improve on an already impressive record

...Exemplifies true meaning of "pride and professionalism" in every facet of
        personal and professional lifestyle
...Starts earlier, works smarter and harder than peers
...Always a step ahead of the others

...Punctuality and strong sense of duty highlight daily performance
...Flexible and cooperative in dealing with others
...Successfully faced all challenges with vim & vigor

...Others routinely draw on abundance of inspiration
...Hard working individual who takes charge and makes positive things
        happen
...Functions particularly well independent of supervision and direction

...Superlative contributions and actions in every respect
...An energetic and highly motivated achiever
...A bold, straight line of dedication and inspiration

...Strong capabilities and abilities across the board
...Duties performed with uncommon quality and timeliness
...A real mainstay to the organization

...Possesses unusually high level of technical expertise
...Actively seeks additional responsibility
...Flawless support and backing of organizational policies and goals

...Astute management of monetary and equipment assets
...Can adjust or adapt to any situation with quality results
...Pursues tasks with a spirit of confidence and relentless drive

...Recognizes opportunities to excel and refuses to be satisfied with anything less than full effort
...Clearly demonstrated ability and desire to assume duties broader in scope and magnitude
...Highly motivated and hard-working individual whose efforts are reflected in the superior performance routinely displayed

...Thrives on important responsibility and maximum action environment
...Keen technical insight, efficient performance, and pleasant manner highlight daily performance
...Always gives unrestrained support to superiors

...Aggressively tackled many demanding challenges and routinely met with success
...Performs well under external stress and pressure
...Work highlighted by profusion and variety

...Quality performer with bright future
...Jobs completed on or ahead of schedule
...Possesses sufficient skill and resource to accomplish most difficult tasking

...Hurdles or bulldozes over obstacles, always gets the job done and doesn't let things get in way
...Finest technical skill available
...Highly self-motivated with successful job accomplishment always the number one priority

...Demonstrates time-tested ability and capacity to perform beyond the range and scope of contemporaries
...Has insatiable appetite for increased responsibility
...Ensures all work performed with exacting quality

...Day-to-day performance routinely exceeds highest professional standards
...Epitomizes those qualities most highly sought in model, career person
...Built superior record of accomplishment based on sound technical expertise and proven leadership principles

...Exhibits the skill, temperament, appearance, and reliability of true professional
...Dynamic and positive approach to everyday problem solving
...Sets the course and speed for peers

...A front-runner in every category

...Demonstrated impressive breadth of experience within technical specialty

...Performs well in all situations and uses sound judgment and logic to solve difficult problems or situations

...Devotion to duty and professional performance without peer

...Meets or exceeds requirements in every facet of assigned responsibility

...Considers no job too difficult

...Every assignment taken as a challenge and is completed with remarkable reliability

...Trains for readiness and the unexpected

...Has uncanny ability to find and fix problem areas

...A high achiever, always attains desired results

...Takes corrective action while others ponder and discuss

...Made substantial, quality contributions to organizational effectiveness

...Always on the ball and ahead of the others

...Does what has to be done without awaiting guidance or instruction

...Relentless drive and motivation without peer

...A "hot runner" with unlimited potential

...True team player with enormous professional capabilities

...Invariably hand-picked for difficult and complex assignments

...Takes necessary degree of personal risk without awaiting orders

...Displays selfless devotion and utmost professionalism

...Steadfast performance and dedication to duty

...Able to rapidly acquire in-depth knowledge of intricate systems and varied operational evolutions

...Unsurpassed devotion to duty highlighted by aggressive assumption of more and more responsibilities with continued quality success

...Has ability to bring together divergent views and devise viable and valuable solutions to any problem at hand

...Takes advantage of every opportunity to improve already high level of personal and team technical expertise

...From the onset, aggressively acted to put principles of "pride and professionalism" on the front burner

...Enthusiastic and proper response to dynamic and critical events routinely lead to successful conclusion or resolution

...Exceeds highest expectations for performance in any difficult
   assignment
...Always delivers wholehearted cooperation and support
...Attention to detail, reliability, and thoroughness to assigned projects are
   most impressive

...Excelled in every endeavor and consistently sought more and more
   challenging assignments
...Epitomizes the highest standards of a well-rounded professional
...Exhibits exceptional degree of accuracy and professionalism in each
   undertaking

...Pursues chosen profession with boundless enthusiasm, knowledge, and
   raw ability
...Filled a most challenging, visible, and responsible position in finest
   sense of the word "professional"
...Rare ability to radiate enthusiasm for menial and complex tasking

...Maintains busy and active civic community interests without detracting
   from professional performance
...Energetic personality, positive "can do" attitude, and a deep pride in job
   accomplishment highlight daily performance
...Performs beyond professional abilities and boundaries of
   contemporaries

...Effort and dedicated achieved exceptional results across the board
...Learns equipment and systems quickly and retains and uses that
   knowledge to maximum advantage
...Performance far exceeds that of others of comparable training and
   experience

...Takes pride in always doing best job possible
...Met all stated objectives successfully
...Put into practice a long list of new initiatives which increased overall
   operational effectiveness

...Experienced journeyman in technical specialty
...At the pinnacle of professional excellence
...The standard bearer for pride and professionalism

...Works without prompting or prodding
...A zealot in performing any assignment
...Pursues all assignments with eager and ardent interest

...Acts with full, complete, and deliberate interest and attention
...Made major contributions of considerable and lasting value
...Gets things done by taking the initiative

...An irreplaceable source of professional knowledge and sound judgment
...Great sense of responsibility for quality of workmanship
...Vast experience further enhanced by intelligence and technical know-
how

...Completes any tasking in truly professional manner
...Symbolizes the top quality professional
...Career underscored by pride, self-improvement, and accomplishment

...Sets standards by which excellence is measured
...Executes tasks expediently and correctly
...Possesses an infectious positive attitude

...Great resource for coping with difficult, trying situations
...Responsive to short-fused tasking and special assignments
...Forward-looking individual who has demonstrated traits most desirable
of a person in positions of high trust and responsibility

...Gives complete, energetic support to superiors
...Demonstrated willingness and ability to strike out in a new direction
...Impressive record of accomplishments

...Diligent, persistent worker with refined, skillful workmanship
...Introduces progressive ideas that work
...Always provides whatever assistance required

...Routinely contributes to higher standards of performance excellence
...Compiled impressive list of individual accomplishments
...Top professional in every respect

...Clearly exceeded all established standards of excellence
...Coordinates diverse events with uncommon success and accuracy
...Sets and achieves high personal standards

...Surmounts problems, gets results
...Highly industrious and doesn't believe in idle time
...Aggressive and meticulous in completion of assignments

...Performance regularly exceeds job requirements
...Aggressive in seeking out answers to developing problems
...Unyielding drive and desire for success

...Enjoys total professional diversity
...Always puts job ahead of personal desires and interests
...Workload is correctly balanced and prioritized

...Maintains an exceptionally high level of performance
...Quick to provide personal effort on special occasions and projects
...Plans and completes ambitious workload

...Top achiever in any task assigned or assumed
...Knows job completely and excels in every facet of its complex parts
...Job aggressiveness, dedication, and cooperation exhibited in all tasks
   are commendable

...Professional contributions noteworthy, in addition to being a highly
   respected technical specialist
...Exceptionally well organized
...Carries out responsibilities of demanding position in highly capable and
   professional manner

...Invariably submits timely and perceptive solutions to personal,
   operational, and staff problems
...Performance always exceeds expectations
...Forward-minded, aggressive performance of nonpareil competence

...Can always be relied upon to give all of considerable talent and effort to
   task at hand
...Uncompromising professionalism
...Proven top quality organizer

...Performance stands out prominently from peers
...Exudes emotional confidence and spirit
...Sets the pattern and example for peers

...Takes difficult and hard to accomplish assignments in full stride
...Deeply devoted to chosen profession
...Confident of personal and professional abilities

...Accumulated a long list of impressive accomplishments
...Aggressively pursues difficult challenges
...Demonstrates remarkable versatility and capability

...Prompt, quick, and correct in action
...Possesses degree of excellence rarely observed within peer group
...Takes pride in equaling or exceeding accomplishments of others

...Pursues, with success, ultimate standards of excellence
...Tackles difficult tasking with joyous exuberance
...Plans well organized and designed, not artificial. Achieves and
      accomplishes more than others

...Intense emotional drive and determination
...Plunges into all assignments, unafraid of hard, long work
...Aspiring performer, sets and achieves high goals

...Exemplifies highest standards of dedication and determination
...Persevering and enduring in completing any assignment
...Always ready, never caught off guard or unprepared

...Completes all assignments with accuracy and dispatch
...Proven technical specialist and successful manager
...Discharges responsibilities with complete professionalism

...Accepts all challenges and responsibilities without wavering
...Work routinely receives high acclaim and praise
...Self-starter with natural ability and aptitude for technically oriented tasks

...Carries out assignments to complete satisfaction
  Ensures superiors are kept aware of matters requiring their attention
...Inspired with a sense of purpose and urgency

...Determined and dedicated with a fruitful career ahead
...Accepts added responsibility and vigorously tackles any assignment
...Articulate in self-expression and ability to think logically

...Attains quality performance in any endeavor
...Highly skilled and well trained
...Frequently sought out for expert opinion

...Boundless energy and great strength of character set highest standards
      of excellence
...Eagerly accepts work assignments others would avoid
...Adapts to varying circumstances and situations with uncommon ease

...Actions and deeds always conform to precise standards
...Always vigorous in pursuit of excellence
...Established reputation for meeting challenges with professional
      excellence and a winning spirit

...Consistently puts forth that extra degree of effort required in fast-paced environment
...Results are always immediate and impressive
...Always has a personal commitment to quality and performance

...Clearly demonstrated capacity to meet challenges head-on
...Recognized flaws and discrepancies and took immediate, positive action without waiting for guidance or direction
...A multi-disciplined individual with a promising future

...Proficient and industrious in performance of duty
...Aggressive in assumption of additional responsibility
...Resourceful and dedicated in fulfilling a variety of jobs

...Has long-standing record of credibility, loyalty, and professional dedication
...Will not retreat in the face of adversity
...Technical ability and skill know virtually no bounds

...Consistently produces outstanding results
...Attains results regardless of complexity or magnitude of tasking
...Every goal met timely and correctly the first time

...Actions well planned and smoothly executed
...Displays keen interest and ability in all tasking
...Anticipates future tasking and doesn't need to push a deadline

...Always gives serious and determined effort
...Completes all assignments with dispatch
...Integrity, skill, and accomplishment are personal keynotes to success

...Seeks opportunities to grow professionally
...Tremendous capacity for professional growth
...Committed determination to achieve high goals

...At the zenith of technical specialty
...Anticipates problem areas and plans accordingly
...Makes decisions after weighing pertinent facts

...Adamantly supports all regulations and superiors
...Ingrained ability to work for and achieve positive results
...Endures and succeeds under stress and pressure

...Refuses to give up in face of opposition or difficulty
...Performs all duties without prompting
...Works hard to make jobs of others easier

...Achieves highest level of performance and effectiveness
...Well rounded and professionally knowledgeable
...Maintains superior rapport at all organizational levels

...Achieves uniformly outstanding results
...Possesses all attributes required to excel in any tasking
...Always in harmony and accord with orders of superiors

...Has complete, concise technical understanding of specialty
...Formulates productive plans that contribute to excellence
...Makes positive, supportable decisions

...Demonstrates superlative professionalism with an abundance of
        personal dedication and self-sacrifice
...Supports and enforces all rules and orders
...Epitomizes standards by which all others should be measured

...Unblemished record of proven performance
...Perseverance and total dedication to all tasking ensured complete and
        continued success
...Carried out multitude of assigned and assumed duties and demonstrated
        a rare breed of reliability and dedication

...Comprehensive and complete technical knowledge
...Set a standard of performance standards unparalleled in recent memory
...Can be counted on to take whatever independent action is required to
        get the job accomplished

...Maintains a punishing and productive work schedule
...Unquenchable thirst for knowledge
...Realizes success requires sacrifice and dedication

...Always busy and involved in something constructive
...Especially strong and effective in the execution of demanding tasks
...An individual of decisive and positive action

...Highly skilled in all facets of technical specialty
...Personal talent and commitment rivaled by few and exceeded by none
...Enthusiasm, dedication to task at hand, and long hours are key
        ingredients to successfully meeting multiple challenges

...Can readily shift time and talent to short-fused matters with admirable
   results
...Adapts to new work environment particularly rapid
...Intense dedication, unexcelled efficiency and cheerful enthusiasm are
   cornerstones to success

...Complete and comprehensive knowledge of technical field
...An asset to organizational effectiveness
...Demonstrates superior knowledge of duties and consistently gives
   quality performance

The following pages contain bullets/phrases without an ending. This allows a drafter to select an appropriate beginning and add whatever ending is desired.

...Did a masterful job in/as...
...Without equal in ability to...
...A top specialist in the field of...

...A foremost authority on/in...
...Preeminent in ability to...
...Excels in ability to...

...Has tremendous natural ability for...
...Indispensable performance in/as...
...Achieved impressive results in/by...

...Successfully carried out...
...Widely respected for ability to...
...Great mental aptitude for...

...Rejuvenated and put new life into...
...Performance goes beyond limits of...
...The leading force and influence in...

...Furthers technical specialty by...
...Gives wholehearted support to..
...A strong advocate of...

...Actively supports and encourages...
...Advanced education and skill in....
...Gives full spirit and support to...

...A perfect example of...
...A remarkably skilled...
...Inexhaustible source of...

...Ever energetic, looks forward to...
...Exhibits all essential features of a...
...Firmly established as the top....

...Masterful ability to...
...Developed a landmark...
...An accomplished, proficient...

...Routinely prevails over others at...
...Has the natural flair and ability to...
...Impressive accomplishments include..

...Rare, extraordinary ability to...
...Has substantial knowledge of...
...Routinely hand picked to...

...Praiseworthy characteristics include...
...Represents the embodiment of...
...Takes exceptional pride in...

...Played vital role in...
...An acknowledged expert in...
...Has natural gift for ability to...

...Achieved resounding success in/by...   ...Has special talents for...
...Successfully carried out...   ...Skilled in art of...
...Maintains highest standards of...   ...The driving force behind...

...Quality leader. Knows value of...   ...Has positive, clear view of...
...Prompt and proper in response to...   ...Has natural aptitude for...
...Provided masterful insight into...   ...Thoroughly understands...

...Maintains high standards in/of...   ...Observes chain of command...
...Displays intense dedication in/to...   ...Stresses importance of...
...Conforms to exacting standards of...   ...Highly specialized in...

...Held in high esteem for ability to...   ...Maintains sharp edge in...
...Has extensive knowledge in/of...   ...An absolute master at...
...Especially skilled and adept in/at...   ...Has excellent talent for/in...

...Contributed to vital interests by...   ...Made marked improvement in...
...Widely recognized for ability to...   ...An indispensable member of...
...Freely spends many off-duty hours...   ...Articulate in ability to...

...Stands above peers in ability to...   ...Uniquely skilled to...
...A recognized expert in field of...   ...Has veracious appetite for...
...Won over subordinates by/with...   ...A dominating force in...

...Remarkable talent/ability for/to...   ...Has a natural curiosity for...
...A champion in the field of...   ...Has a fine touch for...
...Instills loyalty and a drive to...   ...Unlimited capacity to/for...

...Achieved total success in/by...   ...No end to potential for/to...
...Inspires confidence by...   ...Unblemished record of...
...Inspires and encourages other by...

...Top performer. Merits serious consideration for...
...Displays special skill and knowledge in field of...
...Surpasses peers in sheer ability to...

...Has full insight and understanding of...
...Has the knowledge and competence to...
...Transformed below average organization into...

...Totally immersed and involved in successful effort to...
...Established new standards of excellence in...
...Extremely high degree of excellence in...

...Unlimited potential with capacity for...
...Made significant progress and gain when/on...
...A fundamental, essential ingredient to the successful...

...Routinely receives high compliment and praise when...
...Enjoys the especially difficult and complex job of...
...Has acquired the necessary attributes to...

...Cheerfully devotes off-duty time working on...
...Devised procedures that carefully weighed time, personnel, and financial
 procedures that resulted in...
...Assumed greatly expanded responsibilities with/when...

...Personal sacrifice and uncompromising standards of conduct provided
 impetus for...
...Strong leadership, acute management acumen, and technical
 competence resulted in...
...Totally mastered each and every aspect of...

...Spearheaded self-help project to/that...
...Simplified and streamlined procedures for...
...Impressively managed diverse and complex...

...Established and enforced strict controls on...
...Through acute awareness, perseverance, and personal diligence...
...Produced commendable results in/as.

...Successfully managed wide and varied programs in/on...
...Instrumental in successful completion of...
...Personal drive and ambition hastened progress and development of...

...Earned high praise and acclaim by/for...
...Open-minded. Can accommodate wide variety of...
...Quickly surged ahead of contemporaries by/in...

...Fully experienced in practical application of...
...Successfully fused together all elements of...
...Performance reached a peak of intensity when...

...Relaxing personality. Creates favorable relationship with...
...Great deductive power. Insatiable appetite for...
...Unquenchable quest for knowledge in...

...Became a moving force in ability to...
...Created perfect foundation for/to...
...Innovative ideas and close personal supervision of subordinates led to...

...A motivating force in achieving significant improvement in...
...Possesses requisite competence and aptitude to...
...Combined innate sense of leadership and keen foresight instrumental
        to...

...Use of sound and prudent judgment was instrumental in/to...
...Strong spirit of inquiry and drive led to...
...Awareness of people's strengths and capabilities led to...

...Enjoys excitement of devising new ways to...
...Possesses overwhelming capacity to/for...
...Succeeded in reaching new heights in...

...Through diligent effort and patience became proficient in..
...Has decisive advantage over others in ability to...
...Possesses overabundance of energy and...

...Strong spirit and character. Not easily swayed to...
...Personal initiative and dedication directly responsible for...
...Demonstrated creative intelligence and wisdom by...

...Personal liaison efforts particularly effective in...
...Possesses concise knowledge and understanding of every facet of...
...One of the most accomplished expert/specialists in...

...Contributions both substantial and significant in...
...Successfully faced extremely complex...
...Carefully planned, organized, and executed successful...

...Using foresight and exceptional planning ability, put together a
        complicated and comprehensive...
...Personal example has been a positive influence on...
...Especially strong and effective in executing demanding duties of...

...Personal concern and initiative directly responsible for...
...Enthusiasm and dedication instrumental in promoting many innovative
        and progressive programs in...
...Flexibility and initiative responsible for upgrade in/of...

...Despite severe limitations of personnel resources, successfully...
...Carefully monitored diverse component demands on/of...
...Stimulated improved harmony and attitudes on/toward...

...Industrious manner and positive attitude resulted in...
...Successfully overcame potentially serious impediment to...
...Most impressive performer in...

...Places proper and heavy emphasis on...
...Developed superb plan of action and milestones for/in...
...Earned individual distinction by/for...

...Superb academic credentials. A prime candidate for...
...Rendered outstanding support and service to...
...Responded positively and correctly to...

...Technical skill and farsightedness led to early identification and
          correction of...
...Superb common sense and professional knowledge led to...
...Played leading and aggressive role in establishing...

...Voluntarily contributed many off-duty hours to ensure timely and correct
          completion of...
...Proved more than equal to the task of...
...Implemented necessary management techniques and concepts to...

...Met goals across a diverse spectrum by...
...Won wide acclaim for promptness in responding to...
...Demonstrates untiring dedication to duty by...

...Has advanced knowledge and skill in
...Already a quality performer, has not vet reached full potential in/for...
...Takes maximum advantage of opportunities to...

...Has style and finesse. Others always willing to join in...
...A major contributing factor in the success of...
...As testimony to leadership skills, successfully...

...Technical knowledge and curiosity led to...
...Does not necessarily stay in beaten path of others when...
...Applies correct mental approach to...

...Enjoys unparalleled success. Recently emerged as...
...Personal vision and courage led to...
...Possesses a wealth of information in/on...

...Superiors have complete confidence in abilities to...
...Despite ever increasing difficulty, accomplished/completed...
...Good mental capacity. Quick to grasp significance of...

...Gives subordinates enthusiasm and...
...A person on the move who can adjust readily to changes in...
...Rapidly established dynamic and motivating leader image by...

...Remarkable ability to work with people and effectively organize tasks
      and priorities enhanced...
...Personally molded cohesive and dedicated team that...
...Constant personal examples of loyalty and professionalism earned
      complete respect and admiration of/from...

...Personal initiative and managerial skills overcame...
...Direct personal involvement instrumental in/to...
...Unselfishly contributed time and talents to numerous special projects,
      including...

...Skillful employment of manpower enabled...
...Demonstrated clearly a superior ability to...
...Professional knowledge and zeal significantly improved...

The words in the following section are general usage words. Used by themselves, they are not strongly favorable or unfavorable.

GENERAL

ADJECTIVES

ABLE
ACCOMMODATING
ADEQUATE

ABREAST
ACCURATE
AGREEABLE

ACCEPTABLE
ACKNOWLEDGED
AMBIGUOUS

BENEFICIAL
CAREFUL
COMPETENT

CAPABLE
CATEGORICAL
COMPLAISANT

CAREFREE
COMPATIBLE
CONGRUENT

CONSISTENT
CREDIBLE
DEPENDABLE

CONVENTIONAL
CURSORY
DEPENDENT

CORRECT
CUSTOMARY
DEVIATE

DOCILE
EASYGOING
ELEMENTAL

DRUDGING
ECCENTRIC
ELEMENTARY

DULL
EFFECTIVE
ENCOURAGING

EQUABLE
FAIR
FEASIBLE

EQUITABLE
FAITHFUL
FELICITOUS

FACTUAL
FAVORABLE
FLEXIBLE

FRAGMENTARY
GINGERLY
GUILELESS

FUNDAMENTAL
GOOD
HARMLESS

FUZZY
GRADUAL
HEEDFUL

HELPFUL
IMPARTIAL
INCONSPICUOUS

HOPEFUL
IMPRESSIONABLE
INDEFINITE

HUMBLE
INCLINED
INDEPENDENT

INDIRECT
INFREQUENT
INVOLUNTARY

INDULGENT
INNOCENT
INVOLVED

INFORMAL
INTERMITTENT
IRONIC

ISOLATED
LEGITIMATE
LOW-KEY

JUST
LENIENT
LOW-PRESSURE

LABORIOUS
LIABLE
LOW-PROFILE

LUKEWARM	MARGINAL	MATTER-OF-COURSE
MATTER-OF-FACT	MEDIOCRE	MERE
METHODICAL	MILD	MODERATE
MODEST	MORAL	NEAT
NEUTRAL	NONCHALANT	NO-NONSENSE
NORMAL	OBEDIENT	OBLIGING
OBSERVANT	ODD	ONE-WAY
ORDERLY	ORDINARY	ORTHODOX
PARTIAL	PASSABLE	PASSIVE
PATIENT	PECULIAR	PERFECTIBLE
PERFUNCTORY	PERTINENT	PLACID
PLIABLE	POTENTIAL	PRACTICAL
PREFERENTIAL	PREOCCUPIED	PREMATURE
PRESENTABLE	PROPER	PROPITIOUS
PUNCTUAL	PURE	QUALIFIED
QUESTIONABLE	READY	READY-MADE
REALISTIC	REASONABLE	REMEDIAL
RESPONSIVE	RUDIMENTARY	SATISFACTORY
SCRUTABLE	SELF-MADE	SELF-SUFFICIENT
SEMISKILLED	SIMPLE	SLOW
SOPHISTICATED	SPARING	STABLE
STODGY	SUBMISSIVE	SUFFICIENT
SUITABLE	SYSTEMATIC	TEDIOUS
TEMPTING	TOLERABLE	TOLERANT
TRANQUIL	TRIVIAL	UNCOMMON
UNEXCEPTIONAL	UNFAMILIAR	USEFUL
VOLUNTARY	WATCHFUL	WELL-INTENTIONED
WILLING	WILLFUL	WORKABLE
WISHFUL	WOULD-BE	

NOUNS

ABILITY	AMBIGUITY	ATTRIBUTE
COMMITMENT	COMMONPLACE	COMPETENT

COMPLIANCE	COMPOSURE	CONCERN
CONFORMANCE	CONFORMITY	CONGRUITY
CONJECTURE	CREDENTIAL	CREDIBILITY
DECORUM	DEPENDENCE	EFFORT
ENIGMA	EQUALITY	ETHIC
FELLOWSHIP	FIDELITY	FIGUREHEAD
FLIP-FLOP	FOLLOWER	FORMALIZE
FRAGMENT	GOOD	GUIDE
HEARSAY	HUMILITY	IMITATION
HEED	IDEALIST	INDIVIDUALIST
INDULGENCE	INTROVERT	KNACK
LABOR	LEGITIMACY	LENIENCY
LONER	MEDIOCRITY	MODERATION
MODESTY	MORALIST	MORALITY
ODDITY	ORTHODOXY	PARITY
PASSIVISM	PASSIVITY	PATIENCE
PLEASANTRY	PROPENSITY	PLATITUDE
REALIST	RELIANCE	RESERVE
RESISTANCE	RETRIBUTION	ROOKIE
RUDIMENT	SATISFACTION	SCAPEGOAT
SCRUPLE	SENTIMENT	SOLITUDE
STABILITY	STAMINA	SURVIVOR
STYLE	TRANQUILLITY	TREADMILL
TRIVIA	YES-MAN	

VERBS

ABIDE	ACCOMMODATE	AGREE
APPEASE	AVOW	COMPLY
CONFORM	COPE	DABBLE
DEPEND	DEVIATE	DRUDGE
EMPLOY	ENABLE	ENJOY
EXONERATE	FLUCTUATE	GENERALIZE

GUIDE	HOPE	IMITATE
INCLINE	INDOCTRINATE	INTERCEDE
INTERPRET	INTERROGATE	INTROVERT
LABOR	MORALIZE	OBEY
OBLIGE	ORIENTATE	OSCILLATE
PACIFY	PERFORM	PURPOSE
PROPITIATE	PURPORT	QUELL
REGRET	REPUTE	RESERVE
STABILIZE	SUCCEED	SURVIVE
TOLERATE	UNDERSTAND	WANDER

FIXED - LASTING

ADJECTIVES

ADAMANT	CERTAIN	COHERENT
COHESIVE	DIFFICULT	DURABLE
ENDURABLE	FIRM	FORMIDABLE
HABITUAL	HARD-AND-FAST	HARD-SET
HARD-SHELL	IMMOBILE	IMMOVABLE
IMPENETRABLE	IMPERVIOUS	IMPONDERABLE
INCONTESTABLE		INCONTROVERTIBLE
INCURABLE	INDEFECTIBLE	INDESTRUCTIBLE
INDISPENSABLE	INDISPUTABLE	INESCAPABLE
INEVITABLE	INEXORABLE	INFLEXIBLE
INGRAINED	INIMITABLE	INSUPERABLE
INSURMOUNTABLE	INTRANSIGENT	INVARIABLE
INVINCIBLE	IRREFUTABLE	IRREPRESSIBLE
LASTING	LIMITLESS	LITERAL
LONG-LIVED		PREPONDERANT
RENITENT	RESISTANT	RIGID
SOLID	STAUNCH	STEADFAST
STEADY	UNBENDING	UNCOMPROMISING
UNDAUNTED	UNDENIABLE	UNRELENTING

NOUNS

ADHERENCE	CERTAINTY	COHESION
DIFFICULTY	ENDURANCE	PERSISTENCE
RESISTANT		

VERBS

ADHERE	COHERE	ENDLESS
ENDURE	INDURATE	INGRAIN
INUNDATE	PERDURE	PERVADE
RESIST	RIGIDIFY	SOLIDIFY
WITHSTAND		

MORE OR LESS

ABUNDANT (A)	CEILING (N)	COLOSSAL (A)
ENORMOUS (A)	EXCESSIVE (A)	FINITE (A)
EXORBITANCE (N)	EXORBITANT (A)	EXTRAVAGANT (A)
FULL-SCALE (A)	GIGANTIC (A)	GOOD DEAL (N)
GOODLY (A)	GREAT (A)	HUGE (A)
IMMEASURABLE (A)	IMMENSE (A)	IMMENSITY (N)
INCALCULABLE (A)	INFINITE (A)	INNUMERABLE (A)
INNUMEROUS (A)	LARGE (A)	LEAST (A)
LESS (A)	LITTLE (A)	MAMMOTH (A)
MAXIMIZE (V)	MAXIMUM (N)	MEAGER (A)
MINIMIZE (V)	MINIMUM (N)	MINISH (V)
MINOR (A)	MINUSCULE (N)	MINUTE (A)
MONUMENTAL (A)	MULTITUDE (N)	MYRIAD (N)
NEGLIGIBLE (A)	NOMINAL (A)	NAUGHT (N)
PALTRY (A)	PAUCITY (N)	SLACKEN (V)
SLACKER (N)	SMALL (A)	TENUOUS (A)
TREMENDOUS (A)	VAST (A)	WANE (A)

Legend: (A) Adjective (N) Noun (V) Verb

114

UNFAVORABLE APPRAISALS

The structure, content, and format used to document UNFAVORABLE Reports are no different from the FAVORABLE. Refer to the FAVORABLE Section for guidance.

The UNFAVORABLE words and PHRASES/BULLETS used in this section of the book are more than sufficient to draft UNFAVORABLE Reports. As can be seen from the examples on the following pages, describing poor or unfavorable performance is mostly a matter of listing what an individual fails to do, or does not do properly or correctly.

Almost all of the material used in the FAVORABLE Section of this book can be used for UNFAVORABLE comments simply by changing the key FAVORABLE ADJECTIVES, NOUNS, or VERBS to the UNFAVORABLE equivalent.

UNFAVORABLE EXAMPLES

(Name) performance, behavior, adaptability, and attitude took a downward turn at the start of this reporting period and continue to decline. UA (...) times, and disobeyed direct orders of a commissioned officer and other superiors. (Name) is intelligent and clever and regardless of the offense or circumstance he has a ready-made excuse. His recollection of recent conversations with various superiors routinely turns out to be in complete disagreement with those superiors. Constant vigilance is required to keep him at his work site and gainfully employed. A detriment to the morale and good order. Frequent counseling has been fruitless. (Name) is unreliable, untrustworthy, displays no initiative, and he is a burden to this organization.

(Name) performance is substandard across the board. He has been reprimanded by the Commanding Officer (...) times for violation of UCMJ Articles (...). Routinely questioning motives of superiors, he asks for an undue amount of justification when assigned tasks. His frequent display of immaturity, bad judgment, and use of half-truths highlight his inability to adjust to a military lifestyle. He gets a haircut only when directed by superiors and routinely fails personnel inspections. Counseling has been required on numerous occasions for lateness, an attitude problem, and a habit of straying from assigned work area. His lack of enthusiasm, constant complaining, and unwillingness to do his share of work have had a detrimental affect on morale.

(Name) overall performance is below standard. He requires close and constant supervision to complete tasks because he is unable to keep his mind on the job at hand. Tardiness and an inability to pass personnel and room inspections also detract from his performance. He has not demonstrated any ability to perform duties independent of supervision and he possesses no leadership qualities. Frequent counseling in all substandard performance areas has not resulted in any significant, lasting improvement. He is immature in behavior and lacks the mental acuity to think through every day common logic situations. He is unable to work harmoniously with others and does not promote good morale.

(Name) is a competent performer with average technical skills. His effort and attention to detail during the early part of this reporting period was high. However, his performance, across the board, declined during the middle of this period because of personal problems. He had difficulty reporting on time for duty, concentrating on his work, and presenting an acceptable military appearance. Initial supervisory counseling sessions failed to show any positive results. Additional later counseling did improve his performance. More recently his attitude, behavior, and appearance have improved significantly, and have returned to the same high level displayed early in this reporting period.

(Name) is a below average performer. He works diligently to arrive at a satisfactory conclusion of an assigned task, usually getting the necessary response from subordinates. Improvements in his leadership skills are needed. He needs to be more demanding and geared to accept only maximum effort and quality performance. Generally a good worker, he sometimes becomes complacent and requires a reminder to present a more professional attitude and appearance.

PERSONALITY

The following list of words express, define, state, or describe **UNFAVORABLE** personality characteristics, traits, performance, or results.

ADJECTIVES

ABERRANT	ABHORRENT	ABRASIVE
ABSENTMINDED	ADOLESCENT	ALOOF
AMBIVALENT	ANTAGONISTIC	ANTISOCIAL
APATHETIC	APPALLING	ARROGANT
ASTRAY	BASHFUL	BELLIGERENT
BERSERK	BLAND	BLUNT
BOISTEROUS	BRASH	BRASSY
CALLOUS	CARELESS	COCKSURE
COCKY	COLD	COLORLESS
COMPLACENT	CONDESCENDING	CONTEMPTIBLE
CORRUPT	CRASS	CRUDE
CRUSTY	CURT	CYNICAL
DECEPTIVE	DEFIANT	DEPRESSED
DERELICT	DESPAIRING	DESPONDENT
DEVIANT	DEVIOUS	DIE-HARD
DIFFIDENT	DISAGREEABLE	DISCOURTEOUS
DISDAINFUL	DISINCLINED	DISLOYAL
DISREPUTABLE	DISSATISFIED	DRABBER
ENERVATE	EGOCENTRIC	EXANIMATE
FACETIOUS	FAITHLESS	FASTIDIOUS
FATUOUS	FAULTFINDING	FECKLESS
FICKLE	FINICKY	FLACCID
FLAPPABLE	FOOLHARDY	FOOLISH
FOPPISH	FORGETFUL	FRACTIOUS
FRUSTRATED	FURIOUS	FUSSY
GALLING	GAUCHE	GARRULOUS
GRUDGING	HALF-BAKED	HALF-COCKED

HALFHEARTED   HAPLESS   HAPPY-GO-LUCKY
HARDHANDED   HARDHEADED   HARD-HEARTED
HARD-NOSED   HEARTLESS   HEAVY-HANDED

HEEDLESS   HIGH-STRUNG   HIGH-TONED
HOSTILE   HUMORLESS   HURTFUL
HYPERCRITICAL   ILLEGIBLE   ILL-HUMORED

ILL-MANNERED   ILL-NATURED   IMMATURE
IMMODERATE   IMMORAL   IMPATIENT
IMPERSONAL   IMPERTINENT   IMPETUOUS

IMPIOUS   IMPOLITE   IMPRUDENT
IMPUDENT   INANE   INAPT
INARTICULATE   INATTENTIVE   INCOGITANT

INCOHERENT   INCOMPETENT   INCONCEIVABLE
INCONGRUOUS   INCONSIDERATE   INDECISIVE
INDIFFERENT   INDIGNANT   INDISCREET

INDOLENT   INELOQUENT   INEPT
INEXPERT   INEXPLICIT   INFIRM
INFURIATE   INHARMONIOUS   INHOSPITABLE

INHUMANE   INIMICAL   INJUDICIOUS
INSENSIBLE   INSENSITIVE   INSINCERE
INSIPID   INSOLENT   INSUBORDINATE

INSURGENT   INVECTIVE   INVIDIOUS
IRATE   IRKSOME   IRRATIONAL
IRRESOLUTE   IRRESPONSIBLE   IRRESPONSIVE

IRRITABLE   JEALOUS   KINDLESS
LACKADAISICAL   LACKLUSTER   LACONIC
LAX   LETHARGIC   LIFELESS

LIGHT-HEADED   LOATH   LOATHSOME
LOFTY   LOQUACIOUS   LOW-MINDED
LOW-SPIRITED   MALADJUSTED   MALEVOLENT

MALICIOUS   MANNERLESS   MEEK
MERCILESS   MISCHIEVOUS   MISTAKEN
MOODY   NAÏVE   NEGLECTFUL

NERVELESS	OBNOXIOUS	OBSTINATE
OFFENSIVE	OPPRESSIVE	OUTSPOKEN
OVERBEARING	OVERCONFIDENT	PARANOID

PEEVISH	PERMISSIVE	PERT
PERTINACIOUS	PESSIMISTIC	PETULANT
PITILESS	POMPOUS	PORTENTOUS

PREJUDICIAL	PRUDISH	PRYING
QUARRELSOME	REASONLESS	REBELLIOUS
RELUCTANT	REMISS	REMORSEFUL

REMORSELESS	REPREHENSIBLE	REPROBATE
REPUGNANT	REPULSIVE	RESENTFUL
RHETORICAL	RUDE	RUTHLESS

SARCASTIC	SAUCY	SCORNFUL
SELF-CENTERED	SELF-CONSCIOUS	SELF-DEFEATING
SELF-IMPORTANT	SELFISH	SELF-OPINIONATED

SELF-RIGHTEOUS	SELF-SERVING	SHALLOW
SHAMEFUL	SHAMELESS	SHARP-TONGUED
SHIFTLESS	SHIFTY	SHORTSIGHTED

SHORT-SPOKEN	SHORT-TEMPERED	SHY
SLOVENLY	SMALL-MINDED	SMUG
SNIDE	SNUFFY	SOFTHEADED

SORROW	SPIRITLESS	SPITEFUL
SUBTLE	SULLEN	SUPERCILIOUS
SURLY	TACTLESS	TEMPERAMENTAL

TEPID	THANKLESS	THOUGHTLESS
TIMID	TIMOROUS	TROUBLESOME
TURBULENT	UNACCOMPLISHED	UNADVISED

UNAPT	UNCHARITABLE	UNCOMFORTABLE
UNDECIDED	UNDERHANDED	UNFAIR
UNFEELING	UNFIT	UNFRIENDLY

UNGRACIOUS	UNINTERESTING	UNMANNERLY
UNMERCIFUL	UNPLEASANT	UNPOPULAR
UNPRINCIPLED	UNPROFESSIONAL	UNREALISTIC

UNREASONABLE UNRULY UNSCRUPULOUS
UNSEASONED UNSKILLED UNSKILLFUL
UNSOCIABLE UNSTABLE UNSUITABLE

UNTIDY UNTRUTHFUL UNWILLING
VAIN VERBOSE VINDICTIVE
VIOLEN WANTON WEAKHEARTED

WEAK-MINDED WILL-LESS WITLESS
WORDY WRETCH WRETCHED
WROTH WRY

PERSONALITY

NOUNS

ABERRANT ABUSE ALTERCATION
ANTAGONIST APATHY ARROGANCE
AUDACITY BELLIGERENCE BERSERK

CHAOS CHARADE COMPLACENCY
CONDESCENDENCE CONFLICT CONTEMPT
CORRUPTION COVER-UP DECEPTION

DEFIANCE DEGRADATION DERELICTION
DESPONDENCY DISAGREEMENT DISCONTENT
DISFAVOR DISDAIN DISGUST

DISILLUSION DISLOYALTY DISMAY
DISREPUTE DISRESPECT DISSENSION
DISSENT DISSENTER DURESS

EGOISM EGOTISM ENMITY
FAKE FALSITY FATIGUE
FAULTFINDING FAVORITISM FEUD

FLEDGLING FLUSTER FOIBLE
FOLLY FOOLISHNESS FOOT-DRAGGING
FOUL-UP FRACAS FRAUD

FRUSTRATION FUROR FURY
GALL GAMESMANSHIP GARRULITY
GRIEVANCE GRIMACE GRUDGE

GUILE	GUISE	HALF-TRUTH
HATRED	HOSTILITY	ILLITERACY
ILLOGIC	IMPATIENCE	IMPERTINENCE
IMPROPRIETY	IMPRUDENCE	IMPUDENCE
INABILITY	INACCURACY	INAPTITUDE
INCAPACITY	INCERTITUDE	INCOMPATIBILITY
INCOMPETENCE	INDECISION	INDIFFERENCE
INDIGNATION	INDIGNITY	INDISCIPLINE
INDISCRETION	INEPTITUDE	INEQUALITY
INEQUITY	INEXPERIENCE	INGRATITUDE
INHARMONY	INIQUITY	INJUSTICE
INSOLENCE	INSTABILITY	INSULT
INTOLERANCE	IRE	JEALOUSY
KLUTZ	KNOW-IT-ALL	LAXITY
LETHARGY	LOATHING	MALEVOLENCE
MALICE	NONCONFORMIST	
MENACE	MISGIVING	MISUNDERSTANDING
NEGLIGENCE	OBSESSION	OUTBURST
OUTRAGE	PANIC	PARTISAN
PEDANT	PERTINACITY	PESSIMISM
POMPOSITY	PREJUDICE	PRUDE
QUITTER	RAGE	RAMPAGE
REBUFF	REFUSAL	RELUCTANCE
REMORSE	REPRESSION	REPRIMAND
REPROACH	REPUGNANCE	REPULSION
RESENTMENT	RHETORIC	RHETORICIAN
RIDICULE	RIVALRY	SARCASM
SCOFF	SCORN	SELF-CONCEIT
SELF-DOUBT	SELF-INDULGENCE	
SELF-INTEREST	SHAM	SKIRMISH
SOLVENT	SPITE	STUPOR
STYMIE	TEDIUM	TEMERITY
TROUBLEMAKER	TRUANT	TURMOIL

UNREASON   UNTRUTH   WEAKNESS
WILE   WRONGDOER   WRONGDOING

PERSONALITY

VERBS

ABASE	ABUSE	ACCOST
ANTAGONIZE	APPALL	BAFFLE
BALK	BELITTLE	BERATE
BETRAY	BIAS	BLUNDER
CENSURE	CHASTISE	COERCE
CONDEMN	CONFUSE	CONSPIRE
CRITICIZE	DAUNT	DEGRADE
DELUDE	DEMEAN	DEMORALIZE
DEPRESS	DESPAIR	DESPOND
DISACCORD	DISAGREE	DISCORD
DISDAIN	DISGRUNTLE	DISGUST
DISMAY	DISPUTE	DISREGARD
DISRESPECT	DISSATISFY	DISSENT
EMBITTER	ENERVATE	ENRAGE
EQUIVOCATE	FALSIFY	FINAGLE
FLAUNT	FLOUT	FORESTALL
FORFEIT	FORGET	FRET
FRUSTRATE	FUMBLE	GAB
GRIEVE	GRIPE	GROUSE
HARASS	HECKLE	HUMILIATE
IGNORE	IMPERSONALIZE	IMPUGN
INDULGE	INFLAME	INFRINGE
INHIBIT	INSULT	INTERFERE
INTERRUPT	INTIMIDATE	INTRUDE
IRK	JABBER	KNUCKLE UNDER
LOATHE	LOOK DOWN	MALINGER
MEDDLE	MISAPPLY	MISAPPROPRIATE

MISBECOME	MISBEHAVE	MISCALCULATE
MISCONDUCT	MISCONSTRUE	MISFIT
MISGUIDED	MISINTERPRET	MISJUDGE
MISLEAD	MISMANAGE	MISUNDERSTAND
MISUSE	MUDDLE	MUMBLE
OFFEND	OPPOSE	OPPRESS
OSTRACIZE	OVEREXTEND	OVERREACT
OVERSIMPLIFY	PALTER	PAMPER
PARE	PATRONIZE	PERSECUTE
PERTURB	PLOD	PROCRASTINATE
PRY	REFRAIN	RELAPSE
RELENT	RENOUNCE	REPREHEND
REPRESS	REPROACH	REPROBATE
REPUDIATE	REPULSE	RESENT
SCORN	SHIRK	SPURN
SQUABBLE	STUPEFY	STYMIED
SUCCUMB	SUFFER	UNDERMINE
UNNERVE	WANGLE	

UNFAVORABLE

OF OR WITHIN THE MIND

The following list of words express, define, state, or describe
UNFAVORABLE individual intellect, intelligence, knowledge, wisdom,
or reasoning.

ADJECTIVES

ABSURD	CRASS	DENSE
DULL	FEEBLEMINDED	FOOLISH
HALF-SCHOLAR	IGNORANT	ILLITERATE
ILLOGICAL	INANE	INCONSEQUENT
INEPT	INSENSIBLE	INSIGNIFICANT
IRRATIONAL	MEANINGLESS	MINDLESS

123

NESCIENT	OBTUSE	ONE-TRACK-MIND
ORDINARY	RIDICULOUS	SENILE
SENSELESS	SHALLOW	SHORTSIGHTED

SIMPLE	SIMPLE-MINDED	SPECULATIVE
STUPID	SUPERFICIAL	THICK
TRIFLING	UNACQUAINTED	UNAWARE

UNCONVERSANT	UNDISCERNING	UNDISTINGUISHED
UNERUDITE	UNFAMILIAR	UNIMAGINATIVE
UNINFORMATIVE	UNINFORMED	UNINTELLIGENT

UNKNOWING	UNKNOWN	UNLEARNED
UNLETTERED	UNPERCEPTIVE	UNREASONING
UNREFINED	UNSCHOLARLY	UNTAUGHT

| UNTUTORED | UNVERSED | UNWISE |
| VACUOUS | | |

UNFAVORABLE

OF OR WITHIN THE MIND

The following list of words express, define, state, or describe UNFAVORABLE individual intellect, intelligence, knowledge, wisdom, or reasoning.

NOUNS

DULLNESS	IGNORANCE	INCAPACITY
INCOMPREHENSION	INEPTITUDE	INSENSIBILITY
INTELLECTUAL WEAKNESS		IRRATIONALITY

MENTAL DEFICIENCY		MENTAL HANDICAP
MENTAL VOID		MENTAL WEAKNESS
SENILE	SENILITY	SHALLOWNESS

SHORTSIGHTEDNESS		STUPIDITY
SUPERFICIALITY	UNKNOWING	UNPERCEPTIVENESS
UNWITTINGNESS		

NEGATIVE - SHORTCOMING

The following list of words expresses. define, state, or describe **UNFAVORABLE** characteristics, traits, performance, or results not solely individual or personal.

ADJECTIVES

ABNORMAL	ABRUPT	ADVERSE
AMISS	ASKEW	AWRY
CONFLICTING	COSTIVE	CUMBERSOME
DEFECTIVE	DEFICIENT	DESPERATE
DISAPPOINTING	DISPASSIONATE	DISRUPTIVE
DETRIMENTAL	DUBIOUS	EFFETE
EFFORTLESS	ELUSIVE	EQUIVOCAL
EROSIVE	ERRANT	ERRATIC
EVASIVE	ERRONEOUS	FACILE
FALSE	FARCICAL	FARFETCHED
FLAGRANT	FLIMSY	FORBIDDING
FORMLESS	FRAGILE	FRAIL
FRAUDULENT	FRIVOLOUS	FRUITLESS
FUTILE	GLARING	GLOOMY
GLUM	GOOD-FOR-NOTHING	GRAVE
GRIEVOUS	GRIM	GROSS
HAPHAZARD	HARD PUT	HARSH
HELPLESS	HERKY-JERKY	HIT-OR-MISS
HOPELESS	HORRENDOUS	HUMDRUM
HUMILIATING	IDLE	ILL-ADVISED
ILLAUDIBLE	ILLEGAL	ILL-FATED
ILL-GOTTEN	ILLICIT	IMAGINATIVE
IMAGINARY	IMPERFECT	IMPOSSIBLE
IMPOTENT	IMPRACTICABLE	IMPRACTICAL
IMPRECISE	IMPROBABLE	IMPROPER
INACCURATE	INACTIVE	INADEQUATE
INADVISABLE	INAPPROPRIATE	INCAPABLE

INCOMPARABLE	INCOMPATIBLE	INCOMPLETE
INCOMPREHENSIBLE		INCONSEQUENTIAL
INCONSIDERABLE	INCONSISTENT	INCONVENIENT
INCORRECT	INCORRIGIBLE	INDEFENSIBLE
INDEFINABLE	INDISCERNIBLE	INDISTINCT
INDISTINCTIVE	INEFFECTIVE	INEFFECTUAL
INEFFICIENT	INELIGIBLE	INEQUITABLE
INERT	INEXACT	INEXCUSABLE
INEXPEDIENT	INEXPLICABLE	INFERIOR
INOPPORTUNE	INORDINATE	INSECURE
INSIDIOUS	INSIGNIFICANT	INSOLVABLE
INSUBSTANTIAL	INSUFFERABLE	INSUFFICIENT
INSUPPORTABLE	INTOLERABLE	INTOLERANT
INTRACTABLE	INTRUSIVE	INVALID
IRREDEEMABLE	IRREFORMABLE	IRREGULAR
IRRELATIVE	IRRELEVANT	LAST
LAST-DITCH	LIMITED	LOST
LOW-GRADE	LOW-LEVEL	LUDICROUS
MALADROIT	NEGLIGENT	MEANINGLESS
MISERABLE	MUNDANE	NEGATIVE
NONPRODUCTIVE	NULL	OBSCURE
OBSOLETE	OUTCAST	OUTLANDISH
OUT-OF-DATE	OUTRAGEOUS	OVERDUE
PATHETIC	PECCANT	PEJORATIVE
PELL-MELL	PENITENT	PETTY
PLAUSIBLE	POLEMIC	PRECARIOUS
PREPOSTEROUS	PROBLEM	PRODIGAL
PURPOSELESS	REDUNDANT	RESISTLESS
RIGOROUS	ROUGH	RUN-DOWN
RUSTY	SCANT	SCANTY
SHABBY	SHAKY	SKEPTICAL
SKEPTICISM	SLIPSHOD	SLOPPY
SMALL-SCALE	SOMBER	SORROWFUL

SPARSE	SPORADIC	SPOTTY
SPURIOUS	STAGNANT	SUBNORMAL
SUBSTANDARD	SUPERFICIAL	SUPERFLUOUS
THRIFTLESS	TIRESOME	TRICKY
TRITE	UNCERTAIN	UNEASY
UNFAVORABLE	UNFORTUNATE	UNLAWFUL
UNORGANIZED	UNSETTLED	UNSUCCESSFUL
UNTRUE	UNWORTHY	USELESS
VALUELESS	WANTING	WASHED-UP
WASTED	WASTEFUL	WEAK
WEARIFUL	WEARISOME	WEARY
WHIMSICAL	WISHY-WASHY	WORSE
WORST	WORTHLESS	WRONG
WRONGFUL		

NEGATIVE - SHORTCOMING

NOUNS

ADVERSITY	BLEMISH	CHAGRIN
CONFUSION	DEFECT	DEMERIT
DEMISE	DEPENDENCY	DETRIMENT
DEVIATE	DISADVANTAGE	DISAPPOINTMENT
DISASTER	DISCORD	DISCREDIT
DISORDER	DISPARITY	DISSATISFACTION
EBB	EGOIST	ENCUMBRANCE
ERROR	EXCUSE	EYESORE
FAILURE	FATUITY	FAULT
FIASCO	FIZZLE	FLAW
FLUTTER	FORFEIT	FRICTION
FUTILITY	GLITCH	HAPHAZARD
HAPPENSTANCE	HARDSHIP	HARM
HINDRANCE	IMBALANCE	IMPARITY
IMPERFECTION	IMPOSSIBILITY	INACTION

INADEQUACY	INATTENTION	INCONSISTENCY
INCONSONANCE	INCONVENIENCE	INEFFICACY
INEFFICIENCY	INEXPEDIENCY	INFRACTION
INSIGNIFICANCE	INTERFERENCE	INTRUSION
INVALIDITY	IRREGULARITY	LACK
LAG	LAPSE	LEVITY
LIABILITY	LOSER	MEANDER
MISFORTUNE	MISHAP	MIX-UP
NONSENSE	NUISANCE	OPPOSITION
OVERSIGHT	PARODY	PELL-MELL
PITFALL	PROBLEM	QUIBBLE
REGRESS	REGRESSION	RESTRAINT
RIGOR	SHODDY	SHORTCOMING
SHORTFALL	SLOPWORK	TENSION
TRAVESTY	UNCERTAINTY	WASTE

NEGATIVE - SHORTCOMING

VERBS

COLLAPSE	CONCEAL	CONCEDE
CONDESCEND	CRIMP	DEBASE
DENOUNCE	DEPRIVE	DESTROY
DETERIORATE	DILUTE	DIMINISH
DISAPPOINT	DISRUPT	DISTORT
DODGE	DWINDLE	EBB
ELUDE	ENCUMBER	ERODE
ESCHEW	EXACERBATE	EXAGGERATE
EXTENUATE	FADE	FAIL
FAKE	FALTER	FLOP
FLOUNDER	FLUNK	FOIL
FOUNDER	GLOOM	HAMPER
HARM	HINDER	IMMOBILIZE
IMPAIR	IMPEDE	INCAPACITATE
IRRITATE	LACK	LAG

LAPSE	LAVISH	LESSEN
LIMP	LOWER	MAR
MISTAKE	NEGATE	NEGLECT
OBSTRUCT	OUST	PALL
QUIT	REBUT	REFUSE
REJECT	RELINQUISH	REPUGN
RESTRAIN	RETARD	ROUSE
SQUANDER	STAGNATE	SUPPRESS
SWAY	THWART	TRANSGRESS
VEX	VIOLATE	VITIATE
WEAKEN	WEAR OUT	WILT
WORK OVER	WORSEN	

UNFAVORABLE BULLETS PHRASES

...Inexcusable behavior
...Distasteful behavior
...Not fit

...Inconsiderate and uncaring
...Dull, uninspiring leader
...Inappropriate actions

...Of little value
...Not manageable
...Illogical performance and actions

...Indolent, sluggish personality
...Not a potent, effective leader
...Slow to act

...Produces inaccurate, faulty work
...Abrupt manner
...Lacking in knowledge

...Abnormal behavior
...Causes disorder and unrest
...Has defeatist attitude

...Dispassionate leader
...Erratic work habits
...Erodes morale and team spirit

...Weak, ineffective leader
...Shows little or no effort
...Weak, inadequate leader

...Inferior workmanship
...Lacks physical vigor
...Indecisive and evasive

...Not well organized mentally
...Flagrant violation of orders
...Disagreeable personality

...Causes depression and gloom
...Lacks charisma
...Ambiguous and evasive in manner

...Non-productive worker
...Overly bold and assertive
...Attracts trouble

...Stubborn and obstinate
...Crude, coarse personality
...Operates in a vacuum

...Aberrant behavior
...Unstable personality
...Impersonal leader

...Poor planner, great hindsight
...Vague, ambiguous self-expression
...Evasive and indirect manner

...Disagreeable personality
...Emotionally immature
...Antisocial behavior

...Abrupt, blunt manner
...Deviant behavior
...Overly talkative

...Careless in manner and action
...Unprincipled behavior
...Unfriendly disposition

...Careless, untidy appearance
...Indiscreet and thoughtless action
...Lax in performance & behavior

...Accepts orders reluctantly
...Abusive in language and action
...Undisciplined and unruly

...Vain, self-centered personality
...Reluctant, unwilling performer
...Tends to be troublesome

...Bad in manner and disposition
...Short-tempered and arrogant
...Prone to indecisiveness

...Weak, vacillating leadership
...Prankish, childish mannerism
...Impolite and unmannerly actions

...Creates resentment & disharmony
...Impolite, insulting manner
...Insincere, careless manager

...Aggressive, challenging attitude
...Disrespectful to superiors
...Devious and cunning personality

...Inferior performer
...Careless work habits
...Professionally stagnant

...Adolescent behavior
...Arrogant, overbearing manner
...Crude, tactless manner

...Drab, dull personality
...Fails to observe regulations
...Spiritless, lifeless leader

...Unable to master job
...Overbearing and oppressive
...Acts on impulse, not plan

...Indecisive leader
...Benevolent behavior
...Ill-humored personality

...Obstinate and impudent
...Fault-finding to excess
...Misuses position

...Disorderly conduct
...Temperamental behavior
...Maladjusted personality

...Undignified manner
...Provokes arguments
...A problem person

...Careless appearance
...Unpredictable behavior
...Failed to improve

...Loses control
...Totally unconcerned
...Lack of desire

...Completely helpless
...Impedes progress
...Low self-esteem

...Cold, indifferent attitude
...Corrupt, immoral character
...Argumentative toward others

...Boisterous and rude personality
...Unsound management practices
...Misrepresents the facts

...Ineffectual leadership skills
...Interferes with progress
...Easily excitable and troublesome

...Improper behavior and conduct
...Indifferent towards others
...Seriously endangers morale

...Difficult to reason with
...Uncaring in reason or sympathy
...Impervious to counseling

...Subject to daily failure
...Ignores advice of superiors
...Inflexible, rigid taskmaster

...Practices deceit and trickery
...Doubtful, confusing leadership
...Undesirable personality traits

...Corruptive, dishonest nature
...Irritates and annoys others
...Faulty, defective workmanship

...Mundane, methodical leadership
...Concerned with own self-interest
...Discourages team unity

...Contemptible and arrogant
...Unjustly exploits others
...Suppresses subordinate initiative

...Avoids work and responsibility
...Circumvents chain of command
...Hot tempered, easily angered

...Lack of confidence
...Ignores reality
...Threat to morale

...Mentally malnourished
...Shirks responsibility
...Pressures subordinates

...Emotionally immature
...Leadership vacuum
...Mistaken judgment

...A complainer
...Bad judgment
...Carefree attitude

...Incapable and inept
...Distant and impersonal
...Plots and schemes

...Abrasive personality
...Throws weight around
...Wasted opportunities

...Slow and methodical
...Fabricates the truth
...Incites arguments

...Insensitive leadership
...Degrading to others
...Short temper

...Deviates from standards
...Inhibits progress
...Shuns duty

...Unimpressive leader
...Meek and humble manner
...Incompetent manager

...Brash and immature
...Loses emotional control
...Meager productiveness

...Becomes emotionally violent
...Without mercy or compassion
...Lacks proper mental discipline

...Becomes easily frustrated
...Has innate aversion to work
...Not dependable or reliable

...Unpredictable work habits
...Mild learning disability
...Persistently poor performance

...Complete disregard for authority
...Does no more than required
...Less than moderate success

...Arrogant and overbearing
...Finds excessive leisure time
...Quarrelsome, touchy nature

...Unable to control emotions
...Intentionally avoids work
...Deliberately refuses orders

...Lacks depth and substance
...Hostile, aggressive temperament
...Unwilling to obey orders

...Without sorrow or remorse
...Immaturity and bad judgment
...Behavior and attitude problems

...Unimpressive performance
...Prejudicial to good order
...Detrimental to team spirit

...Less than marginal performer
...Fails to monitor subordinates
...Openly disagrees with superiors

...Causes extra work for others
...Lackadaisical attitude
...Continuing discipline problem

...Serious judgment error
...Blatant negligence
...Disruptive influence

...Abnormal behavior
...Imperceptible progress
...Argues to excess

...Mediocre abilities
...Common and ordinary
...Inflexible leader

...Dull, trite personality
...Undermines morale
...Lack of initiative

...Negative attitude
...Openly discontent
...Unacceptable behavior

...Ignores direction
...Not job-aggressive
...Lack of pride in work

...Flouts authority
...Lags behind others
...Becomes easily excited

...Stirs up trouble
...Breaks down morale
...Irregular work habits

...Lacks persistence
...Acts on impulse
...Frequent complainer

...Constantly complains
...Not trustworthy
...Plagued by indecision

...Not reliable
...Unwilling to conform
...Creates problems

...Reluctant to abide by rules
...Unable to stay abreast of job
...Interferes with progress

...Indecisive under pressure
...Obvious lack of motivation
...Disobedient and disrespectful

...Volatile, explosive disposition
...Fails to accomplish tasks
...Negative outlook and disposition

...Lax in carrying out duties
...Requires routine reminders
...Wears down subordinate spirit

...Uses questionable leadership
...Impersonal, detached leader
...Gets less than desired results

...Not receptive to counseling
...Irrational, erratic behavior
...Overly aggressive personality

...Verbally abuses subordinates
...Spreads ill-will and disharmony
...Careless attention to duty

...Non-forgiving leadership traits
...Lack of personal conviction
...Unable to perform routine tasks

...Abusive and offensive language
...Ingrained disrespectful nature
...Fails to achieve consistency

...Lacks knowledge and ability
...A burden to leadership
...Disobedient and belligerent

...Improper counseling techniques
...Spreads discontent and resentment
...Not firm with subordinates

...Exercises bad judgment
...Weak personality
...Abrupt manner

...Apathetic leader
...Not an inspiring leader
...Lacks self-discipline

...Shirks responsibility
...Sloppy workmanship
...Asks undue questions

...Lack of initiative
...Indecisive leader
...Slow, plodding worker

...Erodes good order
...Prone to argument
...Inconsistent worker

...Frequent bad judgment
...Marginal performer
...Exerts minimum effort

...No future potential
...Overly bold and brash
...Emotional difficulty

...Inattentive to detail
...Suppresses subordinate growth
...Gives misguided direction

...Manipulates others to own end
...Of little worth or value
...Lack of confidence in abilities

...Helpless without supervision
...Unable to deal with reality
...Needs continued reminders

...Interprets rules loosely
...Overbearing and intolerant
...Reluctant to accept direction

...Tries hard, accomplishes little
...Frequently in discord with superiors
...Lacks consistency of performance

...Deficient in skill and knowledge
...Inflexible, unimaginative leadership
...Insolent, overbearing personality

...Unwilling to listen to reason or fact
...Instigates and provokes disharmony
...Mechanical, non-inventive leadership

...Failed to live up to expectations
...Unmanageable off-duty activities
...Becomes easily agitated and excited

...Blames others for own shortcomings
...Oppressive in character and action
...Insulting and arrogant personality

...Unable to overcome minor problems
...Lacks orderly mental continuity
...Careless of the feelings of others

...Non-compassionate, harsh leader
...Overreacts to minor situations
...Decisions are open to question

...Weakens or breaks under pressure
...Does not pay attention to instruction
...Increased supervision is required

...Deviates from expected standards
...Wears down spirit of subordinates
...Consistent marginal performance

...Lacks mental depth and soundness
...Noticeable decline in performance
...Displays obvious lack of motivation

...Unpleasant appearance and personality
...Unpredictable attention to duty and detail
...Incapable manager and supervisor

...Chronic financial problems
...Fails to respond to direction
...Low level of self-confidence

...Lackluster, lackadaisical attitude
...Inclined to stray from the truth
...Uncertain, indecisive in action

...Is a complete disappointment
...Not correct and precise in detail
...Acts out of emotion, not reason

...Habitually reports to work late
...Insulting and abusive to others
...Unforgiving leader

...Aimless management
...Lacks plan, order & discipline
...Blames shortcomings on others

...Overly unreasonable
...Indiscreet personal affairs
...Rubs a mistake in, not out

...A prankster, not serious minded
...A liability to the organization
...Relies too heavily on others

...Inconsistent supervisor
...Plagued by indecisiveness
...A less than positive attitude

...Not a self-starter
...Slow and deliberate work pace
...Fails to respond to counseling

...Habitually flouts authority
...Seriously lacking in initiative
...Fabricates the truth

...Incapable of sustained satisfactory performance
...Aimless, errant decision making facilities
...Not a potent, effective supervisor

...Incapable of handling practical matters
...Makes decisions that are not sensible or prudent
...Incompatible, disagreeing personality

...Incompetent without direct, consistent supervision
...Unfair and inequitable treatment of subordinates
...Personal behavior is incompatible with good discipline

...Disruptive to good order and discipline
...Uncertain and doubtful in making decisions
...Intentionally makes minor mistakes

...Lacks personal sincerity and believability
...Frequently makes false or untrue statements
...Organization lacks order and cohesiveness

...Self-indulgent, irresponsible leadership
...Sometimes impatient with subordinates
...Achieves less than moderately successful results

...Can achieve good results only under ordinary conditions
...Deliberately goes out of way to irritate others
...Efforts frequently prove fruitless and unsuccessful

...Shows little forethought or preparation of task at hand
...Criticizes and reprimands subordinates in public
...Lacks good judgment and common sense

...Does not demonstrate a sense of responsibility
...Too submissive and mild mannered to be an effective leader
...Subject to mood changes without warning

...Evades and shirks duty when possible
...Becomes confused and frustrated when forced to choose one of various
        options
...Makes mistakes through lack of attention

...Argumentative with irritating persistence
...Intentional disregard for following orders
...Excessively lenient in handling subordinates

135

...Conveniently misunderstands or misinterprets orders
...Superiors find it difficult to support independently made decisions
...Excessively forceful toward subordinates

...Fails to act according to professional standards
...A bad leader and a worse follower
...Plans lack breadth, originality, and substance

...Lax and careless in performing professional duties
...Off-duty conduct is disgraceful and unacceptable
...Conduct is beyond the bounds of decency

...Frequently breaks rules and disobeys orders
...Overly strict and harsh leadership practices
...Considers all jobs below personal dignity to accomplish

...Apprehensive about accepting any new job or challenge
...Does not abide by rules in an orderly fashion
...Professional development lags behind contemporaries

...Ignores direction and guidance of superiors
...Wasteful and extravagant use of resources
...Alters facts to suit own self-interest

...Strays from work area if not closely watched
...Unable to stay mentally involved with job, becomes preoccupied with
          personal matters
...Deviates sharply from behavioral standards

...Belligerent and hostile personality
...Displays open contempt for authority
...Devoid of hope for improvement

...Has more than a mild dislike for work
...Violates standards of behavior and conduct
...Will violate any rule or regulation not to personal liking

...Written products are not clear and coherent
...Overly harsh and critical of minor mistakes by subordinates
...Blunt and rude in speech and manner

...Unable to choose correct courses of action
...Thoughtless in considering feelings of others
...Insensitive and callous leadership

...Not responsive to guidance or direction
...Destructive to good order and discipline
...Unsophisticated behavior and attitude

...Performance highlighted by neglect and negligence
...Policies are not uniform and consistent
...Unpleasant, objectionable personality

...Unyielding to reason or rationale
...Not a strong leader, too permissive and lenient
...Lacks necessary personal traits to be a successful leader

...Acts without giving due consideration or thought
...Personal problems demand excessive time and energy of others
...Neglectful and forgetful work habits

...Lacking in social grace and courtesy
...Will not work unless prompted or prodded
...Exaggerated self-opinion and self-importance

...Unable to restrain or control emotions
...Stubbornly opposes corrective counseling
...Refuses to yield or relent to change

...Does not objectively evaluate evidence and conditions
...Leadership too tolerant and permissive
...Excessive minor infractions of discipline

...Gross deviation from regulations
...Becomes bogged down in petty, insignificant details
...A slacker, shirks duty when possible

...Administrative and disciplinary burden
...Disrespectful attitude and behavior
...Exhibits lack of desire to conform to standards

...Persistent minor disciplinary infraction
...Exhibits only short periods of success
...Performance a deterrent to good order and discipline

...Shows no desire for improvement
...Frequently deviates from standards
...Behavior goes beyond the bounds of good taste

...Without personal restraint or calmness
...Not straightforward and open in manner
...Unable to distinguish right from wrong

...Passive and submissive in nature
...Unable to overcome personal problems and difficulties
...Fails to maintain harmony and cohesiveness within work group

...Fails to achieve minimum acceptable performance
...Actual performance falls well short of abilities
...Work marked by utter, complete failure

...Has a personality clash with almost all co-workers
...Makes careless, avoidable mistakes
...Work frequently falls short of expectations and abilities

...Failed to live up to expectations
...Suitable for routine, ordinary jobs
...Twists recollection of events to own ends

...Counseled regarding incongruent interaction with others
...Working relationship with subordinates does not reflect the necessary
        tact and maturity required
...Very difficult for others to work with

...Incapable of compassionate leadership
...Neglects personal welfare of subordinates
...Evasive when confronted with shortcomings

...Helpless in meeting new situations without on-the-scene leadership
...Tries very hard but achieves little
...Hesitant and confused in unfamiliar surrounding

...Excuses offered more frequently than productive performance
...Expects success using guesswork and conjecture
...Mechanical, non-inventive or inspiring leadership

...Exerts undue influence and pressure on subordinates
...Routinely doubts and questions superiors
...Works hard only when personally convenient

...Turns simple tasks into complex problems
...Disagreeing personality dims hopes and desires of others
...Agitates others, creates ill-will and discontent

...Unplanned, unforeseen problems hinder professional ability
...Work suffers from plainness and simplicity
...Has a deceptive and deceitful character

...Superficial work doesn't hold up to close examination
...Overly demanding and self-assertive
...Overly concerned with self-image

...Organization out of kilter and does not function properly
...Cannot cope successfully with severe, trying situations
...Discussions frequently turn into heated disputes

...Gives in to pressure during crisis situations
...Opposes improvement efforts of others
...Inability to change or adapt to changing situations

...Unable to stay abreast of events in fast-paced environment
...Does not provide personal touch to leadership responsibilities
...Not clear in thought or reasoning. Clouds or confuses issues

...Cannot articulate in speech, incoherent in writing
...Willful disobedience and open disrespect for authority
...Cannot make proper decisions under pressure

...Dodges work and responsibility at almost every opportunity
...Has strong tendency to stray from normal behavior
...Not job-aggressive, waits for something to happen before taking action

...Below average performer. May come around in due time
...Not overly serious or concerned in doing tasks correctly
...Functions well below level of performance capable and acceptable

...Manipulates people to meet own ends
...Not prudent in personal financial matters
...Displays carefree and reckless abandon attitude

...Routinely displays unacceptable behavior and performance
...Prejudicial to good order and discipline
...Substandard mission performance routinely displayed

...Does not get things done in timely manner
...A "sea lawyer," attempts to walk thin line between right and wrong
...Needs continued reminders about personal hygiene, haircuts, and clean
        uniforms

...Good judgment sometimes impaired by short temper
...Abrasive personality. Has difficulty getting along with others
...Intractable unwillingness to conform to expected standards of behavior
      and conduct

...Premature in judgment. Does not always get all the facts before acting
...Sometimes becomes absent-minded or preoccupied with events not
      related to task at hand
...Interprets rules loosely and usually to personal benefit

...Weak leader, too easily influenced by subordinates
...Becomes withdrawn and distraught when confronted on shortcoming
...Prefers to forsake any personal help or assistance

...Uses improper counseling techniques, often degrading and humiliating
      subordinates
...Will stray or deviate from work standards if not closely watched
...Sometimes overbearing and overly intolerant of mistakes

...Not a strong personality. Overly apologetic and humble
...Erodes good order and discipline
...Abnormally high reluctance to accept direction and guidance

...Argumentative. Opposes all views other than own
...Not capable of continued good performance
...Not firm and resolute with subordinates

...Abrasive personality and abrupt manner stirs discontent and resentment
      among others
...Usually, but not always, in compliance with regulations
...Treatment of subordinates less than desired and expected

...Inconsistent behavior, subject to sudden bursts of anger
...Routinely fails personnel inspections
...Inattentive to routine work procedures, lacks persistence

...Even best efforts frequently prove fruitless or unsuccessful.
...Arbitrarily enforces rules and standards
...Believes job should be subordinate to personal interests

...Poor leader. Unforeseen and unplanned problems routinely arise
...Gives undue consideration and attention to personal likes and priorities
      at the expense of job performance
...Accommodating to subordinate desires to a fault

...Takes uncompromising stand in even minor matters
...Speaks and acts on impulse, does not always think through situation
...Overly challenging and aggressive personality

...Has difficulty getting along with others
...Blames others for own shortcomings
...Condemns or shuns thoughts and ideas of others

...Displays no rational or orderly relationship in planning or assigning tasks
...Cannot be relied upon to take timely, correct action
...Unconventional and unorthodox style of leadership produces less than
    desired results

...Overconfident. Abnormally high self-opinion
...Not receptive to constructive counseling
...Views standing orders as a matter of personal convenience

...Walks on thin edge between right and wrong
...Displays irrational and erratic behavior
...Harsh and coarse in leadership and language

...Possesses ample knowledge and skill to perform routine tasks without
    constant supervision
...Subordinates suffer from lack of own sense of direction and self-
    discipline
...Gets in verbal confrontation with others.

...Abusive language and improper treatment are major flaws in leadership
    skills
...Fails to abide by rules and regulations
...Lacks quality and depth of character

...Weak personality. Frequently concedes point of view without positive
    stand
...Leadership and guidance lacks substance and purpose
...Rigid thinking restricts ability to learn new courses of action

...Unable to cope with difficult situations without assistance
...Improper leadership takes its toll on organizational effectiveness
...Plagued by lack of self-confidence and positive leadership

...Defeatist attitude and lack of personal conviction proved to be a major
    disappointment
...Possesses ingrained disregard for authority
...Leadership style leaves uneasy feeling

...Proposed plans and actions frequently riddled with paradox
...Governs others by overly stern code of own ethics
...Non-forgiving leader. Rubs in mistakes and doesn't forget

...Asks for an undue amount of justification when assigned almost any task
...Exerts only the minimum amount of initiative needed to complete
            assigned tasks
...Fails to properly supervise subordinates

...Assigns work but does not follow-up to ensure finished product
...Has difficulty managing paperwork
...Unable to ensure quality work completed in timely manner

...Not steadfast in commitment, displays reversal of point of view or
            attitude
...Leadership ability is questionable at best and routinely ends in confusion
            and no purpose of action by subordinates
...Inattentive to detail, becomes easily distracted

...Routinely questions motive of superiors
...Reliability and effectiveness oscillates between extreme highs and lows,
            depending on daily mood and attitude
...Has difficulty understanding orders and correctly following direction

...Excels in jobs routine and repetitive in nature
...Superiors waste more hours counseling and documenting substandard
            performance than they receive productive work in return
...Exhibits neither desire nor ability to perform satisfactorily

...Does not always consider gravity of situation at hand
...Tries hard, but sometimes gets carried away with own enthusiasm and
            overlooks routine but necessary details
...Usually in compliance with rules and regulations

...Becomes belligerent and disobedient when given direction by some
            superiors
...Counseling required for sloppy workmanship
...Does not care about the final product

...Performance of duty totally unsatisfactory
...Often leaves work area without permission
...Does not seek, and reluctantly accepts, any responsibility

...Performance marked by inconsistency and incompleteness
...Sporadic in understanding and carrying out directives
...Frequently displays immaturity and bad judgment

...Inability to adjust to expected standards
...Shoddy workmanship, takes not pride in work or job accomplishment
...Half-truths highlight attitude and behavior problems

...Demonstrates little initiative or little desire for improvement
...Adversely affects operations and morale of contemporaries
...Received counseling on numerous occasions for lack of motivation

...Negative attitude toward work and others
...Acceptance of orders depends upon issuing superior
...Late for work on numerous occasions

...Performance, across the board, is unsatisfactory.
...Personal conduct is prejudicial to good order and discipline
...Lateness for work places extra burden on co-workers

...Detracts from otherwise high morale and team spirit
...Performance is all valleys and no peaks
...Impulsive, subject to actions without due thought or consideration

...Considers counseling on off-duty activities an unwarranted intrusion into
        personal life
...Unreliable performance persists despite counseling at various levels
...Negative attitude is reflected almost daily by continued marginal
        performance

...Conduct and performance have degenerated to unacceptable level
...Flagrant violation of direction and guidance seriously detract from
        already low level of performance
...Total lack of amenability to structured work environment

...Displays open discontent toward superiors and job content
...Inconsistent in accepting and reacting to supervision and direction
...Performance well below that expected

...Becomes involved in immediate task at hand and sometimes lets more
        broad-scope matters slip by without due attention
...Less than marginal performer, requires almost constant supervision
...Ignores explicit direction of superiors

...Counseling on substandard performance results in only short-term improvement
...Generally performs to full expectations
...Disruptive to good order and discipline

...Frequently voices displeasure at job assignments
...Not aggressive in meeting established standards or goals
...Performance migrates between acceptable and unsatisfactory

...Exhibits nonchalance and engenders disrespect among peers
...Requires almost constant supervision to accomplish assigned tasks
...Fails to properly monitor and direct activity of assigned personnel

...Continually commits minor offenses as if testing superiors
...A below average performer who causes extra work for others
...Unresponsive to normal and special counseling

...Consistently places higher priority on personal desires than on assigned duties
...Openly voices disagreement with supervision and policy
...Flouts authority despite numerous attempts at counseling on formal and informal basis

...Lackadaisical attitude toward superiors and job
...Becomes withdrawn and disdain when counseled on deficiencies
...Leaves assigned place of work to take care of personal matters without informing superiors

...Has negative outlook and disposition regardless of subject matter
...Complains openly when not assigned tasks to personal liking
...Lack of motivation and frequent short absences cause supervisory and administrative burden

...Continuing discipline problem evidenced in inability and unwillingness to comply with simplest direction and guidance
...Despite extensive training, lacks requisite skill and knowledge required of assigned job
...Unable to simultaneously monitor and control individual operations and functions of a diverse and dynamic environment

...Inconsistent performance. Usually good worker, but at times requires close supervision
...Works without supervision when the mood strikes
...Total lack of enthusiasm, constant complaining, and unwillingness to do personal share of work has detrimental impact on morale

...Has great deal of difficulty following even the simplest of orders
...A marginal performer whose work must remain under constant
       supervision
...Often requires reminders to commence job on schedule

...Counseling on deficiencies results in only short-term improvement
...Marginal performer, requires direct guidance and supervision in routine
       matters
...Immature and undisciplined with no potential for continued, useful
       service

...Reluctance to conform to standards
...Continuous poor attitude and behavior
...Steady and prolonged decline in performance and waning interest

...Consistently failed to take positive, corrective action on shortcomings
...Performance characterized by tension, dissension and half-efforts
...Leadership marred by indecisive and undisciplined practices

...Inadequate performance brought about by inability to gain proficiency in
       functional skills
...Has insufficient motivation to overcome personal deficiencies
...Unable to take constructive criticism and private counseling

...Ineptness in job accomplishment places undue burden on others
...Will not acknowledge mistakes or failures. Always blames others
...Does not exhibit a knack for making positive things happen

...Performance below standard despite ability and well-defined
       assignments
...Attempts to correct deficiencies have been in vain
...Inappropriate behavior and performance

...Unsophisticated reasoning and judgment
...Exhibits unsatisfactory performance in technical specialty
...Slow to learn and develop professionally

The following pages contain bullet phrases without an ending. This allows you, the drafter, to select an appropriate beginning and add whatever ending is desired.

...Habitually gets into trouble by...
...Not mentally capable to...
...Impairs morale by...

...Does not have the ability to...
...Below normal level of skill in...
...Lacks necessary ability to...

...Failed to achieve consistency in...
...Involved in unethical practice of...
...Under emotional strain when...

...Not qualified to be...
...Not worthy of...
...Lacking in ability to...

...Hinders and impedes progress by...
...Is of little or no use in/when...
...Unforgiving nature causes...

...Of little value in/when...
...Behavior not conducive to...
...Unable to grasp meaning of...

...Contemptuous disregard for...
...Slow to learn and develop as a/an...
...Enjoys a low reputation due to...

...Has open contempt for...
...Lacks mental aptitude to...
...Blatant disregard for...

...Will not maintain commitment to...
...Loses composure when/under...
...Becomes agitated and upset when...

...Openly defies and challenges...
...Lacks vigor or force to...
...Not mature enough to...

...Upsets normal operations by...
...A misfit, not suited for/to...
...Lacks the emotional stability to...

...Has not adjusted well to...
...Unable to refrain from...
...Bad habits include...

...Lax in complying and enforcing...
...Made crude attempt to...
...Lacks mental restraint to...

...Unsuitable and unfit for...
...Unsuitable for...
...Strongly opposed to...

...Incompetent in areas of...
...Careless and negligent in...
...Misguided efforts caused...

...Lacks inner discipline to...
...Of little use or value in...
...Has no idea of how to...

...A constant threat to morale by...
...Finds it most difficult to fit in with...
...Inexperienced in matters of...

...Not serious about...
...Has bad habit of...
...Not mentally equipped to...

...Displays marked indifference in...
...Usually drops behind others when...
...Fails to grasp essentials of...

...Has great difficulty in/with...
...Sometimes lax in...
...Stirs up trouble by...

...Helpless when confronted with...
...Does not totally comply with...
...Has chronic weakness of/in...

...Has distorted view of...
...Apathetic towards...
...Unable to fall in line with...

...Unable to deal with reality of...
...Has difficulty with...
...Planned badly for...

...Has not kept pace with...
...Ignores reality. Unable to...

...Unwilling to put forth necessary effort to...
...Does not give required importance to...
...Conduct not fit or becoming of a/an...

...Unable to maintain a stable balance of...
...Becomes hostile when approached about...
...Despite receiving sufficient counseling and supervision, continued to...

...Overall performance declined because of isolated incidence of...
...Lacks mental courage and conviction to...
...Did not exercise sound judgment by/when...

...Shows apathy and indifference to/toward...
...Disenchanted with present duties because...
...Rude and impolite, does not show proper respect to/for...

...Performance has deteriorated to point to...
...Becomes confused and puzzled when...
...Does not satisfy minimum requirements for/of...

...Does not possess the mental vigor and vitality to...
...Interferes with normal functioning of...
...Behavior has declined to point of...

...Has a strong moral weakness in...
...Suffers frequent minor setbacks because of...
...Failure to pay attention to detail caused...

...Has made insignificant progress in...
...Lags behind contemporaries in...
...Unable to take full advantage of...

...A major cause of disappointment because...
...Acts in haste without due regard of...
...Suffered total loss of integrity because of...

...Open distrust of subordinates causes...
...Lacks necessary wisdom and judgment to...
...Does not possess sufficient knowledge to...

...Made false statements concerning...
...Failed to act with promptness and dispatch in/when...
...Sometimes uses ethically dubious means to...

...Displayed improper judgment by/when...
...Refused to accept assistance to...
...Does not posses the necessary self-confidence to...

...Shows only artificial interest in...
...Deliberate lack of consideration for...
...Does not have the will or ability to...

...Excitable temper frequently cause of...
...Not an accomplished or skilled...
...Work characterized by complete absence of...

...Chronic personal and financial problems have lead to...
...Despite ample opportunity, failed to improve...
...Critically undermines morale by...

...Lacks knowledge or comprehension to...
...Impedes work and discipline by...
...Requires routine reminders to...

...Inconsistent and unimpressive performance led to...
...Attitude and performance not in tune with...
...Shows a marked unwillingness to...

...Has exaggerated ego problem which results in...
...Relinquishes control over subordinates when...
...Prone to substandard work because of...

...Becomes intensely excited and aroused by/when...
...Inconsistent work and irregular work habits caused by...
...Occasionally regresses to old habits of...

...Personal doubt and indecision sometimes hinders...
...Acts on spontaneous impulse, without due consideration of...
...Becomes easily distressed when/over...

...Deeply emotional, cannot control urge to...
...Sometimes uses excessive force or pressure to/in...
...Actions and deeds in sharp contrast with...

...Barely satisfactory in ability to...
...Compounds existing problems by...
...Carelessness and inattention to duty caused/led to...

...Belabors on nonessential matters to detriment of...
...Personal desires frequently at contrast with...
...Generally learned but totally inexperienced in...

...Relieved of duties for cause when...
...Suppresses subordinate growth potential by...
...Superiors began to lose trust in abilities when...

...Tries to do a good job, but is hindered by...
...Utterly helpless when it comes to...
...Tends to create a bad relationship with co-workers because...

...Lacks vigor and persistence required to...
...Management plans are without substance and marred by...
...Not reliable to work independently, needs a crutch to...

...Substandard behavior. Frequently engages in...
...Buckles under pressure. Loses control of/when...
...Becomes easily detached from job by...

...Unwillingness and inability to act decisively caused...
...Has difficulty dealing with others because...
...Produced minimal improvement despite...

...Exercised bad judgment and discretion in/by...
...Does not stay in strict compliance with...
...Does not support...

...Experienced isolated incidences of...
...Becomes degradation to morale by...
...Does not demonstrate potential for further useful...

...Failed to achieve consistency in...
...Suspended from regular duties for/because...
...Time after time proved a burden to...

...Positive aspects of performance outweighed by...
...Suffered loss of confidence in/by...
...Spends an inordinate amount of time on...

...Lacks requisite knowledge in/to...
...Has a noticeable imperfection in...
...Demonstrates a lack of interest and concern for...

...Not reasonable and rational in thought. Unable to make sense of...
...Struggles to maintain correct balance of...
...Despite noble intentions, unable to...

...Personal desires and preferences frequently in discord with...
...Despite adequate time, failed to make satisfactory headway in...
...Not open-minded. Has predisposition toward...

PERFORMANCE

DICTIONARY

The following section contains 2000 of the most frequently

used words in the English language to explain, state, define,

or demonstrate individual performance or character.

A brief definition/meaning is also provided.

FOR EXPANDED USE, A DRAFTER CAN USE THE DEFINITION OF THE WORDS.

WORD	CLASS	DEFINITION
-A-		
Abase	Verb	Loss of esteem
Aberrant	Adj./Noun	Substandard behavior
Abet	Verb	Encourage
Abhorrent	Adj.	Disagreeable
Abide	Verb	Tolerate or accept
Ability	Noun	Skill, Competence

Able	Adj.	Capable. Have ability
Abnormal	Adj.	Not normal
Abrasive	Adj.	Irritating
Abreast	Adj.	At standard. Even
Abrupt	Adj.	Cut short without warning
Absentminded	Adj.	Drifting of the mind
Absolute	Adj.	Without doubt, fault
Abstract Thought	Noun	Theoretical thought process
Absurd	Adj.	Obviously, clearly ridiculous
Abundant	Adj.	Plenty
Abuse	Noun	Be improper, misuse
Abuse	Verb	Improper, misuse
Acceptable	Adj.	Allowable. Passable. Adequate
Acclaim	Verb	Praise. Hold in high esteem
Acclaim	Noun	To praise
Accolade	Noun	A praise or acclaim
Accommodate	Verb	Allow. Make room. Fit
Accommodating	Adj.	Beneficial. Help. Assistance
Accomplished	Adj.	Skilled
Accost	Verb	Confront aggressively
Accurate	Adj.	Correct
Ace	Adj.	Top quality
Achieve	Verb	Accomplish. Reach
Achievement	Noun	Something achieved
Achiever	Noun	One who achieves
Acme	Noun	The top, peak, highest point
Activation	Noun	Make or cause action
Acuity	Noun	Keen. Acute
Acumen	Noun	Perceptive. Quickness
Acute	Adj.	Keen or sharp
Acuteness	Noun	Agile, keen mind
Adamant	Adj.	Not moving or flexible
Adept	Adj./Noun	Expert. Skilled

Adequate	Adj.	Satisfactory
Adhere	Verb	Stick to. Abide by
Adherence	Noun	To stick to. Abide by
Admirable	Adj.	In high esteem. Acclaim
Admire	Verb	Hold in high esteem, acclaim
Adolescent	Adj.	Not mature. Immature
Adroit	Adj.	Skillful
Adverse	Adj.	Opposed or opposing
Adversity	Noun	Bad situation
Advocate	Verb	To support, or back
Affable	Adj.	Friendly. Gets along with others
Agree	Verb	In accord. Concur. Agreement
Agreeable	Adj.	Likable. Pleasant
Aggressive	Adj.	Forceful, intense
Agile	Adj.	Skillful and flexible
Agile-minded	Adj.	Mental dexterity, quickness
Agility	Noun	Being quick and agile
Agitate	Verb	Incite or fuel
Agitator	Noun	Someone who incites or fuels
Agog	Adj.	Excitement. Anticipation
Alacrity	Noun	Ready and willing
Alert	Adj.	Perceptive
All-around	Adj.	Versatile. Multi-faceted
Altercation	Noun	Heated and aggressive argument
Ambiguity	Noun	Not definite or precise. Obscure
Ambiguous	Adj.	Not definite or precise. Obscure
Ambivalent	Adj.	Indecisive. Not firm
Amenity	Noun	Friendly
Amiable	Adj.	Likable
Amicable	Adj.	Likable. Harmonious
Amity	Noun	Harmonious
Amiss	Adj.	Awry. Wrong
Analyze	Verb	Study part by part, in detail

Analytic	Adj.	Skillful. Discernible
Analytical	Adj.	Logical analysis
Animate	Verb	Show zest and action
Animator	Noun	Active person. Puts into motion
Antagonist	Noun	One who agitates another
Antagonistic	Adj.	Agitating
Antagonize	Verb	To agitate, incite
Anticipate	Verb	Expect
Antisocial	Adj.	Not social
Anxious	Adj.	Eager
Anxiousness	Noun	Anxious, apprehensive, eager
A1	Adj.	The best. Top. Number one
Apathetic	Adj.	Without interest
Apathy	Noun	Being without interest
Apex	Noun	The uppermost or highest point
Aplomb	Noun	Under control
Appall	Verb	Dismay. Disagreeable
Appalling	Adj.	Be in dismay. Disagreeable
Appealing	Adj.	Pleasing
Appease	Verb	To quell or quiet
Applaud	Verb	Show agreement, approval
Apt	Adj.	Quick to grasp, learn
Aptitude	Noun	Ability, gift
Aptness	Noun	Quick to grasp, learn
Ardent	Adj.	Strong. Passionate
Arduous	Adj.	Hard. Strenuous. Difficult
Arouse	Verb	Excite to action
Arrogance	Noun	Overbearing
Arrogant	Adj.	Overbearing. Feeling egotistical
Artful	Adj.	Of much skill, ability
Articulate	Adj.	Clear. Effective. Highly skilled
Artistic	Adj.	Skillful thought, action
Artistic Imagination	Noun	Skillful, artful mental vision

Arousal	Noun	Move, spark to action
Askew	Adj.	Not normal. Awry. Slanted
Aspiration	Noun	High ambition
Aspire	Verb	Attempt to reach
Assert	Verb	To compel or compelling
Assertive	Adj.	Compel. Compelling
Asset	Noun	Something owned of value
Astray	Adj.	Move from correct, right
Astute	Adj.	Mental alertness
Attitude	Noun	Mental disposition
Attribute	Noun	Possessed trait, ability
Audacious	Adj.	Bold, venturesome
Audacity	Noun	Overly bold
Auspicious	Adj.	Favorable. Successful
Autocratic	Adj.	Self rule. Not democratic
Aversion	Noun	Avoid
Avid	Adj.	Extreme and intense
Avoid	Verb	Keep away from
Avow	Verb	Acknowledge
Aware	Adj.	To have knowledge. Know
Awareness	Noun	Be aware. Have knowledge
Awe	Noun	Mixed feelings
Awry	Adj.	Wrong. Not right, correct

-B-

Baffle	Verb	Confuse. Mix up
Balk	Verb	Hesitate. Delay
Banner	Adj.	Above others
Bashful	Adj.	Introvert. Shy
Behavior	Noun	Conduct. Manner
Belittle	Verb	Make little. Small
Belligerence	Noun	Being aggressive. Hostile
Belligerent	Adj.	Aggressive. Hostile
Beneficial	Adj.	Of use, benefit

Benevolence	Noun	Kind disposition
Benevolent	Adj.	Kind or charitable
Benign	Adj.	Good-natured
Berate	Verb	Scold violently
Berserk	Noun/Adj.	Violent, reckless action
Betray	Verb	To violate. Go against
Bias	Verb	Predetermined. Bent. Swayed
Big-hearted	Adj.	Giving, caring
Bland	Adj.	Dull, uninteresting
Blemish	Noun	To mar or scar
Blithe	Adj.	Gay, cheerful
Blunder	Verb	To mistake or error
Blunt	Adj.	Abrupt. Over candid
Boisterous	Adj.	Openly noisy or rowdy
Bold	Adj.	Forward. Without reservation
Bold Imagination	Noun	Daring, confident mental powers
Bolster	Verb	Support. Enforce. Back
Brainchild	Noun	Product of one's mental thought
Brainstorm	Noun	Fresh, new sudden idea
Brain Trust	Noun	Subject experts
Brash	Adj.	Bold and harsh
Brassy	Adj.	Bold impudence. Brash
Brevity	Noun	Brief, to the point
Bright	Adj.	Quick, keen mind
Brilliance	Noun	Bright, keen intellect
Brilliant	Adj.	Great. Bright
Brisk	Adj.	Lively. Energetic

-C-

Calculating	Adj.	Shrewd, cunning
Callous	Adj.	Insensitive
Camaraderie	Noun	Loyal friendship
Candid	Adj.	Frank. Open
Capable	Adj.	Possessing the ability
Capitalize	Verb	Use to advantage

Carefree	Adj.	Without care
Careful	Adj.	Attention to detail
Careless	Adj.	Without attention to detail
Catalyst	Noun	Spark/stimulus for great change
Categorical	Adj.	Without boundaries
Categorize	Verb	To classify
Ceiling	Noun	Top. Upper most
Censure	Verb	Condemn. Criticize
Certain	Adj.	Correct or true
Certainty	Noun	True without doubt
Chagrin	Noun	Disappointment in mind
Challenging	Adj.	Prompting or stirring action
Champion	Verb	Lead or uphold
Chaos	Noun	Unorganized activity
Charade	Noun	Deceit. Hidden
Charisma	Noun	Magnetic leadership
Charismatic	Adj.	Magnetic leadership
Charm	Verb	Appealing. Personable
Charmer	Noun	Someone with charm, appeal
Charming	Adj.	Greatly appealing or personable
Chastise	Verb	Censure or punish
Cheerful	Adj.	Happy. Gay
Circumvent	Verb	Go around
Clairvoyance	Noun	Extraordinary perceptive powers
Clairvoyant	Adj.	Extraordinarily perceptive
Clarity	Noun	Clear. Lucid
Clear-cut	Adj.	Clear. Not ambiguous
Clear-headed	Adj.	Clear knowledge
Clear-sighted	Adj.	Clear, understanding thought
Clear-witted	Adj.	Clear, keen mental faculty
Clever	Adj.	Skillful wit
Cleverness	Noun	Quick, clever wit
Cocksure	Adj.	Overconfident, sure

Cocky	Adj.	Too self-confident
Coerce	Verb	Compel through strength
Cogent	Adj.	Convince through strength
Cogitate	Verb	Deep meditation, thought
Cogitation	Noun	Of deep thought
Cognizance	Noun	Knowledge. Information
Cohere	Verb	Hold together
Coherence	Noun	Consistency of mind, thought
Coherent	Adj.	Holding or remaining together
Cohesion	Noun	Hold together firmly
Cohesive	Adj.	Held together firmly
Cohort	Noun	Associate. Companion
Cold	Adj.	Lacking in humanity
Collapse	Verb	Fall or fail
Colorless	Adj.	Lacking in personality
Colossal	Adj.	Exceptionally large
Comfort	Noun	Caring aid
Commend	Verb	To merit commendation
Commendation	Noun	Complimentary merit
Commitment	Noun	Obligation
Commonplace	Noun	Ordinary or routine
Common sense	Noun	Judgment with or without logic
Compassion	Noun	Humane sympathy
Compassionate	Adj.	Humane sympathy
Compatible	Adj.	Agreeable. Be, fit together
Compel	Verb	To make unavoidable
Compelling	Adj.	Demanding
Competent	Adj./Noun	Capable, able
Competitive	Adj.	Challenging. Competition
Competitor	Noun	One who challenges
Complacency	Noun	Satisfied to a fault
Complacent	Adj.	Satisfied to a fault
Complaisant	Adj.	Overly obliging

Complexity	Noun	Difficult. Complex
Complex	Adj.	Hard to integrate or answer
Compliance	Noun	Comply. In accord
Complicate	Verb	Add difficulty
Complicated	Adj.	Difficult, complex
Compliment	Noun	Give recognition
Comply	Verb	Adhere or conform
Comportment	Noun	Personal bearing
Composed	Adj.	Calm. Under control
Composure	Noun	Calmness
Comprehend	Verb	Understand
Comprehensible	Adj.	Understandable
Comprehension	Noun	To grasp, understand, know
Comprehensive	Adj.	Extensive or inclusive
Compulsive	Adj.	Uncontrollable urge
Conceal	Verb	Cover. Hide. Omit
Concede	Verb	Give in. Accept. Agree
Conceivable	Adj.	Imaginable in thought
Conceive	Verb	To think up
Concentrate	Verb	Direct, control thought process
Concentrating	Adj.	Focusing one's mental powers
Conception	Noun	Mentally conceiving
Conceptive	Adj.	Ability to mentally conceive
Conceptual	Adj.	Mental grasp, conception
Conceptualize	Verb	Mentally conceive, formulate
Concern	Noun	Of interest
Concise	Adj.	Brief and exact
Condemn	Verb	Find at fault
Condescend	Verb	To degrade, descend lower
Condescendence	Noun	Act of degrading. Patronize
Condescending	Adj.	Degrading
Confidence	Noun	Assured belief
Conflict	Noun	At opposition

Conflicting	Adj.	In opposition
Conform	Verb	In compliance, agreement
Conformance	Noun	Acceptable compliance
Conformity	Noun	Be in compliance
Confront	Verb	Openly challenge
Confuse	Verb	Not in order
Confusion	Noun	Mixed up
Confute	Verb	Refute. False. Useless
Congenial	Adj.	Genial. Friendly
Congruent	Adj.	Agreement. Harmony
Congruity	Noun	In agreement. Harmony
Congruous	Adj.	Harmonious agreement
Conjecture	Noun	Assumption. Something assumed
Conscious	Adj.	Knowing self-awareness
Consciousness	Noun	Self-awareness
Consistent	Adj.	Steady and regular
Consonance	Noun	Harmonious. Agreement
Consonant	Adj.	Harmony. In accord
Conspire	Verb	Plot, plan, act together
Constructive Imagination	Noun	Positive mental creativity
Consummate	Adj.	Complete. Perfect
Contagious	Adj.	Infectious. Spread to others
Contemplate	Verb	Deep thought. Ponder
Contempt	Noun	Having ill-feelings
Contemptible	Adj.	Ill-feelings
Contribute	Verb	Give. Provide. Assist
Contribution	Noun	To give, provide
Contrive	Verb	Formulate with deep thought
Controversy	Noun	Debate. Dispute
Conventional	Adj.	Standard. Routine
Conversant	Adj.	Knowledgeable
Converse	Verb	Talk. Communicate
Convey	Verb	Get meaning across

Convincing	Adj.	To win agreement
Cope	Verb	Able to handle, deal with
Cordial	Adj.	Friendly and sociable
Correct	Adj.	Without error
Corrupt	Adj.	Not pure. Improper
Corruption	Noun	Not pure. Improper conduct/action
Courage	Noun	Strength/will power to overcome
Courageous	Adj.	Displaying courage, bravery
Courteous	Adj.	Consideration
Courtesy	Noun	Considerate behavior
Cover-up	Noun	Hide. Not disclose
Craftiness	Noun	Sly, devious cunning
Crafty	Adj.	Sly. Cunning
Crass	Adj.	Without intelligent decency
Create	Verb	Conceive. Originate
Creative	Adj.	Create. Originate. Invent
Creative Ability	Noun	Intellectual creative power
Creative Imagination	Noun	Intellectual creativeness
Creativeness	Noun	Creative intellect
Creative Power	Noun	Ability to originate, create
Creative Thought	Noun	Mental ability to create
Creativity	Noun	Able to create/originate/invent
Credential	Noun	Reputation or supportive fact
Credibility	Noun	Believable
Credible	Adj.	Believed
Crimp	Verb	Hinder. Impede. Slow down
Crisis	Noun	Extremely important
Crisp	Adj.	Terse. Clear
Critical	Adj.	Extremely important
Criticize	Verb	Announce faults
Crucial	Adj.	Critical. Important
Crude	Adj.	Rough. Crass. Unrefined
Crusty	Adj.	Ill-mannered. Rough

Cultivate	Verb	Nurture. Ignite. Spur on
Cultivated	Adj.	Well refined, developed
Cultured	Adj.	Refined, polished manner
Cumbersome	Adj.	Hard to manage or wield
Cunning	Adj.	Sharp, sly skill
Curiosity	Noun	In interest. Inquisitive
Curious	Adj.	Keenly interested. Inquisitive
Cursory	Adj.	Brief view or interest
Curt	Adj.	Abrupt and offensive
Customary	Adj.	Routinely. Commonly. Usually
Cynical	Adj.	Unbelieving with bad attitude

-D-

Dabble	Verb	Superficial involvement
Daunt	Verb	Unnerve. Discourage. Dismay
Dauntless	Adj.	Unnerving. Intimidating
Debase	Verb	To lessen or diminish
Deception	Noun	Mislead. Trick
Deceptive	Adj.	Mislead. Trick
Decisive	Adj.	Without doubt or question
Decorum	Noun	Respectable behavior or dress
Deduction	Noun	Evaluate with logic
Deductive Power	Adj.	Evaluate by logical reasoning
Deductive Power	Noun	Ability to logically reason
Deep-Thinking	Adj.	Deep, profound intellect
Defect	Noun	Error. Fault
Defective	Adj.	Having error or fault
Defiance	Noun	Go against. Oppose
Defiant	Adj.	Against. Oppose
Deficient	Adj.	Shortcoming. Missing something
Degradation	Noun	Belittle. Lower. Degrade
Degrade	Verb	Lower. Belittle. Take away
Deliberation	Adj.	Full, due consideration
Delude	Verb	Mislead. Trick. Deceive

Delve	Verb	Dig into. Research
Demean	Verb	Belittle. Lessen. Lower
Demeanor	Noun	Behavior
Demerit	Noun	Without merit, good
Demise	Noun	Loss. Decline. Failure
Demoralize	Verb	Great drop in morale
Demure	Adj.	Shy. Modest
Denounce	Verb	Publicly criticize
Dense	Adj.	Slow to pick up, comprehend
Depend	Verb	Rely on
Dependable	Adj.	Reliable. Trustworthy
Dependence	Noun	Dependent or relied upon
Dependency	Noun	Something needing assistance
Dependent	Adj.	Depend or rely on
Depress	Verb	Disheartened. Discourage
Depressed	Adj.	Disheartened. Sad
Deprive	Verb	Do without
Derelict	Adj.	Improper attention
Dereliction	Noun	Knowing improper attention
Despair	Verb	Lose hope. Give up
Despairing	Adj.	Without hope. Despair
Desperate	Adj.	Without hope. Despair
Despond	Verb	Become without hope
Despondency	Noun	Being without hope
Despondent	Adj.	Great hopelessness
Destroy	Verb	Ruin. Tear down
Deter	Verb	To thwart or turn
Deteriorate	Verb	Become less, lower
Determination	Noun	Firm resolve, conviction
Determined	Adj.	Firmly committed
Detriment	Noun	Ill-being. To damage
Detrimental	Adj.	Damaging. Ill-being
Deviant	Adj.	Change downward or for worse

Deviate	Adj./Noun/Verb	Changing from the normal
Devious	Adj.	Conniving, sly deviation
Devise	Verb	Originate. Invent
Devoted	Adj.	Loyal. Faithful
Dexterity	Noun	Mental or physical agility
Dexterous	Adj.	Mental or physical agility
Diction	Noun	Verbally clear, correct
Diehard	Noun	Decidedly against something
Die-hard	Adj.	Positively against something
Differentiate	Verb	Distinguish difference
Difficult	Adj.	Hard. Demanding
Difficulty	Noun	Being hard, demanding
Diffident	Adj.	Self-confident
Dignity	Noun	High esteem. Praiseworthy
Dilute	Verb	Lessen. Reduce
Diminish	Verb	To lessen or reduce
Diplomacy	Noun	Skillfully tactful
Diplomat	Noun	Someone skillfully tactful
Diplomatic	Adj.	Using tact with skill
Dire	Adj.	Desperate. Distressful
Disaccord	Verb	Not in accord or agreement
Disadvantage	Noun	Not to advantage
Disagree	Verb	Against. Opposed
Disagreeable	Adj.	Being against or opposed
Disagreement	Noun	At opposition. Against
Disappoint	Verb	Not to expectation, as expected
Disappointing	Adj.	Not as expected
Disappointment	Noun	To disappoint, not succeed
Disaster	Noun	Great disorder
Discern	Verb	Skillful understanding/judgment
Discernible	Adj.	Mentally recognize & separate
Discerning	Adj.	Skillful understanding/judgment
Discipline	Noun	Self-control. Enforced control

Discontent	Noun	Not content or pleased
Discord	Noun/Verb	Failure to get along
Discourse	Adj.	Verbally communicating
Discourteous	Adj.	Not courteous. Not kind
Discredit	Noun	Without credit, belief
Discreet	Adj.	Prudent judgment
Discriminating	Adj.	Recognize. Distinguish difference
Disdain	Noun/Verb	Low in regard. At distance
Disdainful	Adj.	Showing low regard
Disfavor	Noun	Not in favor, good standing
Disgruntle	Verb	Not happy, satisfied
Disgust	Verb	Sharp disapproval. Dislike
Disgust	Noun	A sharp disapproval, dislike
Disillusion	Noun	Not content, satisfied
Disinclined	Adj.	Not approving or agreeing
Disloyal	Adj.	Not loyal, trustworthy
Disloyalty	Noun	Without loyalty
Dismay	Noun/Verb	Disheartened. Disappointed
Disorder	Noun	Not in order
Disparity	Noun	A difference, fault
Dispassionate	Adj.	Without passion, personal feeling
Dispute	Verb	Disagreement
Disregard	Verb	Without regard or attention
Disreputable	Adj.	Bad reputation
Disrepute	Noun	Low reputation
Disrespect	Noun/Verb	Without respect
Disrupt	Verb	Break up or apart
Disruptive	Adj.	Be out of order, routine
Dissatisfaction	Noun	Not satisfied, pleased
Dissatisfied	Adj.	Not satisfied
Dissatisfy	Verb	Not satisfying
Dissension	Noun	Not in agreement
Dissent	Noun/Verb	Not in agreement

Dissenter	Noun	Someone who disagrees
Distinguished	Adj.	With distinction. High esteem
Distort	Verb	Make cloudy, unclear, uncertain
Diverse	Adj.	Varied. Multi-faceted
Docile	Adj.	Passive. Highly receptive
Dodge	Verb	To go around. Evade
Dominant	Adj.	Commanding or controlling
Dominate	Verb	To command or control over
Domineering	Adj.	Prevail over, above
Drabber	Adj.	Dull. Not lively
Dramatic	Adj.	Extreme effect
Drastic	Adj.	Major effect. Extreme. Harsh
Drive	Noun	Spur to action. Push. Urge
Drudge	Verb	Routine, recurring dull work
Drudging	Adj.	Being routine and dull
Dubious	Adj.	Questionable. Doubtful
Dull	Adj.	Not mentally quick, perceptive
Dullness	Noun	Not mentally quick, perceptive
Durable	Adj.	Long lasting without change
Duress	Noun	Under great pressure or strain
Dwindle	Verb	Continued decline
Dynamic	Adj.	Powerful. Forceful

-E-

Eager	Adj.	Ready. Zealous
Eager Beaver	Noun	Ready volunteer
Eagerness	Noun	Being ready, enthusiastic
Earnest	Noun	Sincere. Serious
Easygoing	Adj.	Carefree. Little effort
Ebb	Noun/Verb	To recede. Diminish
Eccentric	Adj.	Vary from norm, standard
Edit	Verb	Go over. Review
Editorialize	Verb	Communicate own opinion

Educable	Adj.	Able to learn
Educate	Verb	Teach
Educated	Adj.	Advanced education
Educator	Noun	A teacher
Effective	Adj.	Obtain results. Satisfactory
Effervesce	Verb	Lively. Zestful
Effervescent	Adj.	Liveliness. Zest. Zeal
Effete	Adj.	Old. Obsolete
Efficiency	Noun	Doing without needless waste
Efficient	Adj.	Without needless loss, waste
Effort	Noun	Attempt. Try
Effortless	Adj.	Without effort, attempt
Ego	Noun	Self-esteem
Egocentric	Adj.	Concerned with one's self
Egoism	Noun	Overly interested in one's self
Egoist	Noun	An ego person
Egotism	Noun	Overly self-centered
Elaborate	Adj.	Go over in great detail
Elated	Adj.	Elevated, high in thought
Elegance	Noun	Cultured. Respectable
Elegant	Adj.	Greatly cultured, respectable
Elemental	Adj.	Basic. Fundamental
Elementary	Adj.	Basic elements
Elevated	Adj.	Raised. Lifted
Elicit	Verb	Bring forward or out
Eloquence	Noun	Persuasive, fluent communications
Elucidate	Verb	Make clear, lucid
Elude	Verb	Avoid. Escape
Elusive	Adj.	Avoid attention. Escape
Embitter	Verb	Bitter, harsh
Embodiment	Noun	To encompass, embody something
Emerge	Verb	Come to view, focus
Embody	Verb	Encompass, incorporate, include

Eminent	Adj.	Be, stand above
Emotion	Noun	Mental condition or state
Emotional	Adj.	Expressed emotion
Empathetic	Adj.	Humanely sensitive
Empathic	Adj.	Exhibiting empathy
Empathize	Verb	Being humanely sensitive
Empathy	Noun	Humanely sensitive
Emphasize	Verb	Point out with strong attention
Emphatic	Adj.	Express actively and zealously
Employ	Verb	Use. Occupy
Emulate	Verb	Imitate. Try to copy
Emulation	Noun	To imitate, copy, duplicate
Enable	Verb	Make able, ready
Enchant	Verb	Charm. Entice
Enchantment	Noun	Charmed. Enticing
Encourage	Verb	Prompt. Spur on
Encouragement	Noun	Prompting. Spurring
Encouraging	Adj.	To encourage or prompt
Encumber	Verb	Burden. Weigh down
Encumbrance	Noun	Being burdened
Endeavor	Noun/Verb	Try. Attempt
Endless	Adj.	Without end. Unending
Endurable	Adj.	Able to last
Endurance	Noun	To last or hold up
Endure	Verb	To last, hold up
Energetic	Adj.	Zeal, vim, vigor
Energize	Verb	Make energetic
Energy	Noun	Having zeal, vim, and vigor
Enervate	Adj./Verb	Without vim, vigor, vitality
Enforce	Verb	Give force. To back
Engaging	Adj.	Attracting. Pleasant
Engender	Verb	Initiate. Foster. Spur
Engrossing	Adj.	Engaging. Involving

Enhance	Verb	Help. Promote. Add to
Enigma	Noun	Confusing, hard to understand
Enjoy	Verb	Like. Please
Enjoyment	Noun	Being at joy. Pleasing
Enlighten	Verb	Bring to light. Inform
Enlightened	Adj.	Brought to light. Informed
Enlightenment	Noun	To enlighten
Enmity	Noun	Deep, bad feeling or will
Enormous	Adj.	Great amount, size
Enrage	Verb	Angry. Furious
Enrich	Verb	Add, contribute, or give to
Enterprise	Noun	Task or tasking. Project
Enterprising	Adj.	Energetic, vigorous, and ready
Entertain Ideas	Verb	Open to suggestion, thought
Enthuse	Verb	Inspire. Excite
Enthusiasm	Noun	Inspiring. Exciting
Enthusiast	Noun	Someone with enthusiasm
Enthusiastic	Adj.	Being enthused
Entice	Verb	Skillfully tempt or excite
Entrust	Verb	To trust
Enunciate	Verb	Verbal dexterity and clarity
Enviable	Adj.	Having worthy qualities
Envious	Adj.	Possessing worthy qualities
Envision	Verb	See, think within
Epitome	Noun	Best. Ideal example
Epitomize	Verb	Idealize. Representative
Equable	Adj.	Even. Consistent
Equality	Noun	Equal. On par. Even
Equitable	Adj.	Being even, consistent
Equivocal	Adj.	Not definite, certain
Equivocate	Verb	False. Vague
Eradicate	Verb	End. Finish off
Erode	Verb	Wear away. Tear down

Erosive	Adj.	Able to erode
Errant	Adj.	Stray. Wander
Erratic	Adj.	Not regular, consistent
Erroneous	Adj.	Error. Mistake
Error	Noun	Wrong. Incorrect. Not right/true
Erudite	Adj.	Learned. Skilled
Erudition	Noun	Highly learned, skilled
Erupt	Verb	Burst out, forward
Escalate	Verb	Heighten. Increase
Eschew	Verb	Shun. Go around
Esprit de corps	Noun	Strong common spirit or bond
Essential	Adj.	Mandatory part or ingredient
Establish	Verb	Bring into being
Esteem	Noun	High regard. Honored
Ethic	Noun	Moral concepts or views
Ethical	Adj.	In accord, conformance
Etiquette	Noun	Social conduct
Euphoria	Noun	High in feeling
Evasive	Adj.	Evading. Elusive
Exacerbate	Verb	Increase in harshness, bitterness
Exact	Adj.	Precise. Without error
Exacting	Adj.	Demanding. Correctness
Exaggerate	Verb	False or artificial largeness
Exalt	Verb	Favorable rise or raise
Exanimate	Adj.	Without spirit
Exceed	Verb	Go beyond. Surpass
Exceeding	Adj.	Going beyond. Surpassing
Excel	Verb	Surpass. Succeed
Excellence	Noun	High quality
Excellent	Adj.	First rate. Top quality
Exceptional	Adj.	Very top quality
Excessive	Adj.	More than needed, required
Excitable	Adj.	Capable of arousing

Excite	Verb	Arouse. Move to action
Excitement	Noun	Aroused. Moved to action
Exciter	Noun	One who excites
Exciting	Adj.	Arousing. Stimulating
Exclusive	Adj.	Strictly limited
Excuse	Noun	Reason. Explanation
Exemplary	Adj.	Excellent. Finest quality
Exemplify	Verb	Embody. An example
Exhort	Verb	Incite. Urge
Exonerate	Verb	Clear. Free
Exorbitance	Noun	Being exorbitant, in excess
Exorbitant	Adj.	Too much. Excess
Expand	Verb	Increase. Grow
Expectation	Noun	Anticipate. Look forward
Expedience	Noun	Speed-up
Expediency	Noun	Speed-up. Expedient
Expedient	Adj.	Easiest choice
Expedite	Verb	Proceed immediately
Expeditious	Adj.	To expedite, cause action
Experience	Noun	Learned earlier
Experienced	Adj.	Knowledgeable. Skillful
Expert	Adj.	Most experienced or skilled
Expertise	Noun	Possessing experience or skill
Explicit	Adj.	Not ambiguous. Exact
Exploit	Verb	Make use of
Explore	Verb	Check into. Investigate
Explosive	Adj.	Capable or erupting
Expostulate	Verb	Consider. Evaluate
Expound	Verb	Explain. Clarify. Put forth
Extensive	Adj.	To great extent
Extenuate	Verb	Reduce. Lessen
Extra	Adj.	More. Additional
Extraneous	Adj.	Extra. More than enough

Extraordinary	Adj.	Extra to, or above ordinary
Extravagant	Adj.	More than necessary, required
Extreme	Adj.	Beyond reasonable
Exuberance	Noun	Being exuberant, enthused
Exuberant	Adj.	Enthused. Lively. Zealous
Exultant	Adj.	Extreme joy, high thrill
Eyesore	Noun	Repulsive to see

-F-

Fabricate	Verb	Make. Make up
Fabulous	Adj.	Great almost beyond belief
Facetious	Adj.	Unsuccessful wit
Facile	Adj.	Superficial. Without substance
Facilitate	Verb	Aid. Assist
Facility	Noun	Aptitude. Ability. Skill
Factual	Adj.	Truthful. Actual
Faculties	Noun	Possessed ability or capacity
Faculty	Noun	Possessed skill, ability
Fade	Verb	Decrease, lessen with time
Fail	Verb	Without success or gain
Failure	Noun	Perform without success
Fair	Adj.	Without bias or prejudice
Fair-minded	Adj.	Minded without bias or prejudice
Fair play	Noun	Equal and fair
Fair-spoken	Adj.	Light or soft spoken
Faith	Noun	Belief. Believe in
Faithful	Adj.	True in faith
Faithless	Adj.	Without truth or faith
Fake	Noun/Verb	Impostor. Not true
False	Adj.	Not true or correct
Falsify	Verb	Make untrue or incorrect
Falsity	Noun	At or being false
Falter	Verb	Hesitate. Fall short
Fantastic	Adj.	Great. Almost beyond belief

Farcical	Adj.	Ridiculous. Laughable
Farfetched	Adj.	Far out. Hard to believe
Far-reaching	Adj.	Wide or long reaching
Farseeing	Adj.	See far ahead
Farsighted	Adj.	See or plan far ahead
Fascinating	Adj.	Enchanting. Engaging
Fascination	Noun	Being enchanted
Fastidious	Adj.	Overly demanding
Fatigue	Noun	Worn down or out
Fatuity	Noun	Extremely simple
Fatuous	Adj.	Simple. Inane
Fault	Noun	Error. Wrong. Fail
Faultfinding	Adj./Noun	Predetermined to find fault
Faultless	Adj.	Without fault or wrong
Faulty	Adj.	Having fault, error
Favorable	Adj.	Agreeable. Approving
Favoritism	Noun	Showing bias or favor
Fearful	Adj.	In fear from danger
Fearless	Adj.	Without fear. Bold
Feasible	Adj.	Allowable. Acceptable
Feat	Noun	Good or great deed or act
Feckless	Adj.	Without responsibility
Fecund	Adj.	Fertile & productive intelligence
Feeble	Adj.	Weak. Frail
Feebleminded	Adj.	Mentally lacking, deficient
Feeling	Adj.	Emotion. Belief
Feisty	Adj.	Anxious. Exuberant
Felicitous	Adj.	Talk with poise. Suitable
Felicity	Noun	Cheerful. Happy
Fellowship	Noun	Camaraderie. Friendship
Fend	Verb	Defend. Do without assistance
Fertile	Adj.	Reservoir of ability, thought

173

Fertile Mind	Noun	Highly productive mind
Fervent	Adj.	Feeling of friendly warmth
Fervor	Noun	Great passion, emotion
Festive	Adj.	Joyous. Happy. Active
Fetter	Noun	Restrain
Feud	Noun	Long-standing dislike, disagreement
Feverish	Adj.	At a hot pace
Fiasco	Noun	Utter failure
Fickle	Adj.	Not consistent, constant, resolute
Fiction	Noun	Not true or real
Fictitious	Adj.	Being untrue or unreal
Fidelity	Noun	Faithful. In accord
Fiduciary	Adj.	State of high trust
Fierce	Adj.	Intense, active hostility
Fiery	Adj.	Hot, active emotion
Figurehead	Noun	Not actual. In name only
Finagle	Verb	Deceit. False. Trick
Fine	Adj.	Good. Excellent
Finely	Adv	Extremely fine
Finesse	Noun	Mental skill, agility and ability
Fine-tune	Verb	Fine Adjustment for best operation
Finicky	Adj.	Too exacting or petty
Finite	Adj.	Limited. Not infinite
Firm	Adj.	Resolute. Unmoving
First	Noun	Top. Highest. Best
First class	Noun	Classed top, highest, or first
First-rate	Adj.	First or top quality
First-string	Adj.	First-rate
Five-star	Adj.	Best. Tops
Fizzle	Noun	Fade. Fail
Flagged	Adj.	Weak. Without zeal
Flagrant	Adj.	Openly blatant, disagreeable
Flair	Noun	Special knack or skill. Ability

Flappable	Adj.	Not sure, confident
Flashy	Adj.	Superficial. Words without deeds
Flaunt	Verb	Open defiance. Bold
Flaw	Noun	Not correct or perfect
Fledgling	Noun	New. Not mature
Flexibility	Noun	Adaptability. Not rigid
Flexible	Adj.	Adaptable. Able to alter, change
Flimsy	Adj.	Not firm, solid. Weak
Flip-flop	Noun	Not firm. Changes views, opinions
Flop	Verb	Fail
Flounder	Verb	Hesitate. Lose way, direction
Flourish	Verb	Thrive. Excel
Flout	Verb	Open defiance
Fluctuate	Verb	Move back and forth. Oscillate
Fluent	Adj.	Skilled. Learned
Fluid	Adj.	Smooth flowing
Flunk	Verb	Fail. Flop
Fluster	Noun	Thwart. Discourage
Flutter	Noun	Uncertain, non-directed motion
Focus	Noun	Center-in. Key in on
Foible	Noun	Fault. Error
Foil	Verb	Stop. Prevent
Follower	Noun	One who follows. Not a leader
Folly	Noun	Foolish
Foolhardy	Adj.	Ill-advised
Foolish	Adj.	Lack of proper judgment
Foolishness	Noun	Act of improper judgment
Foolproof	Adj.	Without chance of error, fault
Foot-dragging	Noun	Deliberate slowness
Foppish	Adj.	Overly self-concerned, vain
Forbidding	Adj.	Refraining. Prohibiting
Force	Noun	Driving power, influence, strength
Forceful	Adj.	Using force. Exerting pressure

Forcible	Adj.	Able to be forceful
Foremost	Adj.	At the front, top
Foresee	Verb	See forward, ahead
Foresight	Noun	See ahead. Plan ahead
Foresighted	Adj.	Mentally see ahead, future
Foresightedness	Noun	Mentally see ahead, future
Forestall	Verb	To stop or obstruct
Forfeit	Noun/Verb	Give up or away
Forget	Verb	Fail to remember
Forgetful	Adj.	Failing to remember
Forgive	Verb	To let pass. Excuse
Forgiveness	Noun	Letting pass. Excusing
Forgiving	Adj.	To forgive, overlook
Formality	Noun	Official procedure
Formalize	Verb	Make formal, official, complete
Formative	Adj.	Developing. Growing
Formidable	Adj.	Very difficult, discouraging
Formless	Adj.	Without form, order, or shape
Formulate	Verb	Develop. Put together
Forte	Noun	Someone's best trait
Forthright	Adj.	Direct. Frank. Open
Fortify	Verb	To strengthen, build up
Fortitude	Noun	Mental strength and persistence
Fortuitous	Adj.	By accident, chance
Fortunate	Adj.	Lucky. Favorable
Forum	Noun	Free discussion
Forward-looking	Adj.	Look and plan ahead
Foul-up	Noun	Botch. Bungle
Foundation	Noun	Base or founding frame
Founder	Verb	Fail. Fall. Decline
Four-star	Adj.	Top grade, quality
Fracas	Noun	Noisy confrontation
Fractious	Adj.	Unruly. Difficult to control

Fragile	Adj.	Weak. Not strong. Frail
Fragment	Noun	A part or piece of something
Fragmentary	Adj.	Not complete. In parts
Frail	Adj.	Weak. Not strong
Frank	Adj.	Open, forward manner
Frantic	Adj.	Fast, unorganized pace
Fraud	Noun	Knowing deceit
Fraudulent	Adj.	Being or doing deceit
Free-spoken	Adj.	Too openly candid. Speak freely
Freethinker	Noun	Unrestrained, independent thinking
Freewill	Adj.	Spontaneous. Unrestrained
Frenzy	Noun	Unthinking, violent action
Frequent	Adj.	Often. At great frequency
Fresh	Adj.	New energy, vigor
Fret	Verb	Worry. Concerned
Friction	Noun	Disagree. Oppose
Friendly	Adj.	Amicable. Kind disposition
Friendly	Noun	Someone friendly
Frivolous	Adj.	Without importance or value
Fruitful	Adj.	Productive. Successful
Fruitless	Adj.	Non-productive. Without gain
Frustrate	Verb	Thwart. Ineffective
Frustrated	Adj.	Being thwarted or ineffective
Frustration	Noun	Being frustrated
Fulfill	Verb	Accomplish. Complete
Full-fledged	Adj.	Fully completed
Full-scale	Adj.	Maximum limit or scale
Fumble	Verb	Blunder. Clumsy
Fundamental	Adj.	Basic, central elements
Furious	Adj.	Great, heated anger
Furor	Noun	Furious. Angry
Fury	Noun	Anger. Rage
Fussy	Adj.	Finicky. Overly particular

Futile	Adj.	Worthless. Ineffective
Futility	Noun	Being futile
Fuzzy	Adj.	Unclear. Not defined. Blurred

-G-

Gab	Verb	Talk too much or without substance
Gall	Noun	Boldness. Fortitude
Gallant	Adj.	Bold. Energetic. Daring
Galling	Adj.	Annoying. Boldness
Gamesmanship	Noun	Improper advantage or tactics
Garrulity	Noun	Idle, insignificant talk
Garrulous	Adj.	Too much idle, insignificant talk
Gauche	Adj.	Social unacceptance
Generalize	Verb	Vague. Broadly defined
Generate	Verb	Start. Instill
Generous	Adj.	Kind. Giving. Caring
Genial	Adj.	Kind, sympathetic personality
Genius	Noun	Innate superior intellect
Genteel	Adj.	Polite. Poised. Polished
Gentle	Adj.	Soft, kind
Genuine	Adj.	Actual. Real
Gesture	Noun	Express by body movement
Gift	Noun	Talent
Gifted	Adj.	Great natural intellect
Gigantic	Adj.	Extremely large, big
Gimmick	Noun	Shrewd device or scheme
Gingerly	Adj.	Tenderly, tentative
Gist	Noun	Major thought or idea. Overview
Glad	Adj.	Happy. Cheerful. Gay
Glaring	Adj.	Glowing. Gross. Obvious
Glitch	Noun	Problem. Trouble. Setback
Gloom	Verb	Dark, bleak in outlook
Gloomy	Adj.	Bleak, depressed outlook
Glorify	Verb	Make or add glory
Glorious	Adj.	Having, or being, glory

Glory	Noun	High in honor, esteem
Glum	Adj.	Bleak. Gloomy
Good	Adj./Noun	Favorable. Positive
Good	Noun	Something favorable, positive
Good deal	Noun	Great amount
Good faith	Noun	Earnest in faith
Good-for-nothing	Adj.	Worth nothing. Without value
Good-hearted	Adj.	Kind at heart. Kind hearted
Good-humored	Adj.	Positive, cheerful manner
Goodly	Adj.	Great amount
Good-natured	Adj.	Pleasant, helpful manner
Goodwill	Noun	Caring and friendly
Gracious	Adj.	Poised and charming. Thoughtful
Gradual	Adj.	Changing, shifting over time
Grandeur	Noun	Being grand or grandiose
Grandiose	Adj.	Overly impressive. Showy. Grandeur
Gratify	Verb	Pleasing. Satisfying
Gratifying	Adj.	Being pleasing, satisfying
Grave	Adj.	Serious with harmful consequences
Gravity	Noun	Significant in importance
Great	Adj.	Large. Significant. Remarkable
Greathearted	Adj.	Generous and caring
Gregarious	Adj.	Sociable
Grievance	Noun	Gripe. Complaint
Grieve	Verb	Grief. Sorrow
Grievous	Adj.	Grave, serious, painful
Grim	Adj.	Dark. Dreary. Unpleasant
Grimace	Noun	Disapprove by facial gesture
Grind out	Verb	To do methodically, mundane
Gripe	Verb	Complain. Object
Grit	Noun	Strong resolute courage
Gross	Adj.	Bad. Flagrant
Grouse	Verb	Fault-finding. Complain

Grudge	Noun	Get back or even
Grudging	Adj.	With reluctance
Grueling	Adj.	Extremely strenuous or punishing
Guide	Noun/Verb	Oversee, supervise. Point the way
Guile	Noun	Crafty, cagey
Guileless	Adj.	Without guile
Guise	Noun	False cover, front
Gumption	Noun	Common sense. Courage
Gung ho	Adj.	Unbound enthusiasm
Gusto	Noun	Zeal, vigor, vim

-H-

Habitual	Adj.	Recurring as by habit
Half-baked	Adj.	Improper planning, forethought
Half-cocked	Adj.	Improper planning, forethought
Halfhearted	Adj.	Without full support
Half-scholar	Adj.	Not learned, knowing
Half-truth	Noun	Deliberate less than full truth
Halo effect	Noun	Over grading based on few traits
Hamper	Verb	Interfere. Impede. Obstruct
Hands-on	Adj.	Do physically. First hand
Haphazard	Adj./Noun	Without plan. By chance
Hapless	Adj.	Happen without luck
Happenstance	Noun	By chance. Haphazard
Happy-go-lucky	Adj.	Not properly concerned, caring
Harass	Verb	Continued bothering, troubling
Hard-and-fast	Adj.	Firm. Fixed. Unyielding
Hard-handed	Adj.	Overly strict, firm
Hardheaded	Adj.	Unrelenting. Firm. Stubborn
Hard-hearted	Adj.	Without humane concern, sympathy
Hard-nosed	Adj.	Unrelenting. Firm. Stubborn
Hard put	Adj.	With great difficulty
Hard-set	Adj.	Unrelenting. Firm
Hard-shell	Adj.	Not giving or compromising
Hardship	Noun	Great difficulty. Suffering
Harm	Noun/Verb	Cause damage, danger, hurt

Harmless	Adj.	Without harm, damage, danger
Harmonious	Adj.	Be in harmony
Harmony	Noun	Get along. No friction
Harsh	Adj.	Severe. Coarse. Rough
Hasten	Verb	Speed up. Quicken
Hasty	Adj.	Hurried. Quick. Fast
Hatred	Noun	To hate. Extreme dislike
Headlong	Adj.	Without delay, hesitation
Headway	Noun	Gain. Progress
Headwork	Noun	Mental work. Think. Ponder
Hearsay	Noun	Not sure, proven fact
Heartfelt	Adj.	In sincere sympathy
Heartless	Adj.	Without heart, compassion
Hearty	Adj./Noun	Full. Complete. Sincere
Heavy-handed	Adj.	Stern. Harsh. Overly demanding
Heavyhearted	Adj.	Deepest sympathy. Deep felt
Heckle	Verb	Antagonize. Annoy. Impede
Hectic	Adj.	Frantic. Fast-paced
Heed	Noun	To pay attention. Note
Heedful	Adj.	To heed, take notice
Heedless	Adj.	Without attention or heed
Helpless	Adj.	Without help, defense, assistance
Helpful	Adj.	To assist, help. Cooperate
Heritage	Noun	Handed down over time
Herky-jerky	Adj.	Inconsistent. Fluctuating
Hero	Noun	Held in highest esteem, thought
Hidden	Adj.	Not shown. Out of sight
Hierarchy	Noun	Those higher in command, control
Higher education	Noun	Advanced or college education
Higher learning	Noun	Advanced or college learning
High-flying	Adj.	Exuberant. Excessive
High-minded	Adj.	High ideals, principles
High-powered	Adj.	Powerful. Mighty

High-pressure	Adj.	Great pressure. Tense. Demanding
High-spirited	Adj.	Enthusiastic, energetic spirit
High-strung	Adj.	Temperamental. Over bearing
High-toned	Adj.	Arrogant. Elevated principles
Hinder	Verb	Impede. Hamper. Harm
Hindrance	Noun	To hinder, harm, hurt
Hindsight	Noun	Apply after-the-fact knowledge
Hit-or-miss	Adj.	Be by chance. At random
Hone	Verb	To fine tune
Honest	Adj.	True. Truthful. No deceit
Honesty	Noun	Being honest
Honor	Noun	High moral standard
Honorable	Adj.	Having, deserving honor
Hope	Verb	Strong, positive desire
Hopeful	Adj.	Having hope
Hopeless	Adj.	Without hope, chance, desire
Horrendous	Adj.	Extremely bad, distasteful
Hospitable	Adj.	Friendly. Caring
Hostile	Adj.	Not hospitable. Very unfriendly
Hostility	Noun	Aggressive, hostile conduct
Huge	Adj.	Great many. Sizable
Humane	Adj.	Caring, concerned compassion
Humanitarian	Noun	Someone humane in thought, action
Humble	Adj.	Submissive. Subordinate one's self
Humdrum	Adj.	Without vim, vigor. Dull
Humiliate	Verb	To belittle or shame another
Humiliating	Adj.	Demeaning. To humiliate
Humility	Noun	Being humble
Humor	Noun	Pleasing character
Humorless	Adj.	Without humor
Humorous	Adj.	Having humor, wit, charm
Hurdle	Verb	Go over. Not impeded
Hurried	Adj.	Rushed. Hastened

Hurtful	Adj.	Doing hurt, harm, damage
Hygiene	Noun	Personal health, sanitation
Hyper	Adj.	Easily agitated, excited
Hypercritical	Adj.	Over critical

-I-

Idea	Noun	A thought from the mind
Ideal	Adj.	Perfect. Exact. Precise
Ideal	Noun	Envisioned or sought goal

Idealist	Noun	Placing ideals ahead of reality
Idealistic	Adj.	Concerning ideals
Idealize	Adj.	Be ideal, representative

Idle	Adj.	Not busy. Not doing
Ignite	Verb	Fire up. Start. Motivate
Ignorance	Noun	Having lack of knowledge

Ignorant	Adj.	Not knowledgeable
Ignore	Verb	Avoid
Ill-advised	Adj.	Not properly advised

Illaudable	Adj.	Not laudable or praised
Illegal	Adj.	Not legal or lawful
Illegible	Adj.	Not legible, readable

Ill-fated	Adj.	Predetermined bad fate
Ill-gotten	Adj.	Illegal or improperly gotten
Ill-humored	Adj.	Without humor

Illicit	Adj.	Illegal
Illiteracy	Noun	Not literate. Not read or write
Illiterate	Adj.	Not knowing, educated

Ill-mannered	Adj.	Bad manners. Crude
Ill-natured	Adj.	Bad attitude or nature
Illogic	Noun	Being without logic

Illogical	Adj.	Not logical, reasonable
Illustrate	Verb	To show or make clear
Illustrious	Adj.	Commendable actions

Image	Verb	Visualize. See in mind
Imagine	Verb	Mental picture, image
Imaginable	Adj.	Able to imagine or visualize
Imaginary	Adj.	Not real or fact
Imagination	Noun/Adj.	Imagine, visualize in the mind
Imaginative	Adj.	Unreal. Untrue
Imbalance	Noun	Not proper balance
Imitate	Verb	Copy. Duplicate
Imitation	Noun	Not real, fact, true
Immaculate	Adj.	Without flaw. Pure
Immature	Adj.	Not mature or completely developed
Immeasurable	Adj.	Beyond measure
Immediacy	Noun	Being immediate
Immense	Adj.	Vast, huge. Large
Immensity	Noun	Being immense
Immerge	Verb	Immerse. Throw into completely
Immerse	Verb	Become totally absorbed, involved
Immobile	Adj.	Not mobile or movable. Fixed
Immobilize	Verb	Make immobile or fixed
Immoderate	Adj.	Not moderate. Excess. Excessive
Immoral	Adj.	Not moral. Against moral values
Immovable	Adj.	Not movable. Fixed
Impair	Verb	Restrict, restrain, hinder
Imparity	Noun	Inequity. Uneven
Impart	Verb	To pass along. Communicate
Impartial	Adj.	Equal. Fair. No prejudice or bias
Impassioned	Adj.	Great passion, feeling
Impatience	Noun	Not patient. Anxious
Impatient	Adj.	Not patient. Anxious
Impeccable	Adj.	Without flaw or fault. Unblemished
Impede	Verb	Interfere. Harm or slow
Impel	Verb	Push or force forward
Impenetrable	Adj.	Unable to penetrate, enter

Imperfect	Adj.	Not perfect. Flawed. Error
Imperfection	Noun	Being not perfect. Flawed
Impersonal	Adj.	Not personal. Not open, friendly
Impersonalize	Verb	Make impersonal
Impertinence	Noun	Be impertinent
Impertinent	Adj.	Not appropriate or relevant
Impervious	Adj.	Unable to penetrate, enter
Impetuous	Adj.	Impulsive. Acting on emotion
Impetus	Noun	Motivating, or driving force
Impious	Adj.	Improper respect
Implicit	Adj.	Exact, without question
Impolite	Adj.	Not polite or socially acceptable
Imponderable	Adj.	Beyond question or evaluation
Importance	Noun	Being important
Important	Adj.	Of considerable value
Impose	Verb	Force or bring pressure to
Imposing	Adj.	Impressively striking
Impossible	Adj.	Not possible or capable
Impossibility	Noun	To be impossible. Not capable
Impotent	Adj.	Not potent. Unable
Impracticable	Adj.	Not practicable, feasible
Impractical	Adj.	Not practical, prudent or sensible
Imprecise	Adj.	Not precise, correct. Ambiguous
Impress	Verb	Influence. Leave mark. Impact
Impressible	Adj.	Able to impress
Impression	Noun	To influence or impact opinion
Impressionable	Adj.	Easily impressed or influenced
Improbable	Adj.	Unlikely. Not probable
Impromptu	Adj.	Without prior plan
Improper	Adj.	Not proper or correct
Impropriety	Noun	Being or doing improper
Improve	Verb	To make better
Improvement	Noun	Making or doing better

Improvisation	Noun	To improvise
Improvise	Verb	To make do. Impromptu
Imprudence	Noun	Not prudent, wise
Imprudent	Adj.	Not wise or judicious
Impudence	Noun	Being impudent
Impudent	Adj.	Contemptible. Bold. Not reserved
Impugn	Verb	Aggressive, forceful attack
Impulsive	Adj.	Act without thought
Impute	Verb	Accuse. Charge
Inability	Noun	Not able, capable
Inaccuracy	Noun	Not accurate, correct
Inaccurate	Adj.	Not accurate, correct
Inaction	Noun	No action. Motionless
Inactive	Adj.	Not active. Without movement
Inadequacy	Noun	Not adequate, sufficient
Inadequate	Adj.	Not adequate, sufficient
Inadvertence	Noun	By accident, chance. Not intended
Inadvertent	Adj.	By accident, chance. Not intended
Inadvisable	Adj.	Not advised or recommended
Inane	Adj.	Without substance or direction
Inappropriate	Adj.	Not appropriate, acceptable
Inapt	Adj.	Not apt, suitable
Inaptitude	Noun	Lack of aptitude, ability
Inarticulate	Adj.	Not clear, precise in expression
Inattention	Noun	Not giving proper attention
Inattentive	Adj.	Not giving proper attention
Inborn	Adj.	Born with. Natural
Inbred	Adj.	Being in one's nature
Incalculable	Adj.	Not able to calculate or determine
Incapable	Adj.	Not capable, able
Incapacitate	Verb	Make not capable, able
Incapacity	Noun	Without capability or ability
Incentive	Noun	Something providing motive

Incertitude	Noun	Not certain, sure
Incisive	Adj.	Most decisive, direct
Incite	Verb	Stimulate, move, urge
Incitement	Noun	Cause, arouse action, movement
Inclination	Noun	Personal character
Incline	Verb	Lean. Favor
Inclined	Adj.	Leaning. Favoring
Incogitant	Adj.	Without thought or consideration
Incoherent	Adj.	Missing in coherence or presence
Incomparable	Adj.	Not comparable
Incompatibility	Noun	Not able to get along, mix
Incompatible	Adj.	Unable to get along, mix
Incompetence	Noun	Not having capability or capacity
Incompetent	Adj.	Without capability or capacity
Incomplete	Adj.	Not finished, complete
Incomprehensible	Adj.	Not imaginable, believable
Incomprehension	Noun	Unable to understand, grasp
Inconceivable	Adj.	Unable to convince, persuade
Inconclusive	Adj.	Not conclusive, final, complete
Incongruous	Adj.	Not in step, agreement
Inconsequent	Adj.	Not planned, resulting from logic
Inconsequential	Adj.	Of little importance, matter
Inconsiderable	Adj.	Of little value or worth
Inconsiderate	Adj.	Not considerate of others
Inconsistency	Noun	Being inconsistent
Inconsistent	Adj.	Not constant, steady, same
Inconsonance	Noun	Not in agreement, accord
Inconspicuous	Adj.	Not visible, noticeable
Incontestable	Adj.	Without doubt or question
Incontrovertible	Adj.	Not changeable, questionable
Inconvenience	Noun	Not convenient. Out of the way
Inconvenient	Adj.	Out of the way
Incorrect	Adj.	Not correct, accurate, true, right

Incorrigible	Adj.	Not manageable. Not changeable
Incredible	Adj.	Almost beyond belief
Incurable	Adj.	Not changeable, curable
Indecision	Noun	Not decisive, resolute
Indecisive	Adj.	Not decisive, final, complete
Indefectible	Adj.	Without defect, fault, flaw
Indefensible	Adj.	Unable to defend, justify, excuse
Indefinable	Adj.	Unable to define, clarify
Indefinite	Adj.	Not definite or precise
Independent	Adj.	Along. Without assistance or aid
In-depth	Adj.	Complete, comprehensive
Indestructible	Adj.	Not able to destruct, destroy
Indifference	Noun	Being indifferent
Indifferent	Adj.	Not concerned, caring
Indignant	Adj.	Showing indignation
Indignation	Noun	Unjustified anger
Indignity	Noun	Without self-respect
Indirect	Adj.	Not direct or straight
Indiscernible	Adj.	Not identifiable. Not clear
Indiscipline	Noun	Without discipline, control
Indiscreet	Adj.	Not discreet. Too open
Indiscretion	Noun	Not discreet, normal
Indiscriminate	Adj.	Without logic, rhyme, reason
Indispensable	Adj.	Not able to do/be without
Indisputable	Adj.	Without question. Absolutely
Indistinct	Adj.	Not clear, distinct
Indistinctive	Adj.	Not distinct
Individualist	Noun	One going or standing along
Individuality	Noun	One's own character, self
Indoctrinate	Verb	Instruct, train in new areas
Indolent	Adj.	Slow. Lazy
Induce	Verb	Indirect influence
Inducement	Noun	To induce, ignite

Indulge	Verb	Give in, submit
Indulgence	Noun	To indulge, submit
Indulgent	Adj.	To indulge, submit
Indurate	Verb	Hard and fast. Unyielding
Industrious	Adj.	Skillfully and productively active
Industry	Noun	Persistent pursuit
Ineffective	Adj.	Not effective, or as expected
Ineffectual	Adj.	Not effective, or as expected
Inefficacy	Noun	Without sufficient control, power
Inefficiency	Noun	Being inefficient
Inefficient	Adj.	Not best use of resources
Ineligible	Adj.	Not eligible, qualified
Ineloquent	Adj.	Without eloquence
Inept	Adj.	Not competent, fit
Ineptitude	Noun	Being inept
Inequality	Noun	Not equal, even
Inequitable	Adj.	Not equitable, equal, even
Inequity	Noun	Not just, fair
Inerrant	Adj.	Without error, fault, flaw
Inert	Adj.	Not active. Slow
Inescapable	Adj.	Unable to avoid, miss, omit
Inevitable	Adj.	No chance of avoiding
Inexact	Adj.	Not exact, correct. Error
Inexcusable	Adj.	Unable to excuse, overlook
Inexhaustible	Adj.	Unending. Without end
Inexorable	Adj.	Unmoving. Relentless
Inexpedient	Adj.	Not recommended, advisable
Inexperience	Noun	Without experience, training
Inexpert	Adj.	Not expert, trained, skilled
Inexplicable	Adj.	Without explanation, reason
Inexplicit	Adj.	Not explicit, exact, correct
Inextinguishable	Adj.	Unable to stop, end
Infallible	Adj.	Not capable of mistake, error

Infect	Verb	Communicate to, get into
Infectious	Adj.	To infect by spreading
Inferior	Adj.	Below standard, par
Infinite	Adj.	Without end. Unending
Infirm	Adj.	Weak. Not strong or sound
Inflame	Verb	To agitate, excite
Inflexible	Adj.	Not movable, flexible. Rigid
Influence	Noun	Ability to control
Influential	Adj./Noun	To influence, control, power
Informal	Adj.	Not formal, official
Informative	Adj.	Communicate information, knowledge
Informed	Adj.	Knowing. Learned
Infraction	Noun	Violation of rule, law
Infrastructure	Noun	Basic foundation or framework
Infrequent	Adj.	Not frequent. Rare
Infringe	Verb	Violate by entering, intruding
Infuriate	Verb	Make angry, mad
Infuse	Verb	Instill in someone, thing
Ingenious	Adj.	Original in something genius
Ingenuity	Noun	Genius in originating, devising
Ingenuous	Adj.	Open. Not complex, complicated
Ingrain	Verb	To instill, infuse. Put into
Ingrained	Adj.	Deeply rooted within
Ingratitude	Noun	Not grateful in kind, return
Inharmonious	Adj.	Not getting along, fitting in
Inharmony	Noun	Not in harmony, accord, agreement
Inhibit	Verb	Mental restraint, reluctance
Inhospitable	Adj.	Not friendly
Inhumane	Adj.	Not humane, caring
Inimical	Adj.	Not friendly in nature, manner
Inimitable	Adj.	Not able to duplicate
Iniquity	Noun	Not just, fair. Biased
Initiate	Verb	To start, begin

Initiative	Noun	Acting without guidance, direction
Injudicious	Adj.	Not judicious or appropriate
Injustice	Noun	Without justice, fairness
Innate	Adj.	Possessed as natural, inner self
Innocent	Adj.	Not wrong
Innovate	Verb	Originate new ways, means
Innovation	Noun	Doing something new, better
Innovative	Adj.	To innovate
Innuendo	Noun	Subtle hint. Infer indirectly
Innumerable	Adj.	Too many to number, count
Innumerous	Adj.	Too many to number, count
Inopportune	Adj.	Not opportune, convenient, timely
Inordinate	Adj.	Beyond expected limit
Inquisitive	Adj.	Seek information. Ask questions
Insatiable	Adj.	Unending appetite. Never satisfied
Insecure	Adj.	Not steady, secure
Insensibility	Noun	Not perceptive, aware, knowing
Insensible	Adj.	Not sensible, reasonable
Insensitive	Adj.	Without feeling, caring
Insidious	Adj.	Sly. Unsuspecting. Harmful
Insight	Noun	See into and through something
Insightful	Adj.	Mental understanding
Insignificance	Noun	Not significant or meaningful
Insignificant	Adj.	Not significant or meaningful
Insincere	Adj.	Not sincere, honest, true
Insinuate	Verb	Subtle hint. Infer indirectly
Insipid	Adj.	Dull and without interest
Insolence	Noun	Being overbearing, contemptible
Insolent	Adj.	Overbearing. Being in contempt
Insolvable	Adj.	Without solution, answer
Inspiration	Noun	Inspire others to do, move, act
Inspirational	Adj.	Inspire. Influence
Inspire	Verb	Influence, prompt others to act

Inspired	Adj.	Possess inspirational traits
Inspiring	Adj.	Affecting in, to inspire
Inspirit	Verb	Have spirit
Instability	Noun	Not stable, sturdy, sound
Instantaneous	Adj.	Without any delay
Instigate	Verb	To start, spur on or forward
Instill	Verb	To place in or put in
Instinctive	Adj.	Already known, within. Built in
Instrumental	Adj.	A key or important ingredient
Insubordinate	Adj.	In violation of authority
Insubstantial	Adj.	Not substantial, significant
Insufferable	Adj.	
Insufficient	Adj.	Not sufficient enough
Insult	Verb	Openly offend
Insult	Noun	Open indignity
Insuperable	Adj.	Not able to overcome
Insupportable	Adj.	Unable to support, defend
Insurgent	Adj.	Opposed to authority
Insurmountable	Adj.	Not able to overcome
Intangible	Adj.	Not tangible, touchable
Integral	Adj.	Essential, necessary part
Integrate	Verb	To bring together, combine
Integrative Power	Noun	Mental ability to sort, segregate
Integrity	Noun	In adherence. Abiding
Intellect	Noun	Mental capacity, ability
Intellection	Noun	Power, reason of thought
Intellectual	Adj./Noun	Mental power. Intellect
Intellectual Faculty	Noun	Mental, reasoning capability
Intellectual Grasp	Noun	Understand mentally
Intellectual Power	Noun	Mental ability
Intellectual Weakness	Noun	Mentally lacking, deficient
Intelligence	Noun	Mental ability, capacity
Intelligent	Adj.	High mental ability, capacity

Intense	Adj.	Extreme, extensive
Intercede	Verb	To come between
Interested	Adj.	Curious, attentive, involved
Interfere	Verb	Hinder, harm by entering
Interference	Noun	Interfere, obstruct, hinder
Interfuse	Verb	Fuse together. Bind
Intermittent	Adj.	Not regular, constant
Interpose	Verb	Place or put between
Interpret	Verb	Explain. Understand
Interrogate	Verb	Question at length
Interrupt	Verb	To break, cease, interfere
Intestinal Fortitude	Noun	Internal courage
Intimidate	Verb	Threaten
Intolerable	Adj.	Not tolerable, cannot stand
Intolerance	Noun	Not tolerant, bearable
Intolerant	Adj.	Not tolerable, able to stand
Intractable	Adj.	Hard to control, manage
Intransigent	Adj.	Without giving, compromising
Intrepid	Adj.	Without fear. Bold
Intricate	Adj.	Complex. Complicated
Intrigue	Verb	Mind-catching. Suspenseful
Intrinsic	Adj.	Inherent, within
Introvert	Verb	Inward. Not open, outward
Introvert	Noun	Someone not open, outward
Intrude	Verb	Interfere
Intrusion	Noun	To intrude, interfere
Intrusive	Adj.	Intruding, interfering
Intuitive	Adj.	Insight. Intuition
Inundate	Verb	Cover completely. Overwhelm
Invalid	Adj.	Not valid, fact, true, good
Invalidity	Noun	Not valid. Invalid
Invaluable	Adj.	Value beyond calculation
Invariable	Adj.	Not variable, changeable

Invective	Adj.	Verbal attack, abuse
Inveigle	Verb	Lure. Entice
Invent	Verb	To create, devise
Invention	Noun	Invent. Create. Originate
Inventive	Adj.	Able to invent, originate, create
Inventiveness	Noun	Ability to originate, invent
Inventor	Noun	One who originates new ideas
Invidious	Adj.	Not fair, pleasant. Offensive
Invigorate	Verb	Refreshing, lively
Invincible	Adj.	Not able to overcome
Involuntary	Adj.	Not voluntary, by will, choice
Involved	Adj.	Concerned. Into. Part of
Irate	Adj.	Angry
Ire	Noun	Openly angry
Irk	Verb	Annoy. Pester
Irksome	Adj.	To irk
Ironic	Adj.	Say one thing, mean other in wit
Irradiate	Verb	Make clear by intellect
Irradicable	Adj.	Unable to end, get out
Irrational	Adj.	Not rational, normal
Irrationality	Noun	Without reason, rationale
Irredeemable	Adj.	Not able to redeem, save
Irreformable	Adj.	Not able to reform, change
Irrefutable	Adj.	Unable to refute, disprove
Irregular	Adj.	Not regular, customary
Irregularity	Noun	Being irregular
Irrelative	Adj.	Not relative, pertinent
Irrelevant	Adj.	Not relevant, pertinent
Irrepressible	Adj.	Unable to hold, restrain
Irresolute	Adj.	Not firm or sure
Irresponsible	Adj.	Not responsible
Irresponsive	Adj.	Not responsible, timely
Irritable	Adj.	Able to irritate, agitate

| Irritate | Verb | Spark resentment, hate |
| Isolated | Adj. | Infrequent or once |

-J-

Jabber	Verb	Talk on without coherence
Jack-of-all-trades	Noun	Do many things well
Jealous	Adj.	Envious suspicion

Jest	Noun	Joke. Trick. Prank
Jester	Noun	One who jests. A joker
Jocose	Adj.	Witty and humorous

Jocular	Adj.	Jolly, jesting
Jolly	Adj.	Open. Friendly. Cheerful
Josh	Verb	Joke, tease in jest

Journeyman	Noun	Experienced, knowledgeable
Jovial	Adj.	Open, friendly natured
Joy	Noun	Happy, cheerful emotion

Joyful	Adj.	Having happy, cheerful emotion
Jubilant	Adj.	Extreme joy, high thrill
Judgment	Noun	To compare, judge. decide

Judicial	Adj.	Prudent and careful
Judicious	Adj.	Prudent, reasoned, wise
Juggle	Verb	Manipulate. Balance
Just	Adj.	Reasonable. Fair. Right

-K-

Keen	Adj.	Quick. Alert. Sharp
Keenness	Noun	A keen mental faculty
Keen-witted	Adj.	Sharp, keen mental faculty

Keen-wittedness	Noun	Sharp, keen mental faculty
Keynote	Noun	A key or fundamental item
Kilter	Noun	On even keel. In order

Kind	Adj.	Friendly, generous
Kindle	Verb	Ignite, start
Kindless	Adj.	Not kind, friendly

Kindliness	Noun	Being kind, friendly
Kindly	Adj.	Kind, friendly, sympathetic
Kingpin	Noun	Chief person in a group
Kindness	Noun	Showing or exhibiting kind deed
Kink	Noun	Unusual flaw or twist
Klutz	Noun	Someone awkward, clumsy
Knack	Noun	Unusual, ingenious ability
Know	Verb	Clear mental understanding
Know-how	Noun	Possessing knowledge
Knowing	Adj.	Knowledge, knowledgeable
Know-it-all	Noun	Over confident of knowledge
Knowledge	Noun	Possessed wisdom, ability
Knowledgeable	Adj.	Knowing. Learned
Knuckle down	Verb	Earnest effort
Knuckle under	Verb	Quit. Give in
Kudo	Noun	A "well done." Praise

-L-

Labor	Noun	Effort. Exertion. Work
Labor	Verb	To exert effort, work
Laborious	Adj.	Hard work, labor
Lack	Verb	Deficient, missing, short
Lack	Noun	Being deficient, missing, short
Lackadaisical	Adj.	Slow. Without zest, zeal
Lackluster	Adj.	Dull. Without life, energy
Laconic	Adj.	Concise, offensive words
Lag	Noun/Verb	Behind. Slow
Landmark	Noun	First of its kind
Lapse	Noun/Verb	Come overdue, behind. Mistake
Large	Adj.	Big. Many
Largehearted	Adj.	Warm. Caring. Sympathetic
Large-minded	Adj.	Open-minded. Knowledgeable
Last	Adj.	End. Bottom. Lowest

Last-ditch	Adj.	Final. Last
Lasting	Adj.	Continuing on, enduring
Last minute	Noun	Final, ending move, action
Latitude	Noun	Free to act, do, choose
Laudable	Adj.	Commendable. Noteworthy
Laudatory	Adj.	To commend. Commendable
Launch	Verb	Go forth. Start
Laurel	Noun	In high standing, esteem honor
Lavish	Verb	More than necessary
Lax	Adj.	Not firm, resolute
Laxity	Noun	Being lax, not firm
Leading	Adj.	Top. First
Learn	Verb	Obtain knowledge
Learned	Adj.	Knowledgeable. To learn
Learning	Noun	Gaining knowledge
Least	Adj.	Less. Lowest. Last
Legerity	Noun	Mental, physical agility
Legible	Adj.	Understand writing
Legitimacy	Noun	Legal. Lawful
Legitimate	Adj.	Legal. Lawful
Leisure	Noun	Idleness. Lax
Leniency	Noun	Not tough. Ease up. Easy
Lenient	Adj.	Not tough. Ease up. Easy
Less	Adj.	Lower. Below. Decrease
Lessen	Verb	To be less. Decrease
Lethargic	Adj.	Slow. Indifferent
Lethargy	Noun	Being slow, indifferent
Lettered	Adj.	Educated. Knowledgeable
Letter-perfect	Adj.	Without error, flaw
Levelheaded	Adj.	Reasonable in judgment
Levelheadedness	Noun	Even in temperament & rationale
Levity	Noun	Not constant. Changing
Liability	Noun	A disadvantage. Non-asset

Liable	Adj.	Obligated. Responsible
Life blood	Noun	Crucial. Vital
Lifeless	Adj.	Without life, vim, vigor
Life-style	Noun	Way of life
Light-headed	Adj.	Not serious, sound
Lighthearted	Adj.	Carefree. Happy. Joyous
Limelight	Noun	Center of attention
Limited	Adj.	Restrained. Restricted
Limitless	Adj.	Without limit. Continuous
Limp	Verb	Not stout, strong, steady
Limpid	Adj.	Pure. Clear. Not complex
Literacy	Noun	Being literate, educated
Literal	Adj.	Exact. Without error
Literally	Adv	In actuality. Actual
Literary	Adj.	Literate. Well read
Literate	Adj./Noun	Educated. Knowledgeable
Little	Adj.	Small. Less than average
Liveliness	Noun	Active and energetic
Lively	Adj.	Energetic. Alert
Lively Imagination	Noun	Keen, active intellect
Loath	Adj.	Not willing. Reluctant
Loathe	Verb	Intense dislike. Hate
Loathing	Noun	An intense dislike
Loathsome	Adj.	To be loath, detestable
Lofty	Adj.	High above. Overbearing
Logic	Noun	Reasoned deduction. Rational
Logical	Adj.	Skilled logic, systematic
Logical Thought	Noun	Rational, reasoning intellect
Loner	Noun	One avoiding others
Long-lived	Adj.	Lasting. Enduring
Long-range	Adj.	Ahead in time. Future
Look down	Verb	Belittle
Loquacious	Adj.	Excessive talking

Loser	Noun	One unable to win, succeed
Lost	Adj.	No longer possessed
Lower	Verb	Reduce. Make less
Low-grade	Adj.	Below average. Inferior
Low-key	Adj.	Low profile
Low-level	Adj.	Low value. Below average
Low-minded	Adj.	Low thoughts, behavior
Low-pressure	Adj.	Little pressure, tension
Low-profile	Adj.	Low visibility, attention
Low-spirited	Adj.	Dejected, depressed
Loyal	Adj.	Faithful. Dedicated
Loyalty	Noun	Being loyal, dedicated
Lucid	Adj.	Clear knowledge
Lucidity	Noun	Clear understanding
Ludicrous	Adj.	Foolish beyond belief
Lukewarm	Adj.	Mediocre

-M-

Maladjusted	Adj.	Not Adjusted to society
Maladroit	Adj.	No grace or skill
Malevolence	Noun	Grudging, ill will
Malevolent	Adj.	Display grudging, ill will
Malice	Noun	Harmful intent
Malicious	Adj.	Intending harm
Malinger	Verb	Shirk responsibility
Mammoth	Adj.	Massive. Very large
Manage	Verb	Control. Direct
Management	Noun	Managing. Controlling
Manager	Noun	Someone who manages
Managerial	Adj.	Management traits
Manipulate	Verb	Control actions, movements
Manipulation	Noun	Intelligent use, control
Manner	Noun	Behavior

Mannerism	Noun	Standard, expected behavior
Mannerless	Adj.	Bad manners. Rude
Mannerly	Adj.	Good manners. Polite
Mar	Verb	Scar. Fault
Marginal	Adj.	Barely. Minimum
Marvelous	Adj.	Almost above belief
Masterful	Adj.	Most brilliant, skillful
Masterly	Adj.	Display brilliance, skill
Mastermind	Noun	One who plans. Intelligent
Mastery	Noun	Control over. Expert
Matter-of-course	Adj.	Natural events, course
Matter-of-fact	Adj.	Of, to the facts
Mature	Adj.	Developed. Grown full
Maturity	Noun	Being mature, developed
Maxim	Noun	A stated rule, fact
Maximize	Verb	Do to the maximum
Maximum	Noun	Most possible
Meager	Adj.	Small. Little
Meander	Noun	Wander without cause
Meaningless	Adj.	Without meaning, sense
Meddle	Verb	Pry uninvited
Mediate	Verb	Intermediary. Go between
Mediation	Noun	Serving to mediate
Mediocre	Adj.	Barely satisfactory
Mediocrity	Noun	Being mediocre
Meditate	Verb	Mental pondering
Meek	Adj.	Not strong. Weak
Menace	Noun	A threat
Mental	Adj.	The mind or intellect
Mental Alertness	Noun	Quick, alert intelligence
Mental Capacity	Noun	Intellectual limit
Mental Deficiency	Noun	Lacking proper intellect
Mental Faculty	Noun	Intellectual ability, capacity

Mental Handicap	Noun	Intellectually restrained/confined
Mentality	Noun	Mental power
Mental Process	Noun	Intellectual functioning
Mental Void	Noun	Without knowledge, intellect
Mental Weakness	Noun	Lack of intellectual perseverance
Mentor	Noun	A knowing teacher
Merciful	Adj.	Having mercy, compassion
Merciless	Adj.	Without mercy, compassion
Mercy	Noun	Compassionate. Forgiving
Mere	Adj.	The minimum. Only
Merit	Noun	Worthy of praise
Merry	Adj.	Cheerful and lively
Methodical	Adj.	By orderly procession
Meticulous	Adj.	Exacting in detail
Might	Noun	Power. Strength
Mild	Adj.	Even tempered disposition
Mindful	Adj.	Pay heed, attention
Mindless	Adj.	Without knowledge, intelligence
Mingle	Verb	Mix
Minimize	Verb	Reduce. Decrease
Minimum	Noun	Least. Smallest
Minish	Verb	Diminish. Lower. Less
Minor	Adj.	Less. Under
Minuscule	Noun	Extremely small
Minute	Adj.	Extremely small
Misapply	Verb	Misuse. Misapplication
Misappropriate	Verb	Illegal use
Misbecome	Verb	Not becoming, fit, proper
Misbehave	Verb	Wrong behavior
Miscalculate	Verb	Judge badly
Mischievous	Adj.	Minor tricks, pranks
Misconduct	Verb	Bad conduct
Misconstrue	Verb	Misunderstanding

Miserable	Adj.	Bad. Substandard
Misfit	Verb	Not fit, Adjusted
Misfortune	Noun	Bad fortune, luck
Misgiving	Noun	Doubt. Apprehension
Misguided	Verb	Led astray
Mishap	Noun	Unfortunate act
Misinterpret	Verb	Misunderstand
Misjudge	Verb	Bad, wrong judgment
Mislead	Verb	Lead astray, wrong
Mismanage	Verb	Manage badly
Mistake	Verb	Error
Mistaken	Adj.	Be wrong, understand incorrectly
Misunderstanding	Noun	Incorrect understanding
Misuse	Verb	Use incorrectly, wrongly
Mix-up	Noun	Foul-up. Blunder
Moderate	Adj.	Without excess. Reasonable
Moderation	Noun	Be moderate. Without excess
Modest	Adj.	Not boastful, bragging
Modesty	Noun	Being modest
Monumental	Adj.	Great. Tremendous
Moody	Adj.	Uneven temperament
Moral	Adj.	Discern right from wrong
Morale	Noun	Mental spirit
Moralist	Noun	Teach own morals
Moralistic	Adj.	Concerned with rights and wrongs
Morality	Noun	Right and wrong principles
Moralize	Verb	Explain right from wrong
Motivate	Verb	Provide moving force
Motivation	Noun	Emotional drive to action
Motive	Noun	Reason. Driving force
Muddle	Verb	Mix up or confuse
Multitude	Noun	Many. Large amount
Mumble	Verb	Speak indistinctly

Mundane	Adj.	Ordinary.
Myriad	Noun	Infinitely large. Many
Mystique	Noun	Magical intrigue

-N-

Naive	Adj.	Gullible. Simple
Neat	Adj.	In order. Tidy
Negate	Verb	Go or work against
Negative	Adj.	No. Not positive
Neglect	Verb	Omit attention. Ignore
Neglectful	Adj.	To neglect. Ignore
Negligence	Noun	Showing neglect by intent
Negligent	Adj.	Fail to attend to
Negligible	Adj.	Not of much importance
Nerveless	Adj.	Without courage. Not bold
Nescient	Adj.	Without adequate knowledge
Neutral	Adj.	Not negative. Not positive
Nice	Adj.	Friendly. Cordial
Nicety	Noun	Being, doing nice
Nimble	Adj.	Mental agility, quick
Noble	Adj.	High moral correctness
Nominal	Adj.	Slight. Unimportant
Nonchalant	Adj.	Not concerned, interested
Nonconformist	Noun	Not comply to norm
No-nonsense	Adj.	Serious
Nonproductive	Adj.	Not fruitful, productive
Nonsense	Noun	Not serious. Foolish
Normal	Adj.	The norm, standard, average
Notable	Adj.	Worthy of mention
Nought	Noun	Nothing. None
Nourish	Verb	Foster. Feed
Novice	Noun	A beginner. New person
Nuisance	Noun	Annoying
Null	Adj.	No use or value
Nurture	Noun	Help grow, bring up

-O-

Obedient	Adj.	Obeying. Complying
Obey	Verb	Comply. Follow direction
Oblige	Verb	Commit or compel for favor
Obliging	Adj.	To favor. Give favor
Obnoxious	Adj.	Crude. Rude
Obscure	Adj.	Not clear. Hidden
Observant	Adj.	Watchful attention
Obsession	Noun	Uncontrollable desire
Obsolete	Adj.	Out of date
Obstacle	Noun	Something in way of objective
Obstinate	Adj.	Overbearing. Stubborn
Obstruct	Verb	Hinder. Come between
Obtuse	Adj.	Mentally slow to comprehend
Odd	Adj.	Out of the usual. Strange
Oddity	Noun	Being odd, strange
Offend	Verb	Insult. Resent
Offensive	Adj.	Disagreeable. Insulting
Omniscient	Adj.	Limitless knowledge
One-track-mind	Adj.	Handle only one subject at a time
One-upmanship	Noun	Skill of getting one up
One-way	Adj.	Single direction, action
Open-eyed	Adj.	Alert. Awake. Aware
Openhanded	Adj.	Up front. Fair
Openhearted	Adj.	Friendly, open personality
Oppose	Verb	Against
Opposition	Noun	Resisting. Opposing
Oppress	Verb	Restrain by harsh methods
Oppressive	Adj.	Oppress with a force
Optimum	Noun	Ideal or best action
Oral	Adj.	Speak. Speech
Orator	Noun	Skilled speaker
Orchestrate	Verb	Lead. Control
Ordeal	Noun	Trying, hard situation

Orderly	Adj.	Tidy. In proper place
Ordinary	Adj.	Routine. Normal. Common
Organize	Verb	Mesh together. Arrange
Orientate	Verb	Adjust. Become familiar
Original	Adj.	New. Fresh
Originality	Noun	New. Creative. Original
Originate	Adj./Verb	Create. Bring into existence
Orthodox	Adj.	Conventional. Normal
Orthodoxy	Noun	Be orthodox
Oscillate	Verb	Move, go back and forth
Ostracize	Verb	Expel. Cast out
Oust	Verb	Cast out. Expel
Outburst	Noun	Impulsive, offensive action
Outcast	Adj.	Reject. Cast out
Outclass	Verb	Above in excellence
Outdo	Verb	Do better. Excel
Outgoing	Adj.	Open, friendly manner
Outlandish	Adj.	Foolish. Odd
Outlast	Verb	Last longer
Outlook	Noun	View of what is ahead
Outmatch	Verb	To do or be better
Out-of-date	Adj.	Obsolete. Old
Outrage	Noun	Violent anger
Outrageous	Adj.	Extremely violent action
Outshine	Verb	To outdo. Be superior
Outspoken	Adj.	Too freely spoken, disagree
Outstanding	Adj.	Above all others. Preeminent
Outthink	Verb	Out wit. Out smart
Outwit	Verb	Outdo by sly, skill
Overbearing	Adj.	Forceful. Arrogant
Overcome	Verb	Prevail despite obstacles
Overconfident	Adj.	More confident than justified
Overdue	Adj.	Past due. Late

Overextend	Verb	Extended beyond means
Overreact	Verb	React over requirement
Oversee	Verb	Watch over
Overshadow	Verb	Outdo. Outshine
Oversight	Noun	To miss. In error
Oversimplify	Verb	To omit pertinent facts
Overt	Adj.	In the open. Not covered
Overwhelm	Verb	Overcome by force, weight

-P-

Pacify	Verb	To quiet, appease
Pall	Verb	Wear down. Boring
Palter	Verb	Squander without care, concern
Paltry	Adj.	Little. Petty. Without value
Pamper	Verb	Treat too easily. Give in
Panic	Noun	Fear and loss of calmness
Paradox	Noun	Conflicting, true facts
Paragon	Noun	A model of excellence
Paramount	Adj.	Primary or top importance
Paranoid	Adj.	Unreal beliefs, fears
Paraphrase	Noun	Quote in part. Rephrase
Pare	Verb	Cut down. Reduce
Parity	Noun	Equal. Equality
Parlance	Noun	Language style
Parlous	Adj.	Sly and risky
Parody	Noun	Bad double, imitation
Partial	Adj.	Inclined toward. Favoring
Partiality	Noun	Be biased, inclined
Partisan	Noun	Extreme bias, preference
Passable	Adj.	Just adequate
Passion	Noun	Strong seated emotion
Passionate	Adj.	Strong or heated emotion
Passive	Adj.	Inactive. Neutral
Passivism	Noun	Inactive, neutral

Passivity	Noun	Being inactive, neutral
Pathetic	Adj.	Extremely sorrowful
Pathfinder	Noun	One who leads the way
Patience	Noun	Being reserved. Able to wait
Patient	Adj.	Wait calmly
Patriot	Noun	One loyal to country
Patriotism	Noun	Feeling loyal to country
Patronize	Verb	Go along, lowering one's self
Paucity	Noun	Lack of. Little. Small
Peccant	Adj.	Go against rule
Peculiar	Adj.	Unique. Odd
Peculiarity	Noun	Being unique, odd
Pedant	Noun	One lacking in judgment
Peer	Noun	One of same rank, equal
Peerless	Adj.	Without peer, equal
Peevish	Adj.	Immature. Bad humored
Pejorative	Adj.	Become negative, worse
Pell-mell	Adj./Noun	Confusing. Unorganized
Penetrate	Verb	To know, understand
Penetrating	Adj.	Perceptive, discerning
Penetration	Noun	Sharp in mind
Penitent	Adj.	Admit wrong. Regret
Pensive	Adj.	Deep, sad in thought
Pep	Noun	Full of zest, zeal & spirit
Perceive	Verb	To recognize, know, understand
Perception	Noun	To be, make aware. Understand
Perceptive	Adj.	To penetrate, know
Pendurable	Adj.	Durable. Lasting
Perdure	Verb	Enduring. Lasting
Perfect	Adj.	Without flaw. Exact
Perfectible	Adj.	Able to make perfect
Perfection	Noun	Being perfect. Without flaw
Perfectionism	Noun	Reaching for perfection

Perform	Verb	To act or do. Accomplish
Performance	Noun	Performing. Accomplishing
Perfunctory	Adj.	Casual. Indifferent
Permissive	Adj.	Overly allowable, lenient
Perpetual	Adj.	Go on and on. Lasting
Perpetuate	Verb	Cause to go on, continue
Perplex	Verb	Puzzle. Confuse
Perplexed	Adj.	Being puzzled, confused
Perplexity	Noun	Being perplexed, confused
Persecute	Verb	Inflict ill will, trouble
Perseverance	Noun	Enduring, lasting will
Persevere	Verb	To endure, continue on
Persist	Verb	Continue on despite obstacles
Persistence	Noun	Being persistent, enduring
Persistent	Adj.	Continue on despite obstacles
Personable	Adj.	Friendly personality
Personality	Noun	Expressed individual attitudes
Personification	Noun	Embodiment of thing, idea
Personify	Verb	Serve as example
Perspicacious	Adj.	Good perception, judgment
Perspicuous	Adj.	Vivid, clear understanding
Persuade	Verb	Convince
Persuasion	Noun	Ability to convince
Persuasive	Adj.	Be able to convince, persuade
Pert	Adj.	Bold. Brash
Pertinacious	Adj.	Stubborn. Persevere
Pertinacity	Noun	Being stubborn.
Pertinent	Adj.	Applicable. Relevant
Perturb	Verb	Upset. Alarm. Confuse
Pervade	Verb	Permeate. Penetrate. Prevail
Pessimism	Noun	Always think, expect worst
Pessimistic	Adj.	Expect worst. Not optimistic
Petty	Adj.	Meaningless. Worth little

Petulant	Adj.	Insolent. Annoying
Pictured	Verb	Mental image, vision
Pillar	Noun	A mainstay
Pinnacle	Noun	At highest point possible
Pitfall	Noun	Shortcoming. Trap
Pitiless	Adj.	Without pity, compassion
Pity	Noun	Sympathy. Sorrow
Placid	Adj.	Under control. Calm
Platitude	Noun	Ordinary. Common. Trite
Plaudit	Noun	Praise. Approval
Plausible	Adj.	Questionable
Pleasant	Adj.	Pleasing. Agreeable
Pleasantry	Noun	Being pleasant
Pleasing	Adj.	Agreeable. Pleasant
Pleasurable	Adj.	Enjoyable. Gratifying
Pleasure	Noun	Good feeling. Pleasing
Pliable	Adj.	Able to Adjust, Influence
Plod	Verb	Steady, slow, mundane
Poignant	Adj.	Elicit compassion, emotion
Poise	Noun	Refined, dignified style
Polemic	Adj.	Disrupt. Agitate. Incite
Polish	Verb	Social grace, refinement
Polished	Adj.	Having social poise, grace
Polite	Adj.	Courteous and considerate
Politic	Adj.	Possessing prudent skill, wisdom
Polyglot	Adj.	Conversant in language
Pomposity	Noun	Self-indulging or important
Pompous	Adj.	Conceived self importance
Ponder	Verb	Think. Go over. Consider
Ponderable	Adj.	Thinking. Going over. Considering
Popular	Adj.	Widely accepted, liked
Portentous	Adj.	Pretense of self importance
Positive	Adj.	In affirm, favor

Possessive	Adj.	A desire to have, possess
Postulate	Verb	Speculate without proof
Postulator	Noun	Someone who postulates, assumes
Potency	Noun	Ability, potential, capacity
Potent	Adj.	Powerful
Potential	Adj.	Ability. Capacity
Power	Noun	Driving, moving force
Powerhouse	Noun	Mighty. Dynamic
Powerful	Adj.	Mighty. Having great influence
Power of Mind	Noun	Ability to know, think
Power of Reason	Noun	Ability to use ration, reason
Power of Thought	Noun	Ability to think and originate
Practical	Adj.	Sensible. Reasonable
Practical Knowledge	Noun	Realistic/useful mental capability
Practical Wisdom	Noun	Realistic, useful knowledge
Pragmatic	Adj.	Speculate. Conjecture
Praise	Verb	Hold in high esteem. Commend
Precarious	Adj.	Vulnerable. At risk
Precise	Adj.	Exact
Precision	Noun	Being exact and finite
Predominant	Adj.	Dominate without peer
Predominate	Verb	Dominate over, above others
Preeminent	Adj.	Be, exist above others
Preferential	Adj.	Prefer, choose over another
Prejudice	Noun	Judge before hand, facts
Prejudicial	Adj.	Showing prejudice, favor
Premature	Adj.	Before. Prior. Early
Premium	Noun	Extra, added value
Preoccupied	Adj.	Mentally occupied
Prepare	Verb	To get, make ready
Preparedness	Noun	Being prepared
Preponderant	Adj.	Over abundance
Preponderate	Verb	Dominant. Greater

Preposterous	Adj.	Ridiculous. Outrageous
Prepotency	Noun	Very potent, powerful
Presence	Noun	One's bearing, being
Presence of mind	Adj.	Mental clearness to act
Presentable	Adj.	Acceptable to present
Prestige	Noun	Having renown, high stature
Prestigious	Adj.	High honor, esteem, acclaim
Prevail	Verb	To win out, be on top
Prevailing	Adj.	Existing above or superior
Prevalent	Adj.	Dominant. Accepted
Pride	Noun	Esteem. Respect
Prime	Adj.	Most important. First
Privilege	Noun	Special favor, consideration
Privileged	Adj.	Having special consideration
Problem	Noun	Something requiring a solution
Problem	Adj.	Hard to handle, deal with
Procrastinate	Verb	Put-off. Indecision
Prod	Verb	Push, stir to move
Prodigal	Adj.	Overly generous, extravagant
Prodigy	Noun	Someone held in awe, amazement
Produce	Verb	To originate, bring forth
Productive Imagination	Noun	Creative results of the mind
Professional	Noun	One highly skilled
Professionalism	Noun	Exhibiting professional traits
Proficiency	Noun	Highly skilled
Proficient	Adj.	Skilled, productive
Profound	Adj.	Sound, innate mental power
Profound Knowledge	Noun	Broad intellectual depth
Progress	Noun	Improve. Advance. Forward
Progressive	Adj.	Forward thinking
Proliferate	Verb	Multiply, increase rapidly
Prolific	Adj.	Produce great many
Prominence	Noun	Being prominent
Prominent	Adj.	Widely known or acknowledged

Promote	Verb	Foster. Further. Advance
Promoter	Noun	One who promotes or backs
Prompt	Adj.	Quick. Timely
Promptitude	Noun	Being prompt, quick
Propagate	Verb	Spread. Emit
Propel	Verb	Push. Move
Propensity	Noun	Inclination
Proper	Adj.	Correct. Right
Propitiate	Verb	Appease. Please
Propitious	Adj.	Favorable
Propone	Verb	Put forth. Propose
Proponent	Noun	One who backs, promotes
Proposal	Noun	Submitting for view, review
Propriety	Noun	Proper and fit
Prosper	Verb	Flourish. Thrive
Prosperity	Noun	To prosper, succeed
Prosperous	Adj.	Succeed. Flourish
Protégé	Noun	One trained by expert
Prototype	Noun	First of new breed, standard
Proud	Adj.	Holding high esteem
Provident	Adj.	Prudent. Wise
Provocative	Adj.	Agitate. Stimulate. Provoke
Provoke	Verb	Stir up. Agitate. Excite
Provoking	Adj.	To provoke
Prowess	Noun	Outstanding mental agility
Prude	Noun	One overbearing, crass
Prudence	Noun	Being careful, tentative
Prudent	Adj.	Careful. Tentative
Prudential	Adj.	Showing prudence, judgment
Prudish	Adj.	Overly correct and proper
Pry	Verb	Unwanted inquiry, meddling
Prying	Adj.	To pry

Punctilious	Adj.	Excessive about detail
Punctual	Adj.	Timely. On time
Pundit	Noun	Self-proclaimed expert
Pungent	Adj.	Keen of mind
Pure	Adj.	Without defect, impurity
Purge	Verb	Rid of unwanted parts
Purport	Verb	Suppose. Profess
Purpose	Verb	Intend. Reason
Purposeful	Adj.	Having purpose, meaning
Purposeless	Adj.	Without purpose, meaning
Puzzle	Verb	Perplex. Mix-up

-Q-

Qualified	Adj.	Capable. Able
Quality	Noun	A high state, degree
Quantify	Verb	Determine by quantity, amount
Quell	Verb	To stop, silence, end
Query	Noun	Question
Quest	Noun	Venture. Seek. Pursue
Questionable	Adj.	Uncertain. Doubtful
Quibble	Noun	Petty item, concern
Quick	Adj.	Prompt. Fast. Ready
Quicken	Verb	To speed up, hasten
Quickness	Noun	Quick & perceptive mind
Quick-thinking	Noun/Adj.	Quick in mental thought, action
Quick Wit	Noun	Mentally quick & alert
Quick-witted	Adj.	Mentally quick and alert
Quip	Noun	Witty remark
Quirk	Noun	Unforeseen happening, twist
Quit	Verb	Stop. Cease
Quitter	Noun	One who quits too quickly

-R-

Radiance	Noun	Shine with brightness
Radiant	Adj.	Beaming, as goodwill, joy
Radiant	Verb	Emit warmth, goodwill

Rage	Noun	Violent anger
Rally	Verb	Renew, revive effort, action
Rampage	Noun	Violent action, behavior
Rare	Adj.	Unusual. Not ordinary, common
Rarity	Noun	Being rare, uncommon
Rational	Adj.	Sound, logical reasoning
Rationale	Noun	Rational reasoning
Rationalism	Noun	Use of reason
Rationality	Noun	Being rational. Able to reason
Rationalize	Verb	Interpret actions, reasons
Rational Faculty	Noun	Reasoning, rational mind
Ready	Adj.	Prepared. Capable
Ready-made	Adj.	Ordinary. Not original
Ready Wit	Noun	Mentally quick, alert, skillful
Realism	Noun	Being real vice idealistic
Realist	Noun	Practical reality, not idealistic
Realistic	Adj.	Of reality, practical
Reality	Noun	Being real, fact
Realization	Noun	To realize
Reason	Noun	Rational thought
Reasonable	Adj.	Within reason, justifiable
Reasoning	Noun	Rational deduction
Reasoning Facility	Noun	Logical, reasonable mental ability
Reasonless	Adj.	Without reason, logic
Rebellious	Adj.	Defiant. Opposing
Rebuff	Noun	Refute. Brisk refusal
Rebut	Verb	Formal refute, opposition
Recall	Noun	Memory. Memory ability
Receptive	Adj.	Able, willing to learn
Rectify	Verb	Fix. Correct
Redress	Noun/Verb	To right a wrong
Redundant	Adj.	In excess. Too much
Re-examine	Verb	Review again

Reevaluate	Verb	To rethink, reconsider
Refine	Verb	To make better, more pure
Refined	Adj.	Cultured. Learned
Reform	Verb	Change for better. Correct
Refrain	Verb	To hold, keep back
Refreshing	Adj.	New and invigorating
Refusal	Noun	Not accepting
Refuse	Verb	Turn down
Refute	Verb	Prove wrong, false
Regenerate	Adj.	Renew. New vigor
Regress	Noun	Fall back. Lose ground
Regression	Noun	Regress. Move backward
Regret	Verb	Remorse. Sorrow
Regretful	Adj.	To regret, feel sorry
Rehabilitate	Verb	Renew. Put back
Rehash	Verb	Go over again
Reject	Verb	Turn down
Rejuvenate	Verb	Give new, fresh life
Relapse	Verb	Fall back, slip back, to before
Relent	Verb	To give in
Relentless	Adj.	Not giving in, relenting
Reliable	Adj.	Dependable. Trustworthy
Reliance	Noun	Rely. Depend. Trust
Reliant	Adj.	Trustworthy
Relinquish	Verb	Give up
Reluctance	Noun	Being reluctant
Reluctant	Adj.	Not fully willing
Remarkable	Adj.	Unusually good deed, feat
Remedial	Adj.	To remedy, fix
Remedy	Noun	Fix. Correct
Remiss	Adj.	Negligent. At fault
Remorse	Noun	Self sense of guilt
Remorseful	Adj.	Feeling remorse

Remorseless	Adj.	Without remorse, guilt
Renascent	Adj.	Renewed stamina and vim
Renew	Verb	Make new, over
Renitent	Adj.	To resist, oppose
Renounce	Verb	Refuse. Rebut. Disown
Renovate	Verb	To fix up, renew, revive
Renown	Noun	High reputation
Renowned	Adj.	Having high renown, reputation
Renunciation	Noun	To forgo, give up
Reorganize	Verb	Organize over, again
Repercussion	Noun	Reaction to action
Repertoire	Noun	Possessed special skills
Reprehend	Verb	Offend. Criticize
Reprehensible	Adj.	Very offensive, criticizing
Repress	Verb	Suppress. Hold down, back
Repression	Noun	Being repressed
Reprimand	Noun	Official rebuke
Reproach	Verb	Blame for fault
Reproach	Noun	To blame for fault
Reprobate	Verb	Condemn. Disapprove
Reprobate	Adj.	Without moral principles
Repudiate	Verb	Refuse. Deny
Repugn	Verb	Oppose
Repugnance	Noun	Utter dislike
Repugnant	Adj.	Not agreeable
Repulse	Verb	Repel. Reject
Repulsion	Noun	Repel. Dislike
Repulsive	Adj.	Repel. Dislike
Reputable	Adj.	Good reputation
Reputation	Noun	Earned public character, stature
Repute	Verb	Supposed. Assumed
Requisite	Adj.	Requirement
Resent	Verb	Bad feeling. Dislike

Resentful	Adj.	To resent. Have bad feeling
Resentment	Noun	Bad, offensive feeling
Reserve	Verb	To hold back. Keep
Reserve	Noun	Something held back
Reserved	Adj.	Held back, restrained manner
Reservoir	Noun	Place used for storage
Resilience	Noun	Ability to bounce back, recover
Resilient	Adj.	Bounce back. Recover
Resist	Verb	Oppose. Go against
Resistance	Noun	To resist, oppose
Resistant	Adj./Noun	To resist, oppose
Resistless	Adj.	Without resistance, opposition
Resolute	Adj.	Firm. Determined
Resolution	Noun	Firm in resolve
Resolve	Noun/Verb	Firm determination. Decided
Resounding	Adj.	Complete. Unqualified
Resource	Noun	Possessed ability. Resourceful
Resourceful	Adj.	Possessing resource, ability
Respect	Noun/Verb	State of high esteem, regard
Respectable	Adj.	Be held in high esteem, regard
Respectful	Adj.	Being in respect
Responsibility	Noun	Being held accountable
Responsible	Adj.	Accountable
Responsive	Adj.	Ability to respond, answer
Restrain	Verb	Hold back
Restraint	Noun	Something that restrains
Resurge	Verb	Come or surge back
Resurgent	Adj.	Rise or surge back, again
Retard	Verb	Hinder. Slow down
Retentive	Adj.	To retain, remember
Retentivity	Noun	Capacity to retain, remember
Rethink	Verb	Think over again
Retribution	Noun	Due & just reward, punishment

Revive	Verb	Bring back to life
Rhetoric	Noun	Double talk with skill over words
Rhetorical	Adj.	Using rhetoric
Rhetorician	Noun	One skilled in rhetoric
Rich Imagination	Noun	Unending mental originality
Ridicule	Noun	To belittle by joke
Ridiculous	Adj.	Foolish. Outlandish
Righteous	Adj.	Be, act right, proper
Rigid	Adj.	Stiff. Firm. Not flexible
Rigidify	Verb	Be rigid
Rigor	Noun	Hard. Severe. Arduous
Rigorous	Adj.	Hard. Strict. Severe
Rival	Noun	Opponent. Competitor
Rivalry	Noun	Standing rival. Competition
Robust	Adj.	Strong. Healthy. Hardy
Rookie	Noun	A newcomer. Inexperienced
Rosy	Adj.	Promising. Bright
Rough	Adj.	Harsh. Not refined
Rouse	Verb	Agitate. Stir up
Rude	Adj.	Bad in manner
Rudiment	Noun	Not yet fully developed
Rudimentary	Adj.	New. Elementary
Run-down	Adj.	Poor condition. Exhausted
Rusty	Adj.	Not as capable/able as before
Ruthless	Adj.	Without consideration, compassion

-S-

Sacrifice	Noun	Give up or go without something
Sagacious	Adj.	Great judgment, mental ability
Sage	Adj.	Wise and judicious
Sage	Noun	Someone wise and judicious
Salient	Adj.	Main or major aspect
Sane	Adj.	Rational mental faculty
Sanity	Noun	In control of mental facilities
Sapid	Adj.	Pleasant. Interesting
Sapient	Adj.	Wise. Knowing

Sarcasm	Noun	Remark in bad taste. Ridicule
Sarcastic	Adj.	Displaying sarcasm
Satisfaction	Noun	Being satisfied, content
Satisfactory	Adj.	Good. Adequate
Saucy	Adj.	Not in good taste
Savoir-faire	Noun	Verbal wit and tact
Savvy	Verb	Know-how. Knowledge
Scant	Adj.	Not sufficient, satisfactory
Scanty	Adj.	Not sufficient. Meager
Scapegoat	Noun	One taking blame for another
Scarce	Adj.	Rare. Uncommon
Scheme	Noun	A plan, plot
Scholar	Noun	Someone of knowledge
Scholarly	Adj.	Having knowledge. Learned
Scoff	Noun	Contemptible
Scorn	Noun/Verb	Ridicule. Contempt
Scornful	Adj.	Displaying scorn
Scruple	Noun	Indecision of right and wrong
Scrupulous	Adj.	Proper, truthful, and careful
Scrutable	Adj.	Questionable understanding
Scrutinize	Verb	Review closely, carefully
Scrutiny	Noun	Close, careful attention
Seasoned Understanding	Noun	Knowledge acquired over time
Secluded	Adj.	Hidden. Out of view
Second-guess	Verb	Question after the fact
Self-assertion	Noun	Assert one's self. Be insistent
Self-assurance	Noun	Confident in one's self
Self-centered	Adj.	Overly concerned with one's self
Self-composed	Adj.	Having composure. calmness
Self-conceit	Noun	Too high opinion of one's self
Self-confidence	Noun	Confident in one's self
Self-conscious	Adj.	Overly concerned about one's self
Self-control	Noun	Having control of one's self

Self-defeating	Adj.	Something that opposes itself
Self-determination	Noun	Providing one's own will
Self-discipline	Noun	Control of one's own actions
Self-doubt	Noun	Not confident in one's self
Self-esteem	Noun	Pride in one's self
Self-examination	Noun	Study one's own actions
Self-image	Noun	How someone views self
Self-important	Adj.	Feeling overly important
Self-improvement	Noun	Individual effort to improve
Self-indulgence	Noun	Indulge in own desires
Self-interest	Noun	Concerned with one's own interests
Selfish	Adj.	Not share or concerned with others
Selfless	Adj.	Not selfish. Concerned for others
Self-made	Adj.	Made or done by one's self
Self-opinionated	Adj.	Conceited. Hold to own opinions
Self-reliance	Noun	Rely on one's self
Self-respect	Noun	Respecting one's self, values
Self-restraint	Noun	Control over one's self
Self-righteous	Adj.	Showing self as morally better
Self-sacrifice	Noun	Sacrifice for others
Self-serving	Adj.	Serve one's own interests
Self-starter	Noun	Supply own initiative
Self-sufficient	Adj.	Without outside help, assistance
Self-taught	Adj.	Learning by one's self, efforts
Self-will	Noun	Possessed will to do, go forth
Semiskilled	Adj.	Partially skilled
Senile	Adj.	Mental decline due to aging
Senility	Noun	Mental decline due to aging
Senseless	Adj.	Without proper sense, meaning
Sensibility	Noun	Mentally receptive, rational
Sensible	Adj.	Good sense of judgment
Sensitive	Adj.	Compassion for others
Sensitivity	Noun	Being sensitive

Sentiment	Noun	Opinion formed in part by emotion
Sentimental	Adj.	Acting from feeling
Serious	Adj.	Important. Critical
Severe	Adj.	Strict, stern
Severity	Noun	Being severe
Shabby	Adj.	Not appealing, disgraceful
Shaky	Adj.	Not steady, firm, dependable
Shallow	Adj.	Superficial. Without depth/meaning
Shallowness	Noun	Without depth, substance
Sham	Noun	A deception
Shameful	Adj.	Disgraceful
Shameless	Adj.	Without shame. Not with modesty
Sharp	Adj.	Keen, clear
Sharpness	Noun	Mentally quick and keen
Sharp-tongued	Adj.	Harsh spoken
Sharp-witted	Adj.	Quick, keen intelligence
Sharp Wittedness	Noun	Quick, keen mind or wit
Shiftless	Adj.	Unsteady ability, character
Shifty	Adj.	Unstable character
Shipshape	Adj.	Neat and orderly
Shirk	Verb	Evade. Get around
Shoddy	Noun	Bad quality. Inferior
Shortcoming	Noun	Fault. Not to expectation
Shortfall	Noun	Being, falling short
Shortsighted	Adj.	Not looking, thinking ahead
Shortsightedness	Noun	Not thinking, planning ahead
Short-spoken	Adj.	Speak briefly, to the point
Short-tempered	Adj.	Lose temper easily
Shrewd	Adj.	Clever. Cunning
Shrewdness	Noun	Keenly knowledgeable, clever
Shy	Adj.	Quiet, reserved
Significance	Noun	Of some importance
Significant	Adj.	Of importance

Silver-tongued	Adj.	Convincing talker
Simple	Adj.	Not complicated
Simple-minded	Adj.	Mentally deficient, lacking
Simplicity	Noun	Not complicated. Simple
Simplistic	Adj.	Simplify difficult problem
Sincere	Adj.	Honest. Straightforward
Sincerity	Noun	Being sincere
Single-handed	Adj.	Without assistance, help
Skeptical	Adj.	Not convinced, sure
Skepticism	Noun	Being skeptic
Skill	Noun	Proficiency
Skilled	Adj.	Having skill
Skillful	Adj.	Having skill
Skirmish	Noun	Brief conflict
Slacken	Verb	Back-off. Do, become less
Slacker	Noun	One who lets up, slows down
Slipshod	Adj.	Careless
Sloppy	Adj.	Careless. Bad quality
Slopwork	Noun	Careless work
Sloven	Noun	One careless in manner, dress
Slovenly	Adj.	Careless in manner, dress
Slow	Adj.	Not quick
Sly	Adj.	Skillfully clever or devious
Small	Adj.	Little
Small-minded	Adj.	Not open. Narrow
Small-scale	Adj.	Not big. Limited in scale, scope
Smart	Adj.	Intelligent. Sharp
Smartness	Noun	Intellectually sharp, capable
Smooth-spoken	Adj.	Smooth, polished in speech
Smooth-tongued	Adj.	Smooth, eloquent in speech
Smug	Adj.	Complacent. Self-assured
Snappy	Adj.	Lively. Active
Snide	Adj.	Sly and cruel

Snuffy	Adj.	Stuffy. Not agreeable
Sociable	Adj.	Friendly. Gregarious
Social	Adj.	Gregarious. Friendly
Socialize	Verb	Be social with others
Soft-headed	Adj.	Not smart, wise
Softhearted	Adj.	Kindly. Not firm, strict
Solace	Noun	To console, comfort. Kind
Solicitude	Noun	Care. Overly caring
Solid	Adj.	Stout. Firm
Solidify	Verb	Make solid, firm
Solitary	Adj.	Alone
Solitude	Noun	Being alone
Somber	Adj.	Drab. Dull. Boring
Sophisticated	Adj.	Wise, polished or advanced
Sorrow	Noun	Grief. Regret
Sorrowful	Adj.	With, of sorrow
Soundness	Noun	Valid in thought, reasoning
Sound Understanding	Noun	Thorough thought or knowledge
Sparing	Adj.	Not in excess
Spark	Verb/Noun	Initiate. Stir. Stimulate
Sparkle	Verb	Actively clever and lively
Sparse	Adj.	Little. Thin. Shallow
Spartan	Noun	One with high discipline/bravery
Spearhead	Noun/Verb	Leading or moving force
Specialist	Noun	Expert in a skill, field
Specialize	Verb	Develop special skill in area
Specialty	Noun	A particular field of endeavor
Spectacle	Noun	Thing demanding visual attention
Speculate	Verb	Think of options. Ponder
Speculation	Noun	To speculate, guess
Speculative	Adj.	Not sure, certain. Guess
Speedy	Adj.	Quick. Prompt
Spirit	Noun/Verb	Enthusiasm. Drive. Cheer on

Spirited	Adj.	Active. Lively
Spiritless	Adj.	Without spirit. Lifeless
Spite	Noun	Of ill will
Spiteful	Adj.	Vindictive. Hateful
Splendid	Adj.	High worth, value. Great
Spontaneous	Adj.	On impulse
Sporadic	Adj.	Not regular, consistent
Spotless	Adj.	Without flaw or fault
Spotty	Adj.	Not consistent, regular
Spurious	Adj.	False. Not real, true
Spurn	Verb	Contempt. Reject
Spurt	Verb	Short burst of activity
Squabble	Verb	Quarrel. Argument
Squander	Verb	Waste. Waste away
Stability	Noun	Stable. Firm
Stabilize	Verb	Make stable
Stable	Adj.	Unmoving. Fixed. Firm
Staggering	Adj.	Too great, many to imagine
Stagnant	Adj.	Not moving. Inactive
Stagnate	Verb	Become stagnant
Stalwart	Adj./Noun	Strong. Unyielding. Firm
Stamina	Noun	Endure for long periods
Standard-bearer	Noun	One carrying a standard
Standout	Noun	Something superior as to stand out
Star	Noun	Someone who excels or shines
Staunch	Adj.	Firm. Unrelenting
Steadfast	Adj.	Firm. Resolute. Not wavering
Steady	Adj.	Fixed. Constant. Controlled
Stealth	Noun	Undercover. Secretive
Stealthy	Adj.	To be stealth
Stellar	Adj.	Star, outstanding performance
Sterling	Adj.	Of highest quality
Stimulant	Adj.	To stimulate, increase activity

Stimulate	Verb	Ignite, arouse, or spur action
Stimulator	Noun	One who excites increased activity
Stimulus	Noun	Something that excites action
Stodgy	Adj.	Mundane. Standard. Routine
Stoke	Verb	To fuel, stir up
Straight Thinking	Noun	Single direction of thought
Strength	Noun	Strong. Powerful
Strengthen	Verb	Become more strong, powerful
Strenuous	Adj.	Demanding great action, energy
Strict	Adj.	Firm. Solid. Exact
Stringent	Adj.	Being strict
Strive	Verb	Try. Attempt
Strong	Adj.	Strength. Powerful
Strong-minded	Adj.	Determination. Unrelenting will
Strong-willed	Adj.	Determined. Headstrong
Studious	Adj.	Study. Pay attention. Watchful
Stupefy	Verb	To stun, numb, dull
Stupendous	Adj.	Overpowering. Overwhelming
Stupid	Adj.	Not having normal intelligence
Stupidity	Noun	Being stupid, unknowing
Stupor	Noun	Mental dullness. Inattention
Style	Noun	Fashion or manner of something
Stymie	Noun	To interfere, obstruct, get in way
Stymied	Verb	To stymie, interfere
Suave	Adj.	Sophisticated. Poised. Polished
Submissive	Adj.	To submit, yield, give way
Subnormal	Adj.	Below normal, average
Substandard	Adj.	Below standard, expectation
Substantial	Adj.	Great amount. Much. Many
Subtle	Adj.	Not direct or mentally sharp
Succeed	Verb	Complete. Accomplish. Attain
Success	Noun	Complete correctly, favorably
Successful	Adj.	Do with success
Succinct	Adj.	Brief, concise & correct in speech

Succumb	Verb	Submit, yield, give in
Suffer	Verb	Realize pain, unpleasantness
Sufficient	Adj.	Adequate. Enough
Suitable	Adj.	Acceptable. To suit
Sullen	Adj.	Quiet bitterness
Superb	Adj.	Top quality. Without equal. Grand
Supercilious	Adj.	Contemptible. Arrogance
Superficial	Adj.	On the surface only. Shallow
Superficiality	Noun	Not meaningful, profound
Superfine	Adj.	Super good, fine. Top quality
Superfluous	Adj.	Excess. Not needed
Superior	Adj.	Better. Greater. Ace. Top
Superlative	Adj./Noun	Superior, better
Supporter	Noun	One who supports, backs, enforces
Supportive	Adj.	To support, back
Suppress	Verb	Hold down or back. Stop
Supremacy	Noun	Be supreme, superior, above
Supreme	Adj.	Best. Highest
Surly	Adj.	Crass. Crusty. Rude
Surpass	Verb	Go past, beyond. Be superior
Surpassing	Adj.	To surpass, go beyond. Excelling
Survive	Verb	To continue, carry on
Survivor	Noun	One who comes through repetitively
Sway	Verb	Waiver, give way. Change
Swift	Adj.	Fast. Quick. Prompt
Swiftness	Noun	Fast. Quick
Symbolize	Verb	To represent. Be a symbol/standard
Sympathetic	Adj.	Understanding. Express sympathy
Sympathize	Verb	To share in sympathy
Sympathy	Noun	Mutual feeling. Be understanding
Systematic	Adj.	By system or methodical process

-T-

Tacit	Adj.	Quiet. Silent. Without words
Taciturn	Adj.	Tending to be quiet, not talkative
Tact	Noun	Diplomacy skill. Not offending
Tactful	Adj.	Using tact, diplomacy
Tactless	Adj.	Having no tact. Not diplomatic
Talent	Noun	Ability. Skill. Power
Talented	Adj.	Possessing great abilities
Talkative	Adj.	Talk too much, to extreme
Tangible	Adj.	Being able to touch. Definitive
Taskmaster	Noun	One who is demanding, exacting
Teach	Verb	Impart knowledge
Technique	Noun	A particular learned skill
Tedious	Adj.	Tiresome, grueling, boring
Tedium	Noun	Be tedious, tiresome
Temerity	Noun	Too bold, reckless
Temperament	Noun	One's disposition or mood
Temperamental	Adj.	Having excitable, erratic temper
Temperance	Noun	Restrained, reserved, even temper
Temperate	Adj.	Restrained. Even tempered
Tempting	Adj.	Inclined to entice, provoke
Tenacious	Adj.	Firm. Very cohesive. Together
Tenacity	Noun	Firm. Resolute. Cohesive
Tender	Adj.	Considerate. Gentle
Tenderhearted	Adj.	Sympathetic at heart
Tension	Noun	Strain. Stress
Tenuous	Adj.	Thin. Tiny. Little
Tepid	Adj.	Not friendly, feeling
Terrific	Adj.	Great. Super. Outstanding
Terse	Adj.	Eloquent, concise, to the point
Thankful	Adj.	Gratitude. Grateful
Thankless	Adj.	Without thanks, gratitude
Thick	Adj.	Slow to comprehend, learn
Think	Verb	Conceive by mental action

Thinkable	Adj.	Conceivable. Mentally possible
Thinker	Noun	One who think, plans
Thinking	Adj.	Mental thought action
Think-up	Verb	Mentally originate, devise
Thought	Noun	Conceived mental act, process
Thoughtful	Adj.	Showing care, consideration
Thoughtless	Adj.	Without thought or consideration
Thrift	Noun	Careful use of resource
Thriftless	Adj.	Without thrift
Thrifty	Adj.	To be thrift. Not wasteful
Thrive	Verb	Prosper. Flourish. Grow
Thwart	Verb	To intervene, obstruct, spoil
Tidy	Adj.	Neat. Orderly
Timid	Adj.	Shy. Afraid
Timorous	Adj.	Timid. Shy. Afraid
Tiresome	Adj.	Boring. Restless. Being tired
Tolerable	Adj.	To tolerate, allow, bear
Tolerant	Adj.	To bear with, tolerate, allow
Tolerate	Verb	Allow. Bear. Permit
Tough	Adj.	Firm
Tough-minded	Adj.	Tough, strong, firm of mind
Tradition	Noun	Time honored custom
Traditional	Adj.	Being in tradition
Traditionalism	Noun	Being in tradition, custom
Traditionalist	Noun	One upholding tradition
Tranquil	Adj.	At ease, calm
Tranquillity	Noun	Be tranquil, calm, at ease
Transform	Verb	Change to something else
Transgress	Verb	Go beyond established limit
Travesty	Noun	Bad imitation, replacement
Treadmill	Noun	Boring. Repetitive. Monotonous
Tremendous	Adj.	Great. Huge. Large
Trenchant	Adj.	Clear cut. Keen

Tricky	Adj.	Deceitful. Clever
Trifling	Adj.	Superficial. Shallow
Trite	Adj.	No longer valid, fresh. Stale. Old
Trivia	Noun	Unimportant in nature
Trivial	Adj.	Of little value, worth
Troublemaker	Noun	One who routinely makes trouble
Trouble-shooter	Noun	One who looks for trouble to fix
Troublesome	Adj.	Making, causing trouble
Truant	Noun	One who fails to work, perform
Trustful	Adj.	To trust, believe
Trusting	Adj.	To trust, believe
Trustworthy	Adj.	Be able to trust. Reliable
Truthful	Adj.	Being at truth. Honest
Turbulent	Adj.	Violent, disorderly
Turmoil	Noun	Confusion. Not stable
Typical	Adj.	Serving as example of kind, type
Typify	Verb	Be typical

-U-

Ultimate	Adj.	Conclusion. End
Unaccomplished	Adj.	Not accomplished, skilled
Unacquainted	Adj.	Not learned, taught, knowing
Unadvised	Adj.	Done without forethought. Hasty
Unapt	Adj.	Not apt, likely, skilled, able
Unassuming	Adj.	Not forward, aggressive
Unaware	Adj.	Not aware, knowing
Unbeatable	Adj.	Unable to beat, conquer
Unbending	Adj.	Firm. Resolute
Unbiased	Adj.	Not biased, prejudiced
Unbounded	Adj.	Without bounds or limits
Uncanny	Adj.	Unreal, unnatural act or feat
Uncertain	Adj.	Not certain, sure, positive
Uncertainty	Noun	Not certain, sure
Uncharitable	Adj.	Without charity. Not forgiving

Uncomfortable	Adj.	Not comfortable, agreeable
Uncommon	Adj.	Not common, ordinary. Rare
Uncompromising	Adj.	Not giving, relenting. Fixed. Firm
Unconventional	Adj.	Not ordinary or standard
Unconversant	Adj.	Lacking knowledge
Undaunted	Adj.	Not failing, faltering
Undecided	Adj.	Unsure. Not decisive
Undeniable	Adj.	Unable to deny. Without question
Underhanded	Adj.	Not open, above board, honest
Undermine	Verb	To weaken, wear away
Understand	Verb	To know, comprehend
Understanding	Noun	To understand
Understudy	Noun	One who studies under another
Undiscerning	Adj.	No good judgment/understanding
Undistinguished	Adj.	Not looked up to, held in esteem
Uneasy	Adj.	Not comfortable. Anxious
Unequivocal	Adj.	Clear. Plain
Unerring	Adj.	Without error, fault
Unerudite	Adj.	Unlearned. Unskilled
Unexceptional	Adj.	Plain. Common. Ordinary
Unfailing	Adj.	Not fail. Reliable
Unfair	Adj.	Not fair, just, equitable
Unfamiliar	Adj.	Not known, recognized
Unfavorable	Adj.	Not favorable. Against. Adverse
Unfeeling	Adj.	Without feeling
Unfit	Adj.	Not fit, able, capable
Unflappable	Adj.	Composed. Calm
Unfortunate	Adj.	Bad luck
Unfriendly	Adj.	Not friendly
Ungracious	Adj.	Not polite, pleasant
Unimaginative	Adj.	No mental vision, inventiveness
Uninformative	Adj.	Without knowledge, information
Uninformed	Adj.	Not knowing, knowledgeable

Uninhibited	Adj.	Without mental reservation
Unintelligent	Adj.	Lack of intelligence
Uninteresting	Adj.	Dull. Boring
Unique	Adj.	Unusual. One of a kind. Rare
Uniqueness	Noun	Being unique
Unknowing	Adj./Noun	Not known. No knowledge
Unknown	Adj.	Not known, knowing
Unlawful	Adj.	Not within the law. Not legal
Unlearned	Adj.	Not learned, educated
Unlettered	Adj.	Uneducated
Unlimited	Adj.	Without bounds or limits
Unmannerly	Adj.	Bad manners. Rude
Unmerciful	Adj.	Without mercy, pity
Unmistakable	Adj.	Without mistake, error, flaw
Unnerve	Verb	Lose nerve, confidence
Unorganized	Adj.	Not organized, in order
Unparalleled	Adj.	Without peer, match, equal
Unperceptive	Adj.	Not knowing, discerning
Unperceptiveness	Noun	Not keen, penetrating, knowing
Unpleasant	Adj.	Not pleasant, agreeable
Unpopular	Adj.	Not popular, liked
Unprincipled	Adj.	Without moral values
Unprofessional	Adj.	Not professional, proper, correct
Unquestionable	Adj.	Without question
Unrealistic	Adj.	Not realistic, practical
Unreason	Noun	No reason, rationale
Unreasonable	Adj.	Not reasonable, feasible, rational
Unreasoning	Adj.	Without rational reason
Unrefined	Adj.	Lack of culture, social bearing
Unrelenting	Adj.	Not relenting, yielding. Fixed
Unrivaled	Adj.	Without rival, match, equal
Unruly	Adj.	Unable to control, manage
Unscholarly	Adj.	Without knowledge, learning

Unscrupulous	Adj.	Without principles, morals
Unseasoned	Adj.	Not mature, experienced
Unselfish	Adj.	Giving. Caring. Generous
Unsettled	Adj.	Not settled, stable
Unskilled	Adj.	Without skill, ability
Unskillful	Adj.	Without skill, ability
Unsociable	Adj.	Not sociable, friendly
Unstable	Adj.	Not stable, firm. Resolute
Unstoppable	Adj.	Not able to stop, cease
Unsuccessful	Adj.	Without success
Unsuitable	Adj.	Not appropriate, compatible
Untaught	Adj.	Without learning, education
Untidy	Adj.	Not tidy, neat, orderly
Untrue	Adj.	Not true. False
Untruth	Noun	Non-truth. False
Untruthful	Adj.	Be untrue, false
Untutored	Adj.	Unlearned. Uneducated
Unversed	Adj.	Not learned, knowledgeable
Unwilling	Adj.	Not willing. Reluctant
Unwise	Adj.	Not wise, prudent
Unwittingness	Noun	Without wit. Dull
Unworthy	Adj.	Not worthy, deserving, fit
Unyielding	Adj.	Not giving, yielding
Up-and-coming	Adj.	New. Promising
Upright	Adj.	Just. Honest
Useful	Adj.	Of use, benefit
Useless	Adj.	Of no use, benefit

-V-

Vacuous	Adj.	Without intelligence, thought
Vain	Adj.	Empty. Futile
Valuable	Adj.	Be important, meaningful, of value
Valueless	Adj.	Without value or worth
Vast	Adj.	Great. Huge. Immense
Veracious	Adj.	Truth. Honesty

Veracity	Noun	Truthful. Honest
Verbalism	Noun	Word without form, meaning
Verbalist	Noun	Skilled orator, wordsmith
Verbose	Adj.	Too long, wordy
Versatile	Adj.	Adaptable. Multi-dimensional
Versed	Adj.	Experienced. Skilled
Verve	Noun	Exuberant. Energetic
Vex	Verb	Troubling. Irritating
Vigilant	Adj.	Watchful
Vigor	Noun	Vim. Vitality. Strength
Vigorous	Adj.	Lively. Sturdy. Full of energy
Vim	Noun	Vigor. Zest. Vitality
Vindictive	Adj.	Revengeful. Not forgiving
Violate	Verb	To break, penetrate in violation
Violent	Adj.	Physical force, rage
Virtue	Noun	Good moral value
Virtuous	Adj.	Having virtue, high morals
Vision	Noun/Verb	Foresight. See to the future
Visualization	Noun	Foresee by mental picture
Visualize	Verb	Mental picture or image
Vitality	Noun	Vim. Vigor. Energy
Vitalization	Noun	Lively. Vim. Vigor
Vitiate	Verb	Go wrong, faulty, weak
Vivacious	Adj.	Lively, with spirit, vigor
Vivid	Adj.	Clear in vision, picture, thought
Vivid Imagination	Noun	Active, lively mind
Vocabulary	Noun	Word capacity, ability
Voluble	Adj.	Talkative
Voluntary	Adj.	Give freely. Free of will

-W-

Wade	Verb	To plunge into
Wander	Verb	Stray about without reason
Wane	Verb	Become less. Diminish

Wangle	Verb	Trick. Deceive
Wanting	Adj.	Lacking. Deficient
Wanton	Adj.	Without discipline, control
Warm	Adj.	Affectionate
Warmhearted	Adj.	Affectionate. Caring. Giving
Washed-up	Adj.	No longer of benefit, use
Waste	Noun	Ruin. Spoil
Wasted	Adj.	Ruined. Spoiled
Wasteful	Adj.	To waste
Watchful	Adj.	Observant
Weak	Adj.	Not strong, steady
Weaken	Verb	Make weak. Lose strength
Weakhearted	Adj.	Without conviction, courage
Weak-minded	Adj.	Lack will power, judgment
Weakness	Noun	Being weak
Weariful	Adj.	Tired. Weary
Weariless	Adj.	Does not weaken, tire
Wearisome	Adj.	Being weary, tired
Wear out	Verb	Use up. Expend. Exhaust
Weary	Adj.	Drained of strength, energy
Weighty	Adj.	Important. Meaningful
Well-advised	Adj.	Use wisdom, prudence
Well-bred	Adj.	Well raised. Dignified. Sociable
Well-conditioned	Adj.	Being well Adjusted socially
Well-defined	Adj.	Clear, distinct
Well-disposed	Adj.	Good disposition
Well-done	Adj.	Done correctly, properly
Well-founded	Adj.	Based on solid reason
Well-groomed	Adj.	Neat. Orderly. Tidy
Well-grounded	Adj.	Well based knowledge
Well-handed	Adj.	Well managed, controlled
Well-informed	Adj.	Possessing great knowledge
Well-intentioned	Adj.	Intending, meaning well or good

Well-known	Adj.	Widely known
Well-meaning	Adj.	Good meaning, intention
Well-off	Adj.	In good condition
Well-read	Adj.	Well informed. Knowledgeable
Well-rounded	Adj.	Well developed, educated
Well-spoken	Adj.	Speak with skill
Well-taken	Noun	To be well, happy, content
Well-timed	Adj.	Timed to opportunity
Well-versed	Adj.	Having expert knowledge
Whimsical	Adj.	Erratic, unpredictable
Whiz	Noun	A wizard, genius
Wholehearted	Adj.	Sincere & complete support
Wholesome	Adj.	Healthy mind, morals, spirit
Wide-ranging	Adj.	Wide in range, scope, context
Widely-read	Adj.	Knowledgeable in many subjects
Wile	Noun	Deceive. Trick
Willful	Adj.	With one's own free will
Willing	Adj.	With free will. Without reluctance
Will-less	Adj.	Without will
Wilt	Verb	Fade. Grow dim, weak
Wily	Adj.	Skillful. Crafty
Winner	Noun	One who wins, comes out on top
Wisdom	Noun	Knowledge. Wise
Wise	Adj.	Wisdom. Knowledge. Experienced
Wiseness	Noun	Of good judgment, wisdom
Wishful	Adj.	Based on hope
Wishy-washy	Adj.	Not firm, effective, steady
Wit	Noun	Power of mind, reasoning
Wits	Noun	Possess keen mental faculties
Withstand	Verb	Hold up. Oppose
Witless	Adj.	Without wit
Witted	Adj.	Having wit
Witticism	Noun	Sharp, penetrating joke

Witty	Adj.	Having ample wit
Wonderwork	Noun	Successful, skillful undertaking
Wondrous	Adj.	Held in wonder, high esteem
Wording	Noun	Convey in words
Wordplay	Noun	Skillful play at words
Wordsmith	Noun	One skillful at words
Wordy	Adj.	Too many words
Workable	Adj.	Capable. Able
Workaholic	Noun	One filled with capacity for work
Workhorse	Noun	One doing majority of the work
Workmanship	Noun	Quality of product
Work over	Verb	Redo. To do again, over
Workup	Noun	Study. Preparation
Worldly-wise	Adj.	Wise to the way of things
Worse	Adj.	Less desirable or favorable
Worsen	Verb	To do worse
Worst	Adj.	Most faulty, bad
Worthful	Adj.	Of value, worth
Worthless	Adj.	Without worth, value
Worthwhile	Adj.	Worth time, effort
Worthy	Adj.	Having merit, value, worth
Would-be	Adj.	Having potential, ability
Wretch	Noun	One dissatisfied. Bad disposition
Wretched	Adj.	Totally disagreeable personality
Wrong	Adj.	Erroneous. False. Amiss
Wrongdoer	Noun	One who does wrong
Wrongdoing	Noun	To do wrong
Wrongful	Adj.	Being wrong
Wroth	Adj.	Irate. Angry
Wry	Adj.	Grim humor

-Y-

Yardstick	Noun	A standard, reference level
Yes-man	Noun	One always in agreement
Youthful	Adj.	Young, fresh, refreshing

-Z-

Zeal	Noun	Spirit. Vigor. Enthusiasm
Zealot	Noun	One with zeal
Zealotory	Noun	Overfilled with zeal
Zealous	Adj.	Having zeal
Zenith	Noun	Top. Uppermost point
Zest	Noun	Vigor. Enthusiasm
Zestfulness	Noun	Stimulating. Invigorating. Active
Zesty	Adj.	Have zest
Zip	Verb	Swift, speedy. Invigorating
Zippy	Adj.	Having zip

Sentence
Subjects

The Sentence Subjects in this section are intended to give you hundreds of ideas with thousands of possible uses. Notice from the following example some of the ways in which the Sentence Subject can be changed into a variety of uses.

These sentence subjects can also be used to form bullet phrase statements.

<u>Sentence Subject: ABOVE AND BEYOND</u>
> Example: (Name) went above and beyond call of duty in/by .....
> Example: Efforts to ..... were above and beyond that normally expected of .....
> Example: Despite risk of personal injury (name) went above and beyond that normally expected of .....
> Example: (Name) efforts in field/area of ..... were clearly above and beyond standards of .....

<u>Sentence Subject: ABSOLUTE DEDICATION</u>
> Example: (Name) absolute dedication to ..... led to marked improvement in .....
> Example: (Name) absolute dedication exhibited during (period) directly responsible for vast increase in .....
> Example: Superior and successful performance in/as .....were a direct result of his/her absolute dedication to .....

SUBJECT   EXAMPLE USE

Able to size up
> Example: Able to size up any problem area and supply correct fix.

Above and beyond
> Example: Performance above and beyond call of duty

Above board
> Example: Honest and above board at all times.

Absolute confidence
> Example: Has absolute confidence in performance of .....

Absolute dedication
> Example: Absolutely dedicated to improving standards of .....

Absolute faith in
    Example: Others have absolute faith in his/her ability to .....
Absolutely committed to
    Example: Deeply committed to absolute safety of .....
Absolutely essential
    Example: (Name) was absolutely essential in meeting .....
Absorbed in
    Example: Absolutely absorbed in every facet of .....
Abundance of
    Example: Displaying an abundance of energy, he/she .....
Accelerated change
    Example: Quick and accelerated change made possible by .....
Accepted challenge
    Example: Accepted the demanding challenge of .....
Accepted responsibility
    Example: Quickly accepted responsibility for .. and implemented..
Achieved greatness
    Example: Achieved greatness in field of .....
Acquainted with success
    Example: Acquaintance with success instrumental in .....
Across the board
    Example: Across the board success resulted in .....
Acted in concert
    Example: Others acted in concert to aid in .....
Acted prudently
    Example: Acted prudently and decisively in achieving.....
Active role
    Example: Played an active role in the completion of .....
Active support(er)
    Example: (Name) active support in ..... led to .....
Actively engaged in
    Example: Actively engaged in efforts to stem tide of .....
Actively promoted
    Example: Actively promoted new and innovative way to .....
        which led to vast improvements in .....
Acutely aware
    Example: (Name) is/was acutely aware of the necessity for/to.....
Acutely sensitive to
    Example: Performance to duty was exemplary while taking into
        account the acutely sensitive need to/for .....
Adamant in stand
    Example: Showing professional diligence, (name) was adamant in
        stand for/against .....

Added extra dimension

Example: (Name) was able to add the extra dimension needed for the successful conclusion of .....

Added value(s)

Example: (Name) added directly to the value of .....

Address needs of

Example: (Name) never failed to address the needs of .....

Addressed issue(s)

Example: Addressed the sensitive issue(s) of ..... without .....

Admired character(istics)

Example: (Name) has many professional characteristics to be admired, not the least of which is .....

Adopt a course

Example: Adopted a course of action that lead to real improvements in .....

Advanced idea

Example: (Name) was able to advance the idea of ..... which led to dramatic improvements in .....

Advanced state of

Example: Diligent work in area of ..... led to an advanced state of ..... and increased the overall readiness of .....

Adversity

Example: Tackled and successfully completed all ..... despite adversity involved in/with .....

Advocate for

Example: A firm advocate for increased.....

Against all odds

Example: Completed the unenviable task of ... against all odds.

Aggressive agenda

Example: (Name) executed an aggressive work agenda that included .....

Ahead of times

Example: (Name) knowledge and expertise in the field of ..... is ahead of the times.

Alert to possibilities

Example: Always alert to possibilities for improvement in .....

Alive with

Example: His/Her (organization) personnel come alive with energy and excitement when .....

All-out effort

Example: (Name) can always be counted on to give an all-out effort during times of .....

Always eager to
>Example (Name) is always eager and willing to volunteer to
>>assume additional responsibility when/if .....

Always gives 110 percent
>Example: Regardless of the circumstances, (name) always gives
>>110 percent.

Amassed abundance of
>Example: (Name) amassed an abundance of talent that directly
>>resulted in an marked increase/improvement in .....

Amazing speed
>Example: (Name) was able to complete the entire task in amazing
>>speed, despite .....

Ambitious campaign
>Example: (Name) mounted an ambitious campaign in ..... that
>>resulted in a significant improvement/increase in .....

Ambitious initiatives/progress
>Example: Brought into play a broad number of ambitious
>>initiatives that led to .....

Among the best
>Example: His/Her (subject) are among the best I have ever seen.

Analyzed various elements
>Example: Correctly analyzed the various elements of ..... and then
>>proceeded to construct and complete .....

Appetite for
>Example: (Name) has an insatiable appetite for knowledge in a
>>field in which he/she is already considered an expert.

Applaud efforts of
>Example: I have to applaud the personal diligent and efforts to .....

Appreciate uniqueness of'
>Example: Appreciates the uniqueness of each individual's talent
>>and skill and combined this into one of the most
>>impressive .....

Appreciates hard work
>Example: (Name) fully appreciates the hard work and effort of
>>others and rewards this contribution to total team effort by

Architect of
>Example: (Name) was the architect of the highly successful .....

Around-the-clock
>Example: (Name) is willing to work around-the-clock to fulfill
>>mission requirements.

Arouses
>Example:(Name) arouses the spirit and energy of others by.....

Articulate(d) new image
>Example: Shortly after his/her arrival, he/she articulated a new
>>image of the previously sagging .....

241

Ascended to

    Example: (Name) quickly ascended to the top of his/her field through hard work and persistent dedication.

Aspire to excellence

    Example: (Name) aspires to achieve excellence regardless of tasking difficulty or complexity.

Assessment of situation

    Example: Blessed with a rare ability to quickly make an assessment of any tactical/professional situation.

At forefront

    Example: (Name) is at the forefront in the field of .....

At pinnacle

    Example: (Name) is at the pinnacle of his/her profession.

Atmosphere conducive to

    Example: (Name) creates an atmosphere highly conducive to.....

Attention to detail

    Example: Displaying a meticulous attention to detail he/she was able to .....

Attracts followers

    Example: Natural leadership style attracts followers and allows him/her to accomplish more than .....

Attuned to needs

    Example: Ability to stay attuned to the needs of his/her personnel allows him/her to accomplish .....

Awakened spirit(s) of

    Example: Awakened the spirits of others with his/her unique leadership style that resulted in a highly successful .....

Award-winning

    Example: (Name) demonstrated his/her award-winning performance in the area/field of .....

Backbone

    Example: (Name) became the backbone in the organization by.....

Ball of fire

    Example: (Name) is a ball of fire when it comes to .....

Bang up job

    Example: (Name) did a bang up job on/as .....

Bank on it

    Example: When he/she sets out to do something, you can bank on it to be completed completely and on time.

Barely missed a beat

    Example: Despite being undermanned/under funded (etc.), he/she barely missed a beat completing the difficult job of .....

Beacon of hope

    Example: (Name) serves as a beacon of hope for others when .....

Bear down

Example: (Name) can always be counted upon to bear down when it comes to .....

Bear responsibility

Example: (Name) bears the heavy weight of responsibility for ..... without skipping a beat.

Bear the burden

Example: (Name) bears the burden of .....despite handicap of .....

Beat all odds

Example: (Name) beat all odds with his/her completion of .....

Became focal point

Example: (Name) became the focal point for the special project of ..... During this time he/she .....

Became symbol for/to

Example: (Name) became a symbol to others with his/her ability to .....

Beef up

Example: (Name) was able to beef up ..... area despite being .....

Beehive of activity

Example: The (organization) became a beehive of activity in carrying out .....

Began to take form/shape

Example: Showing great care and patience, the ..... began to take form and meet .....

Behind the scene(s)

Example: Someone had to do the lack of credit, behind the scene work on .....(Name) volunteered to tackle this difficult task.

Believability

Example: (Name) never has a believability problem when convincing others to .....

Benchmark

Example: (Name's) work served as a benchmark for .....

Bend over backwards

Example: He/She bends over backwards to maintain good order and discipline between/among .....

Benefits from understanding

Example: Others benefit from his/her total understanding of .....

Best foot forward

Example: (Name) is always ready and willing to help others, putting his/her best foot forward in an effort to .....

Best interest of

Example: (Name) always puts best interest of (organization) first.

Best tradition

Example: The performance of (name) was in the best tradition of.....

Better prepared

       Example: (Name) is always better prepared to meet the
               challenges of ..... than .....

Beyond a doubt

       Example: (Name) is beyond a doubt the best ..... in .....

Blazed new trail

       Example: (Name) blazed a new trail in the area/field of .....

Blessed with

       Example: Blessed with superior ..... ability/talent, name was able
               to complete .....

Blistering pace

       Example: (Name) set a blistering pace in/by .....

Blue ribbon

       Example: (Name) headed up/formed a blue ribbon panel that
               successfully .....

Body of work

       Example: (Name) complete body of work far exceeds .....

Bold new/move

       Example: In a bold move, (name) successfully integrated .....

Boosted spirits

       Example: (Name) always seems to find a way to boost the spirits
               of others when faced with .....

Bottom line

       Example: The bottom line is that (name) simply performs in a
               superior fashion, regardless of complexity of tasking.

Bought into focus

       Example: (Name) is an expert at bringing into focus the diverse
               elements inherent to/in .....

Boyish excitement

       Example: (Name) boyish excitement and zest for work was
               instrumental in gaining the support and loyalty of .....

Brain trust

       Example: (Name) is (organization) brain trust in area/field of .....

Brainchild

       Example: The successful completion of ..... was the brainchild of
               (name), to whom much of the credit is due.

Brainstorm

       Example: During a brainstorm session, (name) suggested the use
               of .....to ..... This proved immensely successful.

Break new ground

       Example: (Name) broke new ground in the area/field of .....when
               he/she .....

Break through

       Example: (Name) work in/as resulted in a major break through in..

Breakneck speed

Example: (Name) completed all work associated with ..... with breakneck speed.

Breakthrough

Example: A real breakthrough in ..... came when (name) suggested the use of ..... in .....

Breath of fresh air

Example: (Name) arrival at (organization) was like a breath of fresh air. He/She brought with him/her a/an .....

Breathed new life

Example: (Name) breathed new life into..... which was previously plagued with .....

Bridged the gap

Example: (Name) was able to bridge the gap between .....

Bright chapter/future

Example: (Name) has a bright future ahead of him/her as a .....

Example: (Name) Brought a bright chapter to (organization) with his/her knowledge and enthusiasm in/on/of.....

Brighten the day

Example: (Name) enthusiasm and zest for .....brightens the day in an otherwise .....

Bring into focus

Example: (Name) penetrating work in/as ..... was able to bring into proper focus the major elements of .....

Bring into line

Example: (Name) was able to bring into line all of the elements involved in/with .....

Broad consensus

Example: (Name) was able to build a broad consensus that led directly to the improvement of .....

Broad stroke

Example: With one broad stroke (name) was able to .....

Broader understanding

Example: (Name) is possessed with a broader understanding of ..... than anyone else in the area/field of .....

Brought about/out

Example: (Name) brought about a major change in ..... which directly led to a dramatic improvement in .....

Brought to life

Example: (Name) brought to life a new chapter in (organization) in which efficiency and production took a decided upward turn, and .....

Brought under control

Example: (Name) brought under control the runaway .....

Build a fire under
>   Example: (Name) was able to bring life to .... by building a fire
>   under the feet of .....

Building blocks
>   Example: (Name) provided the essential building blocks that
>   brought about the extraordinary improvement in .....

Bulldog determination
>   Example: (Name) executed all tasks with bulldog determination.

Burning desire
>   Example: (Name) displayed a burning desire to complete .....

Burst of creativity
>   Example: With a burst of creativity, (name) successfully .....

Bursting with
>   Example: Bursting with pride and determination, (name) was able
>   to .....

Business at hand
>   Example: (Name) ability to focus on the business at hand and
>   eliminate distractions was instrumental in.....

Business-like
>   Example: (Name) business-like professionalism approach to any
>   task allows him/her to .....

By the book
>   Example: A no nonsense who goes by the book person.

Calculated risk/response
>   Example: The risk was calculated response to .....

Call(ed) the signal(s)
>   Example: (Name) took the lead and called the signals in/on a very
>   successful .....

Called upon to
>   Example: (Name) was called upon to .... He/She responded with
>   customary excellence in all aspects of .....

Calm authority
>   Example: (Name) provided the calm presence and authority
>   needed for the successful completion of .....

Came of age
>   Example: (Name) came of age when he/she successfully
>   orchestrated the complex task of .....

Came prepared
>   Example: (Name) came fully prepared for the task of ..... He/She
>   again demonstrated his/her unfailing ability to .....

Came to aid of
>   Example: (Name) came to the aid of ....., and was instrumental in
>   the successful completion of ..... despite .....

Came to fruition

Example: His/Her work came to fruition with the completion of .....
This helped build up what had been .....

Capitalized on

Example: (Name) capitalized on the strength of ..... This allowed
him/her to organize a ..... second to none.

Captured imagination of

Example: (Name) was able to capture the imagination of ... This
in turn resulted in .....

Captured the advantage

Example: (Name) was able to ..... by capturing the advantage
through the use of .....

Career defined by

Example: (Name) career can be defined by the frequent use of
the word "outstanding."

Carefully engineered

Example: (Name) carefully engineered the building/construction
of ..... which in turn allowed him/her to .....

Carefully planned

Example: (Name) carefully planned and brilliantly executed a
program to/that .....

Cares deeply

Example: (Name) cares deeply for the comfort and well being of
others. This was fully demonstrated when he/she .....

Carried forward

Example: (Name) carried forward on a program/project that had
previously been put on hold due to ..... This resulted in ...

Carry through

Example: Always carries through on difficult ..... to

Carry(ied) the ball

Example: (Name) carried the ball for ..... who was out with .....

Carry(ies) weight

Example: (Name) carries his/her weight and helps others at/in.....

Cast a bond

Example: (Name) was able to cast a strong bond with .....

Cast light upon

Example: (Name) research in ..... cast light upon .....

Catalyst of/for

Example: (Name) acted as the catalyst for a new and improved
way to .....

Cemented relationships

Example: (Name) cemented relationship with ..... allowed him/her
to .....

Centerpiece
> Example: (Name) became the centerpiece of activity when it
> became necessary to .....

Certain curiosity
> Example: (Name) has a certain curiosity about him/her that allows
> him/her to find new ways to .....

Chain of events
> Example: The chain of events that (name) started led to real
> improvement in (area)

Chalk up success(es)
> Example: (Name) chalked up another success with the
> implementation of .....

Challenge of change
> Example: (Name) enjoys the challenge of change and seems to
> do his/her best work when .....

Challenges conventional ideas
> Example: (Name) challenged the conventional ideas of ..... and
> then proceeded to revolutionize the .....

Challenges(d) status quo
> Example: (Name) seeks to challenge the status quo while
> searching for new and improved methods of/to .....

Challenging opportunity(ies)
> Example: (Name) thrives on challenging opportunities and difficult
> tasking.

Challenging task(s)
> Example: (Name) faces challenging tasks with a customary zeal
> rarely observed in .....

Champion(s) cause(s)
> Example: (Name) championed the cause of ..... This led to a
> marked upgrade/improvement in .....

Championed efforts to
> Example: (Name) was able to champion the efforts to ..... due to
> his/her .....

Chance to carry on
> Example: (Name) work on/in ..... gave others a chance to carry on
> with continued .....

Changed face of
> Example: (Name) changed the face of ..... with his/her major
> contribution as .....

Changing climate of
> Example: Amid a changing climate of ..... (name) was able to
> successfully overcome .....

Changing times
> Example: In today's changing times, (name) continues to produce
> top quality work by .....

Characteristic enthusiasm
> Example: (Name) characteristic enthusiasm always elicits the
> maximum effort of/from .....

Characterized by
> Example: (Name) performance is characterized by hard work,
> dedication, and .....

Charged ahead
> Example: (Name) charged ahead on .....without awaiting official
> orders or direction. This led to .....

Charisma
> Example: (Name) charisma quickly wins the willing support of .....

Charismatic
> Example: (Name) characteristic enthusiasm for any task has, and
> continues to, lead the way in .....

Charted course
> Example: (Name) charted a course for the future of ..... by his/her
> groundbreaking work in/as .....

Choice of values
> Example: (Name) choice of work and personal values far
> exceeds.....

Clarity of purpose
> Example: (Name) has a focus and clarity of purpose rarely seen
> in.....

Class act
> Example: (Name) is, without doubt, a class act. He/She became
> the first person to .....

Classic example
> Example: (Name) is a classic example of what one person can do
> with .....

Clean and quick
> Example: With one clean and quick stroke (name) successfully ....

Clean slate
> Example: (Name) maintained a clean slate during .....

Clean sweep
> Example: (Name) made a clean sweep of all .....

Cleaned up problems
> Example: (Name) cleaned up problems left by ..... and quickly
> rose to the top of .....

Clear agenda
> Example: (Name) proceeded ahead with a clear agenda on how to
> ..... Noted improvements were quickly noted in.....

Clear picture
> Example: (Name) came up with a clear picture of the problems
> associated with..... He/She proceeded to .....

Clearly articulated

Example: (Name) was able to clearly articulate the workings of .... into .....

Clever idea(s)

Example: (Name) has come up with one clever idea after another for the improvement of .....

Climate of

Example: In a climate of scarce resources and manpower, name was able to .....

Climbed to top

Example: (Name) climbed to the top of ..... with his/her persistence and dedication. This led to an improved .....

Close cooperation

Example: Working in close cooperation with ..... (name) was able to achieve more than .....

Close scrutiny

Example: (Name) gave close scrutiny to the internal workings of ..... then followed up with .....

Close(d) ranks

Example: (Name) closed ranks with other ..... This close-knit working relationship proved highly successful in .....

Coalition building

Example: Behind the scenes coalition building afforded (name) the opportunity to .....

Cohesive group

Example: (Name) formed a very cohesive group of ..... This highly professional group succeeded in .....

Cold analysis

Example: (Name) took a cold analysis look at ..... and dedided to ..... This ultimately led to .....

Collective influence

Example: The collective and continued influence exerted by (name) was the prime reason for .....

Colorful style

Example: (Name) colorful style of leadership allowed him/her to continue the difficult task of ..... with (results)

Come alive

Example: (Name) organization came alive with a flurry of .....

Come to grips with

Example: (Name) came to grips with the problems in/of ..... and took immediate and effective corrective action that led to.....

Comfort level

Example: (Name) is in his/her comfort level when others are in disarray. He/She has a unique ability to .....

Commands attention
> Example: The work of (name) commands the attention of his/her superiors. He/She simply accomplished more than .....

Committed to
> Example: (Name) is fully committed to professional excellence. He/She was able to demonstrate this recently when he/she .....

Common cause
> Example: (Name) always pulls together for the common cause of (organization). Putting ..... ahead of personal needs.

Common effort
> Example: (Name) pulls together the common effort of others into a cohesive .....

Competitive spirit/edge
> Example: (Name) has a competitive spirit. He/She is not satisfied with ..... performance. Instead, he/she looks forward to ...

Complete success
> Example: (Name) tackled various difficult assignments with complete success. One example is .....

Complete turnaround
> Example: (Name) was able to institute a complete turnaround in the ..... Where performance had previously been ..... it is now the front-running organization in .....

Concept became reality
> Example: The concept of ..... became reality when (name) transformed ..... into .....

Concrete benefits
> Example: Tangible, concrete benefits were derived by ..... when (name) .....

Concrete ideas
> Example: (Name) contributed concrete ideas in/for ..... This contribution was instrumental in/to .....

Concrete support
> Example: (Name) gave his/her concrete support in the area of .....

Confidence builder
> Example: (Name) is a real confidence builder. This was most recently demonstrated in/by .....

Confidence restored
> Example: (Name) restored the confidence of his/her (organization). This was accomplished by .....

Confronted challenge(s)
> Example: (Name) confronted the challenges of ..... head-on and without hesitation.

Connects with others

Example: (Name) connects with others with relative ease. This allows him/her to ..... with highly effective results.

Conquered

Example: (Name) conquered the highly complex .....

Example: (Name) conquered the almost insurmountable problem of .....

Conscious effort

Example: In a conscious effort to ..... (name) ventured into the a previously little known .....

Consistent pattern of

Example: (Name) has demonstrated a consistent pattern of ..... This, without doubt led to .....

Constructive attitude

Example: (Name) always maintains a constructive attitude toward ..... None has been more .....

Consummate

Example: (Name) is the consummate professional. He/She was the first person to .....

Content of character

Example: The content of (Name) character was never more evident than when he/she .....

Continued quest for

Example: (Name) continued quest for ..... led him/her to the outstanding .....

Continued success

Example: (Name) continued to demonstrate the success that brought him/her to the forefront of .....

Example: (Name) continued success in ..... serves as an excellent example of how .....

Continued to adapt

Example: (Name) has continued to adapt to the changing environment of ..... with relative ease.

Continued to advance

Example: (Name) has continued to advance the cause of .....

Continuous improvement

Example: (Name) continuous improvement in ..... has led to .....

Contributed to success of

Example: (Name) directly contributed to the success of ..... This was accomplished through the continued display of .....

Controlled response

Example: (Name) controlled response to ..... in a situation where ..... proved highly successful in .....

Conventional barrier(s)

Example: (Name) overcame the conventional barriers of .....

Conventional wisdom
>Example: Despite conventional wisdom, (name) was able to implement and direct a plan that .....

Conveys style
>Example: (Name) has been very successful in the style of ..... he/she conveys to .....

Convinced others
>Example: (Name) convinced others to ..... This led to a dramatic improvement in .....

Cooperative spirit
>Example: The cooperative spirit exhibited by (name) was instrumental in .....

Cornerstone of
>Example: (Name) was the cornerstone of success in the timely completion of ..... that saved (/hours/dollars).

Countless hours/numbers
>Example: (Name) dedicated countless hours working on ..... This was so successful that .....

Courage to face
>Example: (Name) has the courage to face adversity. He/She fully demonstrated this when .....

Courageous act(s)
>Example: (Name) performance was a courageous act of .....

Course of action
>Example: (Name) steered a course of action that led to ..... His/Her rich imagination in this action .....

Coveted award
>Example: (Name) earned the coveted award of ..... His/Her penetrating look at ..... led to .....

Cream of the crop
>Example: (Name) is the cream of the crop in ..... He/She is able to intellectually grasp all the elements of .....

Cream rose to top
>Example: Everyone was given an equal shot at ..... The cream rose to the top as (name) .....

Created (new) process of
>Example: (name) created the new process of .....This logical and comprehensive method led to .....

Created atmosphere/climate
>Example: (Name) created an atmosphere of unparalleled .....

Creative approach to
>Example: (Name) creative approach to ..... was both farsighted and comprehensive.

Creative masterpiece

    Example: (Name) creative masterpiece of ..... was the result of his/her fertile mind and professional .....

Crisis situation

    Example: (Name) performs with uncommon cool and ease in crisis situations, always .....

Critical time/juncture

    Example: At the critical juncture of ..... (name) came to the forefront with his/her recommendation that .....

Critically acclaimed

    Example: (Name) performance in/as ..... has been critically acclaimed by .....

Crown jewel

    Example: (Name) creativeness and understanding of ..... was the crown jewel in ..... It was a brilliant stroke of .....

Crowning achievement(s)

    Example: (Name) crowning achievement in .....was the result of his/her astute awareness of .....

Crucial issue(s)

    Example: Concerning the crucial issue of ..... (Name) aptitude at dealing with ..... was insightful and .....

Crusader's zeal

    Example: (Name) jumped into ..... with a Crusader's zeal. His/Her skillful and artistic response resulted in .....

Crusader for

    Example: (Name) has been a crusader for improvement in .....

Crystal clear

    Example: It became crystal clear that what was needed was ..... (Name) was quick to take the lead in .....

Culmination of

    Example: The culmination of... was a direct result of the bold action taken by (name).

Cushion of safety

    Example: While maintaining a cushion of safety, (name) was able to ..... by creating and applying .....

Customary confidence

    Example: (Name) customary confidence was a cornerstone in expanding virtually every aspect of .....

Cut above

    Example: (Name) performance is a cut above other ..... He/She energized a high-powered .....

Cut teeth on

    Example: (Name) handled the difficult and delicate job of ..... He/She cut his/her teeth on being able to .....

Cutting edge
>Example: (Name) is on the cutting edge of ..... No one in recent memory has .....

Daily challenges of
>Example: Despite the daily challenges of ..... (name) has been able to maintain .....

Dazzling performance
>Example: (Name) dazzling performance as .....led to the orderly and practical completion of ......

Debt of gratitude
>Example: Everyone at ..... owes a debt of gratitude for his/her resounding success in/as/at .....

Deceptively simple
>Example: Despite the difficulty involved, (name) made the job deceptively simple by .....

Decisive action(s)/step
>Example: (Name) took decisive action on the time-critical .....

Dedicated efforts
>Example: (Name) dedicated and matchless efforts culminated in the most successful .....

Deep respect
>Example:(Name) enjoys the deep respect of .....

Defender of
>Example: (Name) is a staunch defender of .....He/She considers no ..... too small or trivial that/to .....

Defined character/essence
>Example: The defined character of (name) can best be summed up as/by .....

Definition of character
>Example: A good definition of character is ..... (Name) has no equal when it comes to .....

Degree of certainty
>Example: Without any measurable degree of certainty, (name) managed to .....

Delicate balance
>Example: (Name) was able to ..... without disturbing the delicate balance of .....

Delivered as expected
>Example: Faced with the prospect of ..... (name) was nevertheless able to deliver as expected the .....

Despite deep cuts
>Example: (Name) was able to complete ..... despite deep cuts in .....He/She is unbeatable in this area.

Develop full potential
> Example: (Name) developed the full potential of ..... This resulted in the superlative .....

Devoted resources to
> Example: (Name) was able to devote scarce resources to the ..... This allowed ..... to .....

Devoted to
> Example: (Name) is devoted to this profession. He/She has become a standout in/at .....

Diehard
> Example: Only (Name) diehard persistence saved the ...

Difficult business of
> Example: (Name) meticulous and unparalleled .....made the difficult business of ..... relatively easy.

Difficult event/circumstances
> Example: Even under the most difficult circumstances (name) manages to produce .....

Diligent patience
> Example: Diligent patience and persistence by (name) led the way when (organization) was faced with ..... He/She always came through with .....

Directly influenced
> Example: (Name) directly influenced ..... with his/her distinguished performance as/in .....

Directly responsible for
> Example: (Name) was directly responsible for the meritorious service of ..... during the time/period of .....

Disciplined passion
> Example: "(Name) tackled (assignment) with disciplined passion which resulted in unparalleled work/improvement in.....

Discovered
> Example: Always alert for ways to improve ..... (Name) discovered a new way to ..... This directly increased .....

Distinct advantage
> Example: (Name) has a distinct advantage over (peers) in the area of ..... because of his/her prowess in/as .....

Distinctively different
> Example: (Name) tried a new and distinctively different way to ..... This top-notch idea turned out to be .....

Distinguished
> Example: (Name) distinguished himself/herself while serving as ..... This sterling performance carried over to .....

Distinguished tradition
> Example: In keeping with the long and distinguished tradition of (organization), Name outmatched .....

Distinguishing characteristic(s)
> Example: One distinguishing characteristic of (name) is his/her
> ability to ....

Diverse background
> Example: (Name) diverse background allowed him/her to venture
> into new areas of ..... with superb results.

Diverse point(s) of view
> Example: After reviewing many diverse points of view, (name)
> decided on a course of action that led to .....

Do great things
> Example: (Name) courageous nature allowed him/her to do great
> things in the area of ....., directly contributing to .....

Dominant force
> Example: (Name) is a dominant force in .....His/Her standout
> performance surpassed .....

Dominated area of
> Example: (Name), a proven expert in ....., dominated the area of
> ..... with his/her .....

Dominated field
> Example: (Name) dominated the field of ..... because of his/her
> ability to ..... and mastery of .....

Down to the wire
> Example: The ..... project went down to the wire on whether or not
> it would succeed. (Name) proved to the deciding
> factor in the ultimate success of .....

Dramatic change/time
> Example: In this dramatic time of change, (name) proved to be a
> journeyman ..... when he/she .....

Dramatic swing in
> Example: (Name) performance produced a dramatic change in
> ..... because of his/her ability to .....

Dramatic turn of events
> Example: A dramatic turn of events caught everyone by surprise.
> (Name) never missed a beat, his/her outstanding
> performance led to a dramatic .....

Dramatically illustrated
> Example: (Name) ability to be a trailblazer in the area/field of .....
> was dramatically illustrated when he/she .....

Draw the line
> Example: (Name) was able to draw the line on ..... Immediate
> and marked improvement in .....quickly followed

Dream come true
> Example: (Name) performance in/as has been a dream come true
> for (organization). He/she is the personification of .....

Drew heavily on/upon

   Example: (Organization) drew heavily on (name) expertise in .....
   This led the perfection of .....

Driving force

   Example: (Name) proved to be a driving force in ..... by
   outclassing the entire field of .....

Dynamic

   Example: (Name) was a dynamic force in ..... His/Her energy
   never skipped a beat and resulted in .....

Eager anticipation

   Example: (Name) always looks in eager anticipation for the most
   challenging and the most difficult tasking.

Eager to

   Example: (Name) has shown by ..... that he/she is eager to.....

Ear marked for

   Example: (Name) should be ear marked for tasks involving .....
   His/Her expertise in the field of ..... identifies him/her
   as the best ..... around.

Earned place in

   Example: (Name) earned a place in the hearts of ..... because of
   his/her ability to .....

Eclipsed previous record

   Example: (Name) eclipsed the previous record of ..... which had
   stood for ..... with the faultless execution of .....

Electrified

   Example: (Name) electrified everyone with his/her remarkable
   ability to ..... Prior to this no one had .....

Element of risk

   Example: Despite a high element of risk, (name) top-notch work
   on/as ..... led the way to an unprecedented level of .....

Elevated to level of

   Example: (Name) was elevated to the level of .....by
   demonstrating an exceptional level of .....

Eliminated all

   Example: (Name) sterling performance as ..... eliminated all waste
   sometimes associated with .....

Eliminated need for

   Example: (Name) virtually eliminated the need for ..... using his/her
   superb level of .....

Elite

   Example: (Name) is one of the elite members of .....because of
   his/her impeccable talent for .....

Embarked upon

   Example: (Name) embarked upon the strenuous task of ..... which
   brought his/her supreme talents of ..... to the forefront of...

Embodies unique

    Example: (Name) embodies the unique qualities of .....

Embraced the concept

    Example: (Name) was quick to embrace the concept of .....and took the lead in action that eventually led to .....

Embraced with enthusiasm

    Example: The (organization) embraced with enthusiasm (name) proposed concept to .....

Emerging

    Example: (Name) is an emerging superstar in the field of .....

Employing strategy of

    Example: Employing the strategy of ..... (name) was able to achieve supreme results in/as .....

Endless possibilities

    Example: (Name) concept of ..... brings almost endless possibilities into play in the area of ..... which should prove to become the standard-bearer in .....

Enduring place in

    Example: (Name) earned an enduring place in the hearts of ..... for his/her exemplary ability to .....

Energy devoted to

    Example: (Name) devoted much energy to .....the difficult task of ..... and distinguished himself/herself by .....

Engaged in

    Example: Being well versed in all aspects of ....., (name) engaged in the more difficult task of ..... and proved more than equal to the task by .....

Engineered path of future

    Example: (Name) diligently engineered a path of the future by personally ....., culminating with the successful .....

Enhanced image

    Example: (Name) enhanced the image of ..... through his/her unselfish devotion to duty and .....

Enjoys(ed) increase(d)

    Example:(Name) enjoys the increased responsibilities as/of ..... and responded with this assignment by .....

Enriched the lives

    Example: (Name) has enriched the personal and professional lives of ..... by .....

Enthusiasm ran high

    Example: When the task of ..... arose, enthusiasm ran high throughout (organization) because of (name) belief and trust in .....

Enthusiastic support

Example: (Name) gained the enthusiastic support of ..... when he/she .....

Entirely new perspective

Example: (Name) brought an entirely new perspective to the table on the subject of ..... With the benefit of his/her expertise the (organization) was able to .....

Entrenched position

Example: (Name) was able to pull people from their old-way entrenched positions of ..... and bring them forward to a point of .....

Entrusted with

Example: (Name) was entrusted with the unenviable task of ..... He/She responded with customary excellence in completing .....

Envisions the future

Example: (Name) envisionment of the future allowed him/her to bring excellent foresight and planning abilities that .....

Epitome of

Example: (Name) is the epitome of a true professional. He.She always responds to ..... with unwavering .....

Equal to challenge

Example: (Name) was equal to the challenge when faces with .....

Equal to task

Example: (Name) was equal to the task of ..... with his/her positive mental attitude and outlook.

Equitable distribution

Example: (Name) received more than an equitable distribution of the work load when/during ..... He/She responded without missing a beat

Escalation of

Example: Despite an escalation of the workload in ....., (name) invigorated and impassioned others to .....

Especially significant

Example: (Name) performance was especially significant during ..... when .....

Essential element/trait(s)

Example: (Name) exhibits the traits most needed to ..... Without him/her the job of ..... would not have been .....

Established foothold

Example: (Name) established a foothold in the mountain of work left to him/her by.....His/Her invigorating spirit resulted in .....

Established legacy/stability
        Example: (Name) was able to establish stability in the area of ....
            which had been plagued by .....

Ever ready to
        Example: (Name) is ever ready to accept new challenges and
            proved up to the task when given the responsibility to .....

Ever-expanding obligations
        Example: Faced with the ever expanding obligations of .....
            (name) has managed to successfully .....

Ever-present/growing
        Example: Facing an ever growing expansion of ..... (name)
            powerhouse performance overcame .....

Every possible avenue
        Example: After evaluating every possible avenue of ..... (name)
            settled on ..... His/Her stimulus to others turned the tide
            on .....

Every step of the way
        Example: Faced with stringent guidelines on ....., (name) was
            able to ..... every step of the way.

Examined all aspects
        Example: (Name) examined all aspects of ..... and with swift and
            sustained action he/she transformed .....

Example of
        Example: (Name) is a sterling example of ....., continually leading
            the way in actual performance and .....

Exceeded expectations
        Example: (Name) accomplishes more in the morning than most
            people do all day, exceeding all expectations of .....

Excellence grew
        Example: (Name) excellence grew in ..... with his/her standard-
            bearer performance.

Exciting accomplishment(s)
        Example: (Name) many exciting accomplishments include his/her
            unparalleled performance in/as .....

Exciting development
        Example: (Name) came up with an exciting development that .....
            This has increased the .....

Exciting possibilities
        Example: (Name) proposed many exciting possibilities that could
            lead to a dramatic improvement in ..... Some of these
            have already .....

Exercise(d) best judgment
        Example: (Name) exercised the best judgment possible when
            he/she ..... At this critical juncture .....

Exerted influence
>   Example: (Name) exerted a positive influence on .....

Expended great energy
>   Example: (Name) expended a great deal of energy in the
>   completion of ..... This wide-ranging (task/project)
>   became the best .....

Experienced viewpoint
>   Example: The experienced viewpoint put forth by (name) resulted
>   in a dramatic increase in .....

Exploited
>   Example: (Name) exploited the weakness in/of ..... which proved
>   extremely helpful in .....

Exploits noteworthy
>   Example: Many of (name) noteworthy exploits in ..... are the result
>   of a special talent he/she has for .....

Explore new direction(s)
>   Example: (Name) wide and diverse background allowed him/her
>   to explore new directions in .....

Explore(d) new methods
>   Example: (Name) is not afraid to explore new methods of .....
>   He/She never ceases to stay on top of the latest .....

Extended range
>   Example: (Name) was able to extend the range of .....using
>   his/her superior ..... talent.

Extensive analysis
>   Example: (Name) completed an extensive analysis on ..... and
>   found a way to increase efficiency by .....

Extra motivation
>   Example: When extra motivation is needed, (name) is the person
>   to see to .....

Extraordinary challenge(s)
>   Example: Faced with the extraordinary challenge of ..... (Name)
>   was able to ..... without missing a beat in the progress
>   of .....

Extreme measures
>   Example: Despite the extreme measures faced by (Name) as a
>   result of ....., he/she proved equal to the task by .....

Extremely delicate
>   Example: During the extremely delicate ..... (Name) brilliantly
>   executed .....

Exuberant
>   Example: (Name) exuberant personality was instrumental in .....

Eye on future
>   Example: With an eye on the future, (name) transformed the
>   workplace from ..... to ....

Face challenge(s)
>
> Example: (Name) faced the new challenges of ..... with his/her
> customary .....

Face up to
>
> Example: (Name) faced up to the mammoth undertaking by .....

Face(d) issue(s) head on
>
> Example: (Name) faced the issue head on. His/Her first important
> task was to overcome .....

Faced tall odds
>
> Example: The task/project faced tall odds at succeeding.
> However, (name), who thrives on new challenges, was
> able to .....

Far and away
>
> Example: (Name) is far and away the best ..... in .....

Far more reliable
>
> Example: (Name) developed a/an ..... that was far more reliable
> than .....

Far-reaching
>
> Example: (Name) far-reaching work in ..... lead others to .....

Farsighted
>
> Example: With (name) farsighted approach to ..... the
> (organization) was able to .....

Fast-moving
>
> Example: (Name) enjoys a fast-moving work environment and is
> at his/her best when .....

Faultless
>
> Example: (Name) faultless performance in/as ..... resulted in .....

Fertile imagination
>
> Example: (Name) has an active mind and a fertile imagination.

Feverish activity
>
> Example: The feverish activity brought about by ..... did not phase
> (name), for he/she was able to .....

Few and far between
>
> Example: People like (name) are few and far between.

Fierce determination
>
> Example: (Name) fierce determination and great ability to ..... led
> to .....

Fill the bill
>
> Example: (Name) was able to fill the bill of/as ..... with great
> success.

Final touch(es)
>
> Example: When (name) put the final touches on ....., he/she had
> developed a/an ..... that set an outstanding example.

Fine detail

> Example: (Name) ability to pay close attention to the fine detail involved in ..... led to the high standards of performance of .....

Finest

> Example: (Name) is the finest example .....

Finest tradition

> Example: (Name) performance were in keeping with the finest tradition of .....

Firm constructive element

> Example: One constant during the recent ..... was the firm constructive element of (name).

Firm conviction

> Example: (Name) sets the finest example for others because of his/her firm conviction in/that .....

Firm position/resolve

> Example: (Name) ability to hold on to his/her firm resolve was directly responsible for the marked improvement in .....

First and foremost

> Example: First and foremost (name) is the most successful ..... in .....

First ever

> Example: (Name) was the first person ever to .....

First in long line of

> Example: (Name) success in/at ..... was the first in a long line of successes that culminated in .....

First rank importance

> Example: What ranks of first importance in (name) is his/her ability to .....

First stabilized, then reversed

> Example: (Name) first stabilized and then reversed the decline of .....

First step(s)

> Example: (Name) all-important first steps in ..... proved invaluable in/for .....

Firsthand experience

> Example: (Name) firsthand experience in/at ..... allowed him/her to successfully .....

Flag bearer

> Example: (Name) became the flag bearer for ..... because of his/her ability to .....

Flawless

> Example: The flawless execution of ..... by (name) set an outstanding example for .....

Flawlessly executed
> Example: (Name) flawlessly executed the critical duties of .....
> with uncommon perception and .....

Flourish in face of
> Example: (Name) flourishes in the face of ..... where others would
> flounder and fall.

Flourishes in environment of
> Example: (Name) flourishes in an environment of .....

Focus attention on
> Example: (Name) has the rare ability to be able to focus due
> attention on the important issues and .....

Focus(es) on
> Example: With his/her focus on ..... (name) was able to .....

Focused and re-doubled efforts
> Example: (Name) focused and re-doubled efforts to ..... despite
> being .....

Followed footsteps
> Example: (Name) followed the footsteps of the highly successful ..

Foothold in
> Example: (Name) gained a foothold in area of ..... by .....

For good measure
> Example: (Name) successfully completed ..... and then for good
> measure he/she .....

For others to emulate
> Example: (Name) performance is a model for others to emulate.

Force in
> Example: (Name) was a real force in ..... when he/she .....

Forever changed
> Example: (Name) performance in/as has forever changed .....

Forged ahead
> Example: (Name) forged ahead in ..... despite the inherent
> problems associated with.....

Forged united effort
> Example: (Name) and his/her people forged a united effort to .....

Formed diverse
> Example: (Name) formed a diverse group that was able to .....

Formed the foundation
> Example: (Name) formed the foundation of/for (area). This was a
> resounding success because of his/her .....

Formidable
> Example: (Name) was a formidable force in ..... with his/her
> masterful accomplishment of .....

Formula for success
> Example: (Name) found the formula for success in ..... He/She is
> recognized as the most .....

Forward-looking

    Example: (Name) is a forward-looking individual with a
        phenomenal record in/as .....

Foster(s) sense of

    Example: (Name) fosters a strong sense of pride among .....

Fostered improved

    Example: (Name) fostered an improved understanding of .....
        with his/her stellar performance as .....

Fought diligently

    Example: (Name) fought diligently to .....with unequaled success.

Fought long and hard

    Example: Disregarding the obstacles involved, (name) fought long
        and hard to .....

Found satisfaction

    Example: (Name) found great satisfaction when he/she
        transformed .....

Foundation built on

    Example: (Name) leadership is built on a strong foundation based
        on .....

Founder of

    Example: (Name) was the founder of a/the highly successful .....

Fragile situation

    Example: When a fragile situation arose in ..... (name) diplomatic
        approach resulted in .....

Frank assessment

    Example: A frank assessment was made in the problem area of
        ..... (Name) was selected to ..... He/She contributed
        significantly to the immediate improvement of ....

Frantic pace

    Example: (Name) maintained a frantic pace in the on-time
        completion of .....

Free of incident

    Example: The (area) was completed free of incident due in large
        part to the effort(s) of (name).

Free rein

    Example: (Name) was given a free rein in making improvements
        in ..... He/She immediately responded by rejuvenating ....

Free-spirited

    Example: (Name) free-spirited personality made him/her ideally
        suited to tackle the problem of ..... His/Her high
        standards of excellence quickly came to the forefront
        when he/she .....

Frequent contributor

    Example: (Name) is a frequent contributor the excellent .....

Fresh new
> Example: The fresh new ideas put forth by (name) quickly won the
> support of .....

Fresh page in
> Example: (Name) arrival at (organization) was a fresh page in an
> otherwise .....

Fresh start
> Example: (Name) was given a fresh start in/as ..... His/Her
> relentless drive and ..... were instrumental in .....

From the onset
> Example: From the onset (name) proved to be .....

Fruitful
> Example: (Name) has been a fruitful contributor to .....

Fruits of labor
> Example: The fruits of (name) labor materialized as .....

Fuel the imagination
> Example: (Name) is able to fuel the imagination of others and .....

Full cooperation
> Example: (Name) enjoys the full and complete cooperation of .....
> This has allowed him/her to .....

Full court press
> Example: (Name) put a full court press on the problem of .....

Full extent/measure
> Example: (Name) contributed full measure to .....

Full force
> Example: (Name) put his/her full weight of force behind .....
> resulting in consistently superior performance.

Full of hope
> Example: (Name) is always full of hope and enthusiastic in the
> completion of .....

Full of possibilities
> Example: (Name) innovative suggestions in the area of ..... are
> full of possibilities.

Full range of
> Example: (Name) has a full range of skills in .....

Full steam ahead
> Example: (Name) believes in full steam ahead, choosing to
> conquer instead of just tackling difficult tasks/projects.

Full-grown
> Example: Tackled the full-grown and mature problem of .....

Full-time job
> Example: Despite an already full-time job of/as ..... he/she
> tackled the .....

Fully prepared to/for
> Example: (Name) is always fully prepared for any eventuality.

Fundamental principal/values

Example: (Name) holds close to the fundamental values of .....

Fundamentally sound

Example: (Name) always offers fundamentally sound suggestions and ideas in .....

Furthered cause

Example: (Name) furthered the cause of ..... my personally .....

Future-oriented

Example: A future oriented person. This was demonstrated recently when he/she .....

Gain(ed) ground

Example: (Name) was able to gain ground where others had failed in the area/field of .....

Gained admiration

Example: (Name) recently gained the admiration of ..... by his/her achievement/accomplishment on/in .....

Gained favor

Example: (Name) gained the favor of ..... with his/her ability to .....

Gained foothold

Example: (Name) gained a foothold in the correction of .....

Gained notoriety

Example: (Name) gained notoriety for his/her recent work in .....

Gave birth to

Example: (Name) gave birth to a new procedure in ..... This was so revolutionary that .....

Gave rise to

Example: (Name's) work in ..... gave rise to ..... which in turn led to a vast improvement in .....

General order of things

Example: (Name) changed the general order of the way things operated in/by ...... This led to vast improvements in .....

Generous assistance

Example: (Name) provided generous assistance in the successful completion of ..... ahead of schedule, and saving (manhours/dollars, etc.)

Generously gave

Example: (Name) gave generously of his/her normal off time to work in the time-sensitive .....

Genuine act of/article

Example: (Name's) genuine act of .....resulted in vast improvements in .....

Genuine desire

Example: (Name) displays(ed) a genuine desire to/for .....

Get a fix on

> Example: (Name) was able to get a fix on the nagging problem of ..... and then took immediate action to/that .....

Get a grip on

> Example: (Name) quickly got a grip on the problem(s) of ..... through his/her experience in/as .....

Get to heart of

> Example: (Name) is able to get to the heart of any problem in short order and find an effective solution.

Giant step forward

> Example: (Organization) took a giant step forward when (Name) identified and corrected .....

Give(n) blank check

> Example: (Name) was given a blank check to fix ..... He/She responded with .....

Glaring reality

> Example: Faced with the glaring reality of ..... (Name) was able to .....

Glimmer of hope

> Example: Despite a glimmer initial of hope, (Name) successfully fought his/her way though .....

Go along with

> Example: (Name) is not content to go along with the crowd. Instead, he/she took the lead in .....

Go extra mile

> Example: (Name) always goes the extra mile to ensure that all projects are completed correctly and ahead of schedule.

Go hand-in-hand

> Example: (Name) knows experience and ..... go hand in hand. This allowed him/her to .....

Go to bat for

> Example: (Name) is always willing to go to bat for ..... This enhances his/her .....

Go to limit(s)

> Example: (Name) always goes to the limit to ..... He/She leaves no stone unturned in .....

Golden opportunity

> Example: (Name) was able to take full advantage of a/the golden opportunity to .....

Good first step

> Example: (Name) made a good first step toward ..... when he/she .....

Good fortune/measure

> Example: (Name) completed ..... ahead of schedule and then for good measure tackled the problem of .....

Got jump on

    Example: (Name) got a jump on others by/when he/she .....

Grace under fire

    Example: (Name) kept his/her composure and grace under fire when he/she .....

Gracefully accepted

    Example: (Name) gracefully accepted .....

Graduated to level

    Example: (Name) has graduated to a level above contemporaries. He/She is truly a level above .....

Grand scale

    Example: (Name) was able to complete ... on a grand scale rarely seen in (organization)

Grass roots

    Example: (Name) quickly gets to the grass roots of problem areas and .....

Gratifying

    Example: It was a gratifying experience having (Name) working with ..... on .....

Gravitate toward(s)

    Example: While others tend(ed) to gravitate toward(s) ..... (Name) was ultimately successful in/by .....

Gravity of situation

    Example: (Name) immediately saw the gravity of the situation and took correct corrective action by .....

Great chapter in history

    Example: (Name's) arrival was a great chapter in the history of (organization). He/She brought with him/her .....

Grew in intensity

    Example: The problem of ..... grew in complexity and intensity. (Name), however, was able to .....

Grew in sophistication

    Example: (Name) (organization) grew in size of scope and structure. This did not slow down his/her efforts to .....

Grew in wisdom and stature

    Example: (Name) grew in wisdom and stature when he/she .....

Groomed to/for

    Example: (Name) has been well groomed to take the helm of .....

Ground breaking

    Example: (Name's) ground breaking work in/as ..... led to the ultimate development of .....

Ground floor

    Example: Working from the ground floor up, (Name) quickly became the person to see when/if .....

Guide the way
>
> Example: (Name) was able to guide the way for others in .....

Guided change
>
> Example: (Name) guided the change from ..... to ..... without a
> decrease in efficiency.

Guiding hand
>
> Example: (Name) was always available, giving a guiding hand to
> others while maintaining a steadying influence on .....

Guiding light/vision
>
> Example: (Name's) superlative effort in/as ..... served as a
> guiding light to/for .....

Had free rein
>
> Example: (Name) had a free rein in ..... His/Her trailblazing effort
> led to distinct improvements in .....

Hallmark
>
> Example: (Name's) work has become a hallmark of excellence.

Hammer away
>
> Example: Despite the hectic work schedule (Name) hammered
> away at ..... until .....

Hand picked
>
> Example: (Name) was hand picked to ..... This turned out to be
> an excellent choice as he/she .....

Hand-in-hand
>
> Example: (Name) worked hand-in-hand with .....   Their efforts
> led to standout improvements in .....

Handled delicate issue(s)
>
> Example: (Name) handled the delicate issue of ..... with the skill
> normally observed in .....

Handled with respect
>
> Example: (Name) handled with respect the subject of ..... while
> displaying a preeminent .....

Hands full
>
> Example: (Name) already had his/her hands full in (area) when
> he/she tackled the unenviable task of .....

Hands-on person
>
> Example: (Name) is a hands-on person. He/She leaves nothing
> to chance.

Hard-earned
>
> Example: (Name) has a hard-earned reputation for .....

Hard-pressed
>
> Example: When others become hard-pressed to ....., they know
> they can always call on (Name) to give them a helping
> hand and a .....

Hardy attitude
>
> Example: (Name) has a hardy attitude for .....

Harm's way

> Example: (Name) is unafraid of going in harm's way. He/She will tackle and successfully complete any .....

Harmonious relationship(s)

> Example: (Name) established a harmonious relationship with ..... which led to laudatory improvements in/with .....

Hats off to

> Example: Hats off to (Name) for his/her faultless performance in/as ..... which led to a masterful .....

Head(ed) off

> Example: (Name) headed off a potential ..... with his/her quick action and unbeatable combination of .....

Headed in right direction

> Example: (Name) moved things off center and got the (organization) headed in the right direction.

Healed wounds

> Example: (Name) healed the wounds of ..... caused by ..... with his/her exceptional .....

Heart and soul

> Example: (Name) is the heart and soul of (organization) with is/her tireless efforts and exemplary .....

Heavy burden

> Example: (Name) was able to carry the heavy burden of ..... because of his/her unique .....

Hectic schedule

> Example: Despite an already hectic schedule, he/she successfully assumed the duties of ..... and performed them with the characteristic .... we have come to expect of (Name)

Heightened activity

> Example: In a period of heightened activity because of ..... (Name) was able to surpass .....

Held firm

> Example: (Name) held firm in his/her convictions despite heavy pressure from .....

Helped build

> Example: (Name) helped build ..... from the ground up. His/Her unequalled performance resulted in .....

Helped inspire

> Example: (Name) helped inspire confidence and dedication in an organization previously ham strung by .....

Helped solidify

> Example: (Name) helped solidify the gains made in ..... by .....

Helping hand
> Example: (Name) is always willing to give a helping and to .....
> and frequently works passed normal hours to ensure .....

Herculean effort
> Example: (Name) gave a Herculean effort in ..... despite having to
> deal with the additional hardship fo .....

Hidden qualities
> Example: (Name) has many hidden qualities that do not show up
> in his/her daily activities, including .....

High gear
> Example: (Name) turned his/her ..... in to high gear and
> completed ..... on time despite .....

High hope(s)
> Example: (Name) has high hopes and high goals and always
> follows through on .....

High stress environment
> Example: (Name) enjoys working in a high stress environment.
> Some of his/her best work comes when .....

High/Low profile
> Example: (Name's) ability to keep a low profile while/as/in ..... is
> especially noteworthy..

Higher goal(s)
> Example: (Name) has set and reached higher goals than ..... due
> to his/her exceptional ability to/as .....

Highly developed
> Example: (Name) has a highly developed .....

Historic event
> Example: (Name) became the first person ever to ..... This is
> considered a historic event because .....

History of
> Example: (Name's) performance in/as ..... is the best in the recent
> history of .....

Hit the books
> Example: (Name) works a full day at ..... and hits the books to
> study/learn ..... during off-work hours.

Hit the mark
> Example: (Name's) suggestion hit the mark on how to ..... This
> resulted in a savings of .....

Honed to perfection
> Example: (Name's) skills at ..... have been honed to perfection.

Honest feedback
> Example: (Name) can always be depended upon to give an
> honest and complete feedback on .....

Hope for future
>Example: (Name) brought new hope for the future of (organization) by his/her .....

Host of problems
>Example: Faced with a host of problems, (Name) nevertheless succeeded in .....

Hot spot
>Example: When a hot spot occurs in/at ..... (Name) is the person to see for quick, effective action.

Hours on end
>Example: (Name) spend hours on end of off-work time perfecting the ..... This resulted in .....

Hunger for
>Example: (Name) has a hunger for knowledge rarely seen in .....

Ideal conditions
>Example: The ideal conditions that exist at ..... are the direct result of (Name's) skill and dedication to .....

Ideal for
>Example: (Name) is the ideal person for ..... He/She has the requisite skills for/to .....

Ignited fire in/to
>Example: (Name) ignited a fire in the spirits of .....

Illustrious career
>Example: (Name) illustrious career was recently highlighted when he/she .....

Immediate impact/success
>Example: (Name) has had an immediate impact on the operation of .....

Immediate turnaround
>Example: Shortly after his/her assignment to ..... an immediate turnaround in ..... was noted.

Immersed in
>Example: (Name) is totally committed to and immersed in his/her chosen field. He/She routinely .....

Impassioned
>Example: (Name's) impassioned talk to ..... paved the way for. ....

Impeccable timing
>Example: (Name) has impeccable timing. He/She always seems to be able to .....

Impeccably prepared
>Example: (Name) approaches any task impeccably prepared.

Impending disaster
>Example: Despite an impending disaster in ..... (Name) was able to .....

Impetus to/for

Example: (Name) provided the impetus for the highly
successful .....

Implemented blueprint

Example: (Name planned and implemented a blueprint for .....
This has been used as a model to/for .....

Important first step

Example: (Name) took the important first step in/to .....

Important point(s)

Example: (Name) is able to incorporate the important points of
..... into his/her daily work schedule with relative ease.

Important source of

Example: (Name) is an important source of ..... in the field of .....

Impressed with

Example: I have been totally impressed with the skill and
dedication demonstrated by ..... during .....

Impressive

Example: (Name) has set an impressive record in/as .....

Improved lives

Example: (Name's) ability to ..... has measurably improved the
lives and working environment of .....

Improved quality of

Example: (Name) efforts to ..... improved the quality of .....

In a nutshell

Example: (Name) is, in a nutshell, simply the best ..... in
(organization), bar none.

In face of

Example: (Name) performance in the face of ..... was admirable.

In full stride

Example: (Name) accepts temporary setbacks in full stride and
never misses a beat in .....

In great measure

Example: The success of ..... was, in great measure, the result of
(Name's) boundless .....

In high gear

Example: (Name) managed to put his/her organization into high
gear recently when the problem of ..... was .....

In line with

Example: (Name's) performance was in line with ..... Further,
he/she exceeded all expectations in/for .....

In mainstream

Example: (Name) clear sighted efforts to ..... were in the
mainstream with (organization's) goals to .....

In short supply
>
> Example: People the caliber of (Name) are in short supply.
> He/She has the astounding ability to .....

In spotlight
>
> Example: Being in the spotlight or on the hot seat does not
> adversely affect (Name) performance in/as .....

In step with
>
> Example:(Name) is always in step with (organization) policies and
> goals. In fact, he/she .....

In the face of
>
> Example: (Name's) performance in the face of adversity is without
> equal.

In the prime
>
> Example: (Name) is in the prime of his/her .....

In touch with
>
> Example: (Name) stays in touch with reality. He/She keeps a
> level head and always stays calm during .....

In wake of
>
> Example: In the wake of disaster in/at ..... (Name) was able
> to .....

Increased appetite for
>
> Example: (Name) continues to have an increased appetite for .....

Increasing number of
>
> Example: (Name) continues to come up with an ever increasing
> number of innovative ideas in/for .....

Increasingly clear
>
> Example: It is becoming increasingly clear that (Name) is one of
> the best ..... in .....

Incredible level/sense of
>
> Example: (Name) has an incredible level of ..... This was most
> recently demonstrated when he/she .....

Indebted to
>
> Example: (Organization) is indebted to the efforts of (Name).
> He/She has shown a remarkable ability to .....

Independent thinking
>
> Example: (Name's) independent thinking on the subject of .....
> was a major cornerstone for the improvement of .....

Indispensable to
>
> Example:(Name) has been indispensable to (organization)
> because of his/her ability to .....

Inexhaustible energy
>
> Example: The inexhaustible energy (Name) beings to a job has
> helped (organization) to/in .....

Inextricably connected

> Example: This (organization's) success is inextricably connected to the efforts and diligence of (Name).

Influence on

> Example: (Name) has been a positive influence on .....

Influential presence

> Example: (Name's) influential presence in/as ..... has won merit and praise from .....

Infuse(d) fresh ideas

> Example: (Name) infused fresh new ideas into the workplace and is directly responsible for .....

Ingenuity

> Example: (Name's) foresightedness and ingenuity led to laudable improvements in .....

Inherent danger

> Example: Despite the inherent danger associated with ..... (Name) formulated and implemented .....

Inherited unsuccessful

> Example: (Name) inherited an organization largely unsuccessful. However, he/she quickly and efficiently .....

Injects life

> Example: (Name) injects life and excitement into others with his/her ability to .....

Innovative new way/solutions

> Example: '(Name) found a new and innovative way to ..... This led to dramatic improvement(s) in/of .....

Inquisitive

> Example: (Name's) inquisitive nature and ..... lead to the highly successful .....

Ins and outs

> Example: (Name) knows the ins and outs of (organization) and uses this knowledge to .....

Insatiable appetite

> Example: (Name) has an insatiable appetite for ..... This, coupled with his/her ability to ..... led to .....

Inspiration to all

> Example: (Name) talent and work on .....has been an inspiration to .....

Inspired by

> Example: Others are inspired by the efforts and ..... of (Name)

Instinct for

> Example: (Name) has a certain instinct for finding and fixing .....

Instituted measures

> Example: (Name) instituted measures that quickly turned around ..... into an organization that .....

Integral part of
>   Example: (Name) has become an integral part of (organization)
>   because of his/her multi-talented skills in/as .....

Intense dedication/work
>   Example:(Name's) intense dedication and work ethics made
>   him/her an overwhelming choice to become .....

Intense pressure
>   Example: Despite the intense pressure inherent with/to .....
>   (Name) has been able to .....

Intimate knowledge
>   Example: (Name's) intimate working knowledge in/of ..... led to
>   ground-breaking advancements in .....

Intricately involved
>   Example: (Name) has been intricately involved in all facets of .....

Introduce(d) new life
>   Example: (Name) introduced a new breath of life into a once
>   failing ..... and (results).

Invaluable contribution(s)
>   Example: (Name's) many invaluable contributions to
>   (organization) have led to .....

Invested talent/time
>   Example: (Name) invested his/her considerable time and talent
>   on ..... with results that .....

Investment in future
>   Example: (Name) made an investment in the future of
>   (organization). This investment paid off with interest
>   when/by .....

Invigorating program
>   Example: (Name) started an invigorating ..... program that
>   completely turned around .....

Iron will
>   Example: Through sheer iron will and determination (Name)
>   completed .....

Jolt of adrenaline
>   Example: (Name) provided a much need jolt of adrenaline into
>   (organization) that (results)

Jump-start
>   Example: (Name) was able to jump start an ailing ..... which
>   quickly won acclaim from .....

Keen awareness
>   Example: (Name) had a keen awareness of ..... and he/she
>   confidently developed a/an ..... that (results)

Keen grasp of
>   Example: (Name) has a keen grasp of ..... which allows him/her to
>   set and achieve clear-cut .....

Keen observation

    Example: (Name's) keen powers of observation were instrumental in ..... which resulted in .....

Keep an eye on

    Example: (Name) managed to keep an eye on ..... while at the same time achieving complete success in/by .....

Kept cool head

    Example: (Name) kept a cool head in the face of adversity when he/she ..... This flawless ..... personifies (Name).

Kept on toes

    Example: (Name) is the leading ..... at (organization) He/She kept on his/her toes when .....

Key element/ingredient(s)

    Example: (Name) provided the key ingredient to ..... This brought about a logical and ..... which won praise from .....

Key juncture

    Example: At a key and important juncture (Name) was able to infuse .....which led to faultless .....

Key part of

    Example: (Name) continues to be a key part of (organization) while at the same time demonstrating .....

Key role in

    Example: (Name) played a key role in the successful completion of ..... which became an overwhelming success.

Key to success

    Example: (Name's) work in/as was the key to success in/at ..... This masterful undertaking led to .....

Knack for

    Example: (Name) has a real knack for getting the job done where others fail. This was never better demonstrated than when he/she .....

Know-how

    Example: (Name) is an ace ..... He/She has the know how to .....

Labor of love

    Example: (Name) approaches each and every task with a labor of love that is unequalled in (organization).

Labored hard

    Example: (Name) labored long and hard to complete ..... The successful completion led to a real improvement in .....

Ladder of success

    Example: (Name) has climbed the ladder of success through personal ..... and .....

Laid foundation/groundwork

    Example:(Name) laid the foundation for ..... by ..... This multi-talented individual further .....

Laid to rest
>Example: (Name's) stellar performance in/as ..... laid to rest any
>questions concerning .....

Landmark
>Example: (Name's) landmark work on/in/as ..... unquestionably
>led the way in .....

Lasting contribution(s)
>Example: (Name) has made significant and lasting contributions
>to (organization).

Lasting impact
>Example: (Name's) performance in/as will have a lasting impact
>on (organization) and will serve as a springboard to/for ....

Launched new
>Example: (Name) successfully launched a new ..... that will
>unquestionably surpass .....

Lead the way
>Example: With unerring accuracy (Name) led the way in/to.....

Leading the way
>Example: (Name) has an unsurpassed ability in leading the way
>in/to ..... with his/her versatility and .....

Learned first-hand
>Example: I was fortunate enough to see first hand (Name's)
>sterling work/performance in/as ..... This versatile
>individual is one of the finest ..... in .....

Least number of
>Example: (Name) had the least number of ..... of anyone in
>(organization). His/Her well grounded work and vision .....

Leave no stone unturned
>Example: (Name) will leave no stone unturned in his/her efforts to
>..... This unflagging dedication .....

Left a mark
>Example: (Name) left a mark on (organization) that will not soon
>be forgotten. His/Her remarkable talent .....

Left legacy
>Example: (Name) left a legacy at (organization) that is worthy of
>praise and ..... His/Her sensational work in as .....
>resulted in .....

Lend a hand
>Example: (Name) is never too busy to lend a hand to help .....

Lengthy process
>Example: The lengthy process of ..... never deterred (Name) from
>his/her goal(s) of ..... He/She with unmatched .....

Level best
>Example: (Name) ability to do his/her level best at any
>assignment demonstrated a remarkable talent for/to .....

Life-long passion for
>   Example: (Name's) life-long passion for ..... revolutionized the
>   way (organization) does .....

Lifeblood
>   Example: (Name) performance in/as .....has been the lifeblood of
>   (organization)

Lifted heavy weight
>   Example: (Name) lifted a heavy weight off the back of
>   (organization) because of his/her ability to .....

Light the way
>   Example: (Name) was able to light the way for (organization) to
>   accomplish .....aided by his/her masterful accomplishment
>   of .....

Lighten the burden
>   Example: (Name) lightened the burden of (organization) by
>   personally meritorious service that included .....

Lightening quick
>   Example: (Name's) lightening quick response to events in critical
>   situations resulted in .....

Like clockwork
>   Example: (Name) completed ..... like clockwork. He/She never
>   wavered or missed a step.

Long and arduous
>   Example: (Name) worked many long and arduous hours
>   completing ..... This led to a dramatic improvement in ....

Long be remembered
>   Example: The work on ..... performed by (Name) will long be
>   remembered for his/her skill in/at .....

Long haul/journey
>   Example: (Name's) invincible determination led the way in the long
>   journey from ..... to .....

Long periods of
>   Example: There is none better than (Name) during long periods of
>   ..... His/Her superior talent at ..... was instrumental in .....

Long, hard road
>   Example: The long hard road to success was orchestrated by
>   (Name). His/Her flawless performance was a level
>   above.....

Long-lasting/-standing
>   Example: The long-standing record of ..... was surpassed by
>   (Name) because of his/her .....

Long-term approach
>   Example: (Name's) long-term approach to ..... brought about
>   unparalleled success in .....

Long-term commitment

Example: (Name's) long-term commitment to the improvement of ..... proved him/her to be a top innovator in/at .....

Looked up to

Example: (Name) is look up to as one of the best ..... in .....

Looks beyond

Example: (Name) has the ability to look beyond ..... and focus on the more important long-range .....

Made a difference

Example: (Name) made a difference at (organization) because of his/her ability to .....

Made good use of

Example: (Organization) made good on its goal of ..... thanks to the super efforts of (Name).

Made inroads

Example: Significant inroads were made into ..... because of (Name's) unique ability to .....

Made it easy for

Example: (Name) made it easy for (organization) to ..... thanks to his/her matchless talent in/at .....

Made short work of

Example: (Name) made short work of the difficult task of ..... and proved himself/herself a shining example of .....

Made the best of

Example: (Name) made the best possible use of .....demonstrating an unending ability to .....

Made to order

Example: The difficult task of ..... was made to order for (Name) He/She has the tremendous individual drive necessary to .....

Made way through

Example: (Name) made his/her way through the difficult task of ..... by demonstrating a banner performance in/as .....

Magnitude of situation

Example: The difficulty or magnitude of a situation never occurs to (Name). He/She cannot be distracted by .....

Maintained course

Example: (Name) maintained a steady course during the difficult time of ..... and again proved his/she was .....

Major challenge(s)

Example: (Name) faced the major challenge of ..... with skill and ..... The results were .....

Major contributor

Example: (Name) made a major contribution to the success of ..... with his/her unerring ability to ...

282

Major obstacle
>   Example: (Name) overcame all major obstacles in the staggering
>   (area) with a stellar performance.

Major transition
>   Example: (Name) made the major transition from ..... to ..... with
>   his/her customary spotless .....

Make best of
>   Example: (Name) was able to make the best of a bad situation of
>   ..... by his/her revolutionary use of .....

Make good (on)
>   Example: (Name) made good on his/her effort to .....

Make short work of
>   Example: (Name) was able to make short work of the delicate
>   task of ..... despite.....

Make the grade
>   Example: (Name) was able to make the grade in the difficult .....
>   because of his/her unbelievable ability to .....

Makes things work
>   Example: (Name) simply makes things work better. He/She is the
>   best ..... at (organization)

Massive undertaking
>   Example: The massive undertaking of ..... was successfully
>   completed by (Name) with a seasoned .....

Master stroke
>   Example: (Name's) work on ..... was a master stroke that added
>   ..... to (organization)

Master the situation/problem
>   Example: (Name) was able to master the problem in/of ..... with
>   his/her zealous work and .....

Mastered details of
>   Example: (Name) was able to master all the intricate details of ....

Mastermind(ed)
>   Example: (Name) masterminded the most difficult task of ..... with
>   a standout performance and .....

Masterpiece
>   Example: At the zenith of his/her career field, (Name) was able to
>   ..... with unmatched .....

Matter of principle
>   Example: As a matter of principle, (Name) refuses to accept
>   anything less than .....

Maximum capacity
>   Example: (Name) always functions at maximum capacity
>   regardless of the complexity or difficulty of .....

Measure of success
> Example: The measure of success demonstrated by (Name) far exceeds(ed) .....

Meet demands
> Example: (Name) meets the highest demands of ..... with .....

Meet new challenges
> Example: (Name) meets new challenges head-on in a totally impressive way.

Meet the needs
> Example:(Name) meets the needs of ..... and is a master at .....

Memorable event/work
> Example: The memorable work (Name) did in/on ..... will further the advance of .....

Mere words fail to
> Example: Mere words fail to describe the accomplishments of (Name). He/She became the standard-bearer in/as .....

Merit(s) special praise
> Example: (Name's) performance in/as ..... merits special praise.

Met criteria
> Example: (Name) met all criteria for ..... in less than half the normal/allotted time.

Meticulous
> Example: The meticulous attention to detail demonstrated by (Name) went far and beyond .....

Milestone(s)
> Example: (Name) passed many milestones on his/her way to .....

Mission accomplished
> Example: (Name) has an astounding success rate of getting the mission accomplished during .....

Modeled after
> Example: All of the operations of (organization) are modeled after (Name's) extremely successful .....

Monumental
> Example: (Name) completed the monumental task of ..... with flawless performance and .....

More important aspect
> Example: (Name) completed one of the more important aspects of ..... in .....

Moved expeditiously
> Example: (Name) moved expeditiously to correct ..... which had been a long-standing problem in/at.....

Moved in positive direction
> Example: (Name) moved in a most positive direction to ..... The results were .....

Multi-faceted/talented

      Example: (Name) is a multi-talented individual with a special knack for .....

Muster up courage/strength

      Example: (Name) mustered up the courage to tackle ..... with results which/that .....

Narrow(ed) the gap

      Example: (Name) narrowed the gap between ..... and .....
      He/She was able to do this because of his/her .....

Natural choice for

      Example: With (Name's) ability to ....., he/she was the natural choice to .....

Natural enthusiasm

      Example: (Name) brings with him/her a natural enthusiasm for ....

Near perfection

      Example: (Name's) performance in/as ..... was near perfection.

Necessary for future of

      Example: (Name) completed the massive task of ..... which was absolutely necessary for the future of .....

Needed shot in the arm

      Example: (Name) gave a much needed shot in the arm to .....
      This resulted in .....

Never gave up

      Example: (Name) never gave up on his/her quest to ..... The end result was the best .....

Never wavered/faltered

      Example: (Name) never faltered in his/her efforts to .....
      The results were extraordinary.

New and challenging

      Example: (Name) is always looking for new and challenging ways to ..... He/She was personally responsible for .....

New and exciting

      Example: (Name) brought a new and exciting ..... to (organization) He/She was able to .....

New approach

      Example: The new approach of ..... to ..... by (Name) helped solve the longstanding problem of .....

New horizons

      Example: (Name) has opened new horizons in the area/field of ..... with his/her unique ability to .....

Newfound

      Example: (Name's) newfound method to/of ..... led the way in the resurrection of .....

Nick of time

Example: The serious problem of ..... was discovered and fixed by (name) just in the nick of time.

No end in sight

Example: There was no end in sight on the problem of ..... (Name) was able to fix the problem with his/her multi-skills of .....

No stranger to

Example: (Name) is no stranger to hard work. He/She worked ..... hours to fix/repair .....

Nose to the grind stone

Example: (Name) put his/her nose to the grind stone to complete the complex task of ..... ahead of time. This resulted in .....

Notable exception

Example: (Name) has been a notable exception to an otherwise ..... He/She completed ..... using .....

Nothing left to chance

Example: (Name) left nothing to chance in his/her efforts to ..... The results were nothing less than outstanding.

Nothing short of

Example: (Name's) performance was nothing short of .....

Nourished

Example: (Name) nourished the new idea of ..... The results were a marked improvement in .....

Off to fast start

Example: (Name) got off to a fast start on/as ..... and never stopped or slowed down.

On cutting edge of

Example: (Name) is on the cutting edge of ..... His/Her ability to ..... is far beyond .....

On guard for/against

Example: (Name) always stays on guard for .....

On the ball

Example: (Name) is a person on the ball and on the move upward. He/She is always .....

On-going process/problem

Example: (Name) was able to solve the on-going problem of .....

Once-over

Example: (Name) gave the problem a once-over look and quickly .....

Onward and upward

Example: (Name) is an "ideas" person, always looking onward and upward to/for the next .....

Opened door/gate
>
> Example: (Name's) work in/on ..... revolutionized the way
> (organization) does .....

Opened new horizon
>
> Example: (Name) opened new doors and new horizons with
> his/her recommendation for .....

Opportunity to create
>
> Example: (Name) was given an opportunity to create a new .....
> He/She responded with a/an .....

Optimistic appraisal/outlook
>
> Example: (Name) always maintains an optimistic outlook
> regardless of the circumstances. This helps him/her to ...

Orchestrated
>
> Example: (Name) orchestrated a demanding ..... that required
> dexterity in .....

Outcome never in doubt
>
> Example: When (Name) is in charge of a project the outcome is
> never in doubt. This was never more amply
> demonstrated than when he/she .....

Over and above
>
> Example: The work of (Name) is always over and above that of
> ..... He/She has the creative craftsmanship to .....

Over the top
>
> Example: (Name) was able to get (organization) over the top of
> ..... with his/her .....

Overcame all obstacles
>
> Example: (Name) overcame all obstacles with his/her .....

Overcame difficulties
>
> Example: (Name) overcame all difficulties associated with .....
> with his/her artful .....

Overshadowed
>
> Example: (Name's) work overshadowed that of ..... with his/her
> contribution in .....

Overwhelmingly positive
>
> Example: (Organization) received an overwhelmingly positive
> response to ..... This was a direct result of (Name's) .....

Paid the price
>
> Example: (Name) has paid the price for his/her success by .....

Painstaking work
>
> Example: With painstaking work (Name) was able to overcome ...

Part and parcel
>
> Example: (Name's) work in/on ..... is part and parcel the best ....

Particularly productive
>
> Example: (Name) has been particularly productive in the
> area/field of ..... because of his/her ability to .....

Passed with flying colors

        Example: (Name) passed muster on ..... with flying colors.
             His/Her noteworthy accomplishments outmatched .....

Pat on the back

        Example: (Name) deserves a pat on the back for his/her work
             on/as ..... He/She personifies what is right about .....

Path of growth

        Example: (Name) path of growth to ..... included the difficult
             job/task of ..... which he/she mastered in .....

Paved the way

        Example: (Name) paved the way for others when he/she .....
             These contributions exceeded .....

Pay attention

        Example: (Name) always pays close attention to detail especially
             when ..... He/She was able to measurably improve .....

Peak of

        Example: (Name) is at the peak of his/her professional skills.
             He/She can only improve by being placed in more
             demanding and complex jobs/tasks.

Perfect blend/choice

        Example: (Name) was the perfect choice to assume ..... because
             of his/her remarkable ability to .....

Perfect example

        Example: (Name) is a perfect example of invincible
             determination. He/She has an enormous capacity for .....

Perfect opportunity

        Example: (Name) took full advantage of the perfect opportunity to
             ..... His/Her banner performance was highlighted by .....

Pick the brain(s)

        Example: Others routinely pick the brain of (Name) because of
             his/her unparalleled expertise in .....

Pick up the pieces

        Example: (Name) was able to pick up the pieces of the previous
             disaster of ..... He/She proceeded to discover new ways
             of/to .....

Picture perfect

        Example: (Name's) performance in/as ..... was picture perfect.
             He/She provided the cornerstone of/for .....

Pillar of strength

        Example: (Name) was a pillar of strength during the entire
             (event/evolution). His/Her exceptional performance
             earned him/her .....

Pinnacle

        Example: (Name) is at the pinnacle of his/her profession. His/Her
             sustained superior performance has .....

Pinpoint accuracy
>   Example: With pinpoint accuracy, (Name) was able to .....

Pioneer in field/spirit
>   Example: (Name) is a pioneer in the field of ..... His/Her
>   unequaled success in ..... led to .....

Pioneering spirit
>   Example: (Name) has the pioneering spirit needed to assume the
>   demanding responsibilities of ..... with his/her .....

Pitch(ed) in
>   Example: (Name) pitched in to lend a helping hand to ..... which
>   proved to be the turning point for .....

Pivotal situation
>   Example: During a pivotal situation when ..... (Name) enormous
>   capacity for ..... carried the day.

Placed emphasis on
>   Example: (Name) correctly placed the main emphasis of ..... on
>   ..... which proved particularly effective in/at .....

Places high premium
>   Example: (Name) places a high premium on ..... There is none
>   better at .....

Played full part
>   Example: (Name) played a full and active part in the ..... He/She
>   personally improved .....

Played important role
>   Example: (Name) played an important role in the completion of
>   ..... Without him/her .....

Pleased with
>   Example: (Organization) has been more than pleased with the
>   performance of (Name). He/She always .....

Poised for
>   Example: (Name) is poised and ready for increased
>   responsibilities now. He/She is the resident expert in/at .....

Policy maker
>   Example: (Name) has become a policy maker in/at ..... because
>   of his/her tremendous .....

Positive movement
>   Example: The positive movement in/on ..... made by (Name) was
>   the centerpiece in ..... that proved a model in/for .....

Positive response
>   Example: The positive response given by (Name) when asked to
>   ..... led the way for .....

Positive thinking
>   Example: (Name's) positive thinking and ..... demonstrated
>   unparalleled professionalism in .....

Positive Feedback
>Example: The positive feedback on ..... given by (Name) led to (organization's) extraordinary ability to .....

Potent
>Example: (Name's) potent work on/at ..... brought praiseworthy reviews by .....

Potential crisis
>Example: (Name) averted a potential crisis in ..... by .....

Potential risk(s)
>Example: Sidestepping the potential risk of ..... (Name) was able to ..... because of his/her .....

Pounced upon
>Example: (Name) pounced upon the opportunity to ....., thus demonstrating his/her never ending capacity for/to .....

Power-packed
>Example: (Name's) power packed performance in/as ..... His/Her never-ending capacity for/to .... was largely responsible for .....

Powerful tool
>Example: (Name's) use of ..... proved to be a powerful tool in improving/controlling .....

Practical application
>Example: (Name) upgraded the capacity/capability of ..... with his/her practical application of .....

Precious little/few
>Example: With precious few resources (Name) was able to .....

Precious source of
>Example: (Name) has become a precious source of .....because of his/her ability to .....

Precision
>Example: (Name's) use of precision ..... made measurable improvements in .....

Presence of mind
>Example: Fortunately, (Name) had the presence of mind to ..... which averted a potentially .....

Press(ed) hard
>Example: (Name) pressed hard for improvements in ..... He/She personally devised a/an ..... that .....

Press(ing) ahead
>Example: (Name) continues to press ahead regardless of the difficulties. During one recent problem, he/she .....

Pressing matters
>Example: Despite pressing matters in ..... (Name) continued to ..... with uncustomary zeal and .....

Pressure-cooker situation

>Example: (Name) enjoys being in a pressure cooker situation. The immediacy of urgent items brings out the best in him/her.

Priceless

>Example: (Name's) priceless help as a top ..... was extremely helpful in .....

Pride of accomplishment

>Example: (Name) takes a personal pride of accomplishment in everything he/she does.

Primary objective

>Example: (Name) stays focused on the primary objectives and does not get sidetracked with matters of minor importance.

Prime mover

>Example: (Name) is a prime mover of ..... in (organization). In one recent event he/she .....

Prime reason

>Example: (Name) is a prime reason (organization) enjoys the good standing and reputation it has today.

Prized position

>Example: (Name) was offered the prized position of ..... He/She responded with his/her customary standard-bearer effort.

Problem prevalent to

>Example: (Name) overcame the problem prevalent to ..... by developing new procedures that .....

Problem solver

>Example: (Name) is a real problem solver. He/She is particularly strong in/at .....

Productivity increased

>Example: (Organization) productivity increased dramatically when (Name) was placed in charge of .....

Professional triumph

>Example: (Name's) professional triumph in/at ..... demonstrates his/her unending ability to succeed at .....

Professional vigor

>Example: (Name's) professional vigor is without equal in/at (organization). He/She can always be depended upon to .....

Profited by/from

>Example: The entire (organization) profited from (Name's) ability to .....

Profound influence/impact

>Example: (Name's) performance as ..... has had a lasting and profound influence in/on .....

Profound respect

> Example: (Name) has won the profound respect of ..... by/with his/her measurable improvements in/on .....

Progressive new

> Example: (Name's) progressive new way of ..... has led to the upgraded capability of .....

Prominent

> Example: (Name) has become a prominent figure in ..... with his/her exceptional ability to .....

Proof positive

> Example: (Name's) dependable and innovative nature are proof positive of his/her .....

Proper balance

> Example: (Name) is able to put a proper balance on ..... and ..... because of his/her outstanding ..... knowledge in .....

Properly handled/prepare

> Example: (Name's) ability to properly prepare for ....., coupled with his/her ability to ....., has made singularly outstanding contributions to .....

Proud to serve

> Example: Anyone would be proud to serve with (Name). He/She exhibits a remarkable ability to .....

Proved fruitful

> Example: (Name's) ability to ..... proved fruitful in the ..... He/She has left his/her mark in .....

Proved mettle

> Example: (Name) proved his/her mettle when he/she was assigned to/as ..... by personally .....

Provided insight into

> Example: (Name) provided valuable insight into ..... This allowed (organization) to .....

Prudent balance of

> Example: The prudent balance of ..... was made possible by (Name) when he/she .....

Pulled out all stops

> Example: (Name) pulled out all the stops to ..... His/Her inexhaustible source of ..... led to .....

Pulled together

> Example: The (organization) all pulled together and completed ..... in time for ..... due to (Name's) .....

Pursue all avenues

> Example: (Name) pursues all possible avenues and courses of action when .....

Pursued with tenacity

     Example: (Name) pursued with unending tenacity the ..... His/Her admirable ability to ..... led to unsurpassed .....

Push(ed) forward

     Example: (Name) pushed forward on ..... despite continued interference/trouble from .....

Pushed to limit(s)

     Example: (Name) pushed the limits of ..... to ..... and met with success rarely observed in/by .....

Put (back) on track

     Example: (Name) was able to put back on track the ..... with a thoroughly meticulous .....

Put finger on

     Example: (Name) quickly put the finger on the problem of ..... and .....

Put in a good word

     Example: (Name) is never too busy to put in a good word for .....

Put in order

     Example: (Name) put in order the complex and difficult ..... in dramatic fashion.

Put lid on

     Example: (Name) put the lid on ..... and ..... The results added a new dimension to .....

Put measures in place

     Example: (Name) put measures in place to ..... This put the finishing touches on his/her distinguished record in/as .....

Put to the test

     Example: (Name's) talents were recently put to the test when ..... He/She responded with .....

Quantum leap

     Example: (Name) made a quantum leap in the improvement of ..... There is none better at .....

Quest for

     Example: (Name's) quest for ..... led to .....

Quick to

     Example: (Name) is always quick to take the lead in ..... His/Her unbeatable ..... distinguishes him/her from .....

Quickly soared to top

     Example: (Name) quickly soared to the top of ..... with his/her enormous capacity for .....

Radiates

     Example: (Name) radiates enthusiasm and ..... in everything that he/she does.

Radical change
>Example: (Name) brought about a radical change to ..... that
>increased .....

Raised new issues
>Example: (Name's) inputs raised new issues that had not
>previously considered. These inputs contributed to .....

Raised state of the art
>Example: (Name') performance in/as ..... raised the state of the
>art in .....

Range of performance
>Example: The range of performance in/on ..... demonstrated by
>(Name) far exceeds .....

Rapid evolution
>Example: (Name) made the rapid evolution from ..... to .....
>with unusual ease and .....

Rare insight
>Example: The rare insight into ..... brought in by (Name) was
>crucial to the success of .....

Rational expectation(s)
>Example: (Name's) performance in/as ..... exceeded all rational
>expectations.

Razor-sharp mind
>Example: (Name) has a razor-sharp mind and .....

Reached milestone
>Example: (Name) reached the major milestone of ..... with his/her
>unequalled ability to .....

Reached new heights/summit
>Example: (Name) reached new heights in area of ..... thanks to
>his/her excellent ..... and .....

Reached peak of
>Example: (Name) is a skilled ..... and has reached the peak of ....

Readily available
>Example: (Name) is always readily available to ..... His/Her
>revitalized ..... has had a profound impact on .....

Real change
>Example: (Name) has made real and significant changes to .....
>This is one of the most sophisticated ..... in .....

Realize fullest potential
>Example: (Name) is one of the few people in ..... to realize
>his/her full potential in/as .....

Reasonable solution
>Example: (Name) always offers a reasonable solution to difficult
>problems. His/Her tireless, top-quality work in .....
>has .....

Rebounded from

Example: (Name) rebounded from a slow start in/as ..... to transform ..... into .....

Recipe for success

Example: (Name) has a simple recipe for success.. He/She always ..... while achieving remarkable .....

Recognized stewardship

Example: (Name's) recognized stewardship in/as ..... is unmatched in (organization) in recent years.

Record breaking/shattering

Example: (Name's) record breaking performance in/ as ..... surpassed .....

Record of

Example: (Name) has a steady and consistent record of ..... His/Her meritorious work furthered .....

Redeeming qualities

Example: (Name) has many redeeming qualities. Among the most notable are .....

Redefined concept

Example: (Name's) work in/as ..... has redefined the traditional concept of .....

Refreshing thought(s)

Example: (Name's) new and refreshing thoughts about/on ..... led to immeasurable .....

Refuses to accept

Example: (Name) refuses to accept mediocre performance. His/Her meticulous attention to ..... led to .....

Reinforced action(s)

Example: (Name) reinforced the actions of ..... with a multi-talented ..... and laudatory performance in/as .....

Rejuvenated

Example: (Name) single-handedly rejuvenated (organization) with the best .....

Relaxed confidence

Example: (Name) displays a relaxed confidence that .....

Relentless pressure(s)

Example: Despite the relentless pressures placed on (Name), he/she performed ..... in an exemplary fashion.

Relentless pursuit

Example: (Name's) relentless pursuit of ..... has led to ..... thanks to his/her exacting .....

Rendered obsolete

Example: (Name) rendered obsolete the old/previous ..... This resulted in a first-rate .....

Renowned for
> Example: (Name) is renowned in (organization) for his/her
> ability to .....

Repeated successes
> Example: (Name's) repeated successes in any variety of jobs in
> (organization) are noteworthy and .....

Reputation
> Example: (Name) has earned a top-notch reputation for being able
to ..... where others routinely fell short.

Reservoir of experience
> Example: (Name) is a reservoir of experience. This was clearly
> evidenced during a recent ..... when .....

Reshaped
> Example: (Name) personally reshaped ..... with his/her
> extraordinary .....

Resilient
> Example: Nothing can keep (Name) down. His/Her resilient
> personality always .....

Resounding success
> Example: (Name's) efforts in/at ..... were a resounding success.

Respectable showing
> Example: (Name) gave much more than a respectable showing
> in/as ..... when he/she .....

Respected figure
> Example: (Name) has become a respected figure in (organization)
> because of his/her ability to .....

Responded in full measure
> Example: (Name) responded in full measure to ..... with .....

Revamped a sagging
> Example: (Name) revamped a sagging ..... and led it to .....

Revitalized
> Example: (Name) was able to revitalize (organization) from .....
> to ..... with his/her .....

Revolutionary (new) idea(s)
> Example: (Name's) revolutionary new idea on/about ..... led to the
> immediate improvement of .....

Revolutionized
> Example: (Name) revolutionized the way (organization) .....
> resulting in .....

Rich past experience(s)
> Example: (Name) brought a rich past experience in/to .....
> This quickly became evident when he/she .....

Rich tradition/variety
> Example: (Name) has a rich variety of talents, including .....

Richly deserved
> Example: (Name) earned ....., a richly deserved honor for
> his/her work in/as .....

Rigorous standards
> Example: (Name's) rigorous work standards led the way in .....
> He/She always .....

Rise to the occasion
> Example: (Name) was able to rise to the occasion recently when
> he/she was tasked with ..... The results were .....

Root of problem
> Example: (Name) is able to get to the root of any problem.
> He/She always finds a way to .....

Rose from depths of
> Example: (Name) rose from the depths of ..... to ..... because of
> his/her unique ability to .....

Rose to the occasion
> Example: Despite the demanding duties of ..... (Name) not only
> rose to the occasion, he/she also .....

Run circles around
> Example: (Name) can run circles around ..... with his/her all-
> around ..... and considerable talent in/as .....

Run down
> Example: (Name) took a run down ..... and raised it to .....

Safely weathered
> Example: (Name) safely weathered the problem of .... thanks
> to his/her boundless .....

Saved the day
> Example: (Name's) experience in ..... saved the day when .....

Search of excellence
> Example: In his/her search for excellence, (Name) was able to
> ..... This innovation saved .....

Searches for opportunities
> Example: (Name) continuously searches for opportunities to
> improve himself/herself.

Seasoned veteran
> Example: (Name) is a seasoned veteran at ..... He/She is
> a valuable addition to .....

Second to none
> Example: (Name) is second to none when it comes to .....
> He/She served as a role model for .....

Seed(s) of success
> Example: The seeds of success to ..... were sewn by (Name)
> when he/she created a new .....

Seize the opportunity
> Example: (Name) seized the opportunity to ..... His/Her sheer

willpower and boundless energy .....

Sensation(al)

Example: (Name) is a sensational ..... His/Her performance in/as
..... was totally impressive from start to finish.

Sense of

Example: (Name) takes a great sense of personal responsibility
for ..... He/She is a real professional.

Sense of purpose

Example: (Name) takes a real sense of purpose into each job.
He/She is a consummate .....

Serious contender

Example: (Name) should be considered as a serious contender
for the job of ..... because of his/her .....

Serious situation

Example: The serious situation caused by ..... could have led to
problems in ..... Instead, (Name) was able to .....

Seriously strengthened

Example: (Name) seriously strengthened (organization's) ability to
..... His/Her flawless performance resulted in .....

Served to

Example: (Name's) performance as ..... served to strengthen
the (organization) in .....

Set apart

Example: (Name) set himself/herself apart from ..... because of
his/her considerable talent in/as .....

Set course for future

Example: (Name) set the course for the future of ..... with a
matchless ability to .....

Set in motion/place

Example: (Name) set in motion procedures that ..... and should
bring uniformly outstanding .....

Set new precedent

Example: (Name) set a new precedent in (area) with contributions
to ..... that .....

Set sights on

Example: When (Name) sets his/her sights on something, it is as
good as accomplished. He/She has the unique ability
to .....

Set the stage

Example: (Name) set the stage for progress in ..... when he/she
led a dramatic increase in .....

Set up and take notice

Example: (Name's) performance is outstanding. He/She has the
ability to make people set up and take notice of his/her
talents in/as .....

Shape(d) the
> Example: (Name) shaped the future of .....by demonstrating
> considerable talent in/as .....

Shaped events
> Example: (Name's) performance in/as ..... shaped future events
> that led to .....

Sharp increase
> Example: There was a sharp increase in ..... thanks to (Name's)
> enormous capacity for .....

Sharply focused
> Example: (Name) always stays sharply focused on the task at
> hand. He/She has a natural aptitude for .....

Sheer energy
> Example: Through sheer strength and energy (Name) was
> able to.....

Shore up weak points
> Example: (Name) was greatly successful at ..... by shoring up the
> weak points in/at .....

Shot in the arm
> Example: (Name) brought a welcomed shot in the arm to
> (organization) by his/her .....

Shouldered responsibility
> Example: (Name) shouldered the awesome responsibility of .....
> by his/her .....

Significant changes/gains
> Example: (Name) made significant changes in ..... which resulted
> in unequalled gains in/that .....

Significant milestone
> Example: (Name) reached a significant milestone in ..... when
> he/she .....

Simple and straight-forward
> Example: (Name's) simple and straight-forward way of doing .....
> has won praise throughout (organization).

Simply the best
> Example: (Name) is simply the best ..... at (organization). His/Her
> performance is underscored by .....

Sincere honor
> Example: It has been a sincere honor to serve/work with .....
> His/Her unblemished record .....

Single-minded purpose
> Example: (Name) approached the task of .... with a single-minded
> purpose. He/She is a real go-getter who can .....

Singled out for
> Example: (Name) has been singled out for special recognition for
> his/her work in/as .....

Sink teeth into
> Example: (Name) was able to sink his/her teeth into the difficult job/task of ..... and produce results that were .....

Sit up & take notice
> Example: (Name) made others sit up and take notice of his/her ability to .....

Size up situation
> Example: (Name) was able to quickly size up the critical situation of ..... and proceeded to .....

Solely responsible
> Example: (Name) was solely responsible for the success of .....

Solid base/foundation
> Example: (Name) built a solid foundation of ..... by staying up to date on the latest developments of .....

Solid contributor
> Example: (Name) has been a solid contributor in/to ..... with his/her capacity to/for .....

Solidified
> Example: (Name) solidified his/her hold on ..... with a performance that .....

Someone special
> Example: (Name) is truly someone very special. His/Her knowledge and efficiency in/at ..... is .....

Sorely needed
> Example: (Name) brought sorely needed ..... to (organization) with an energetic personality that .....

Sought after by
> Example: (Name) is routinely sought after by ..... because of his/her invaluable .....

Source of knowledge/light
> Example: (Name) is the resident expert on ..... He/She is considered the main source of knowledge for .....

Sparked innovation
> Example: (Name's) knowledge in/of ..... sparked the innovation of ..... and led the way to/for .....

Spawned new
> Example: (Name) spawned new frontiers in the effort to .....

Spearhead effort(s) to
> Example: (Name) volunteered to spearhead efforts to .....

Special feel for
> Example: (Name) is an expert in/at ..... He/She has a special feel for .....

Special gift
> Example: (Name) has a special gift for .....

Special quality(ies)
        Example: (Name) has some special qualities in the area of .....
Spirit of cooperation
        Example: (Name's) spirit of cooperation far exceeds .....
Splendid record
        Example: (Name) has built a splendid record of ..... based
                on his/her performance in/as .....
Spotless
        Example: The spotless record of (organization) is due in large
                part to the work of (Name).
Spurred action/growth
        Example: (Name's) response to ..... spurred action on ..... and
                led to a vast improvement in .....
Staggering range of talent
        Example: (Name) has a staggering range of talent. In a recent
                ..... he/she completely turned around .....
Stainless record
        Example: (Name) has a stainless record in all aspects of .....
Stands tall
        Example: When it comes to ..... (Name) stands tall. He/She
                offers the highest caliber performance.
Started from scratch
        Example: (Name) started ..... from scratch and built up a/an .....
                that is unprecedented in .....
State of the art
        Example: (Name) introduced a state of the art ..... to .....
                His/Her keen technical abilities led to .....
Stated objective(s)
        Example: (Name) met all stated objectives and then some.
                He/She was the first person to .....
Steady stream of
        Example: (Name) offered a steady stream of new ideas. This
                allowed (organization) to reach new heights in .....
Step ahead of
        Example: (Name) is always a step ahead of the action. His/Her
                ability to plan and ..... is totally impressive.
Stepped forward
        Example: When the challenge of ..... surfaced (Name) stepped
                forward and, with keen ..... abilities proceeded to .....
Stick it out
        Example: (Name) has the ability to stick it out in tough situations.
                He/She has set a benchmark of excellence in .....
Story of dedication
        Example: (Name) work habits are a story of dedication. He/She
                springs into action and exerts total dedication when.....

Straighten up

Example: (Name's) efforts to ..... straightened up a previously
..... and resulted in a smooth and flawless .....

Strain put on

Example: The additional strain put on (organization) because of
..... was staggering, but (Name) was able to .....

Strengthened resolve

Example: When things go wrong, (Name's) strengthened resolve
allows him/her to .....

Strenuous schedule

Example: Despite an already strenuous work schedule, (Name)
still manages to .....

Stretched boundaries/limits

Example: (Name) stretched the limits of ..... because of his/her
strong technical background in .....

Stretches the imagination

Example: (Name's) ability to ..... stretches the imagination.
He/She directly contributes to the success of .....

Striking improvement

Example: (Name) has brought a striking improvement to
(organization) by his/her ability to successfully .....

Striking results

Example: (Name) striking results in/as .....was instrumental
in/to .....

Stroke of genius

Example: (Name's) plan to ..... was a stroke of genius. He/She
unparalleled productivity has .....

Strong background

Example: (Name) brings a strong background in ..... to
(organization). With this he/she was able to .....

Strong will

Example: (Name's) strong will and professional ..... resulted
in an exceptionally well/good .....

Stunning results

Example: (Name) was able to achieve stunning results in .....
because of his/her .....

Substantial impact/number

Example: (Name) has had a substantial impact on/in .....
His/Her solid professional performance led to .....

Substantially improved

Example: (Name) has substantially improved the operation of .....
He/She always gives 100 percent.

Success story

Example: (Name's) performance in/as ..... has been a success
story from start to finish.

Supportive fashion
> Example: The supportive fashion in which (Name) helped .....
> led to improvements in .....

Surge in activity
> Example: The surge in activity in (organization) can be directly
> attributed to (Name) and his/her ability to .....

Surpassed all expectations
> Example: (Name's) performance in/as ..... surpassed all
> expectations and resulted in .....

Sustained commitment
> Example: (Name) gave a sustained commitment to the
> improvement of ..... by his/her .....

Sweeping changes/reform
> Example: (Name) brought sweeping changes to (organization).
> The results of .... were always impressive and .....

Tackle(s) any
> Example: (Name) can successfully tackle any and all assignments.
> He/She is highly proficient and .....

Take the lead
> Example: (Name) was able to take the lead in ..... The results
> were impressive and contributed to .....

Take to heart
> Example: (Name) takes to heart his/her responsibilities as/of .....
> with a dedication rarely observed in .....

Task at hand
> Example: (Name's) ability to focus on the task at hand is
> noteworthy. He/She is exceptionally well
> organized and .....

Temporary setback
> Example: (Name) takes temporary setbacks in full stride. His/Her
> resilient and energetic personality .....

Testimony to
> Example: (Name's) ability to ..... is testimony to his/her .....

Tests new ideas
> Example: (Name) tests new ideas and ways of doing things. In a
> recent action he/she .....

Thirst for
> Example: (Name) has a thirst for knowledge and can always be
> found .....

Threshold of
> Example: (Name's) ability to ..... has put him/her on the
> threshold of .....

Thrives in/on
> Example: (Name) thrives on ..... His/Her solid professional
> competence always .....

Through thick and thin

> Example: Through thick and thin (Name) can always be
> relied upon to ..... regardless of .....

Thumbs up

> Example: (Name) has earned two thumbs up for his/her
> work in/on .....

Time of transition

> Example: During the time of transition from ..... to ..... (Name)
> irreplaceable dedication .....

Time-tested

> Example: (Name) is highly successful at ..... because he/she
> uses time-tested methods to .....

Tireless efforts

> Example: (Name's) tireless efforts dedicated to the improvement
> of ..... was unmatched in .....

Took advantage of

> Example: (Name) took full advantage of ..... His/Her impressive
> .... and dedication were truly impressive.

Took on added responsibility

> Example: (Name) took on the added responsibility of ..... despite
> an already full work load in/as ..... and performed
> with unmatched .....

Top speed

> Example: (Name) proceeded with top speed to ..... using his/her
> endless energy and .....

Top to bottom

> Example: (Name) revamped ..... from top to bottom. The results
> led to uncommon ..... and .....

Top-level performance

> Example: (Name's) top-level performance in/as .....shows an
> unusually high standard of .....

Top-notch

> Example: (Name) is a top-notch ..... demonstrating the energy
> and resourcefulness .....

Tough act to follow

> Example: (Name) is a tough act to follow. He successfully
> faced the demanding challenge of ..... with .....

Toward the future

> Example: (Name) always looks toward the future. He/She
> continuously seeks to improve .....

Track record

> Example: (Name) has a very successful track record in/of .....
> He/She is self-motivated and always .....

Transformed
        Example: (Name) single-handedly transformer (organization)
              from ..... to ..... without a single .....

Tricky business
        Example: (Name) was able to handle the tricky business of .....
              with a great amount of .....

Tried and true
        Example: (Name's) tried and true methods of ....., coupled with
              his/her innate talent to .....resulted in .....

True pioneer
        Example: (Name) is a true pioneer in the field of ..... His/Her
              qualifications in/as ..... are truly first class.

Trusted completely
        Example: (Name) can be trusted completely. He/She is a
              self-starter who can be depended upon to always .....

Turn the tables
        Example: (Name) turned the tables on the complex/difficult
              ..... with the energy and resourcefulness of .....

Turnaround
        Example: (Name) engineered a complete turnaround of .....
              which had previously been plagued by/with .....

Turning point
        Example: With unusual skill and dexterity, (Name) was able
              to provide the turning point in/for .....

Ultimate success/test
        Example: The ultimate success of ..... was a direct result of
              (Name's) performance/work on .....

Unbeatable combination
        Example: (Name's) unbeatable combination of ..... and .....
              broke new ground in/on .....

Unbreakable spirit
        Example: The unbreakable spirit exhibited by (Name) set
              the stage for the highly successful .....

Uncharted territory
        Example: (Name's) work has entered uncharted territory. His/Her
              technical abilities far exceed .....

Under any circumstances
        Example: (Name) is the best ..... under any circumstances. No
              one is better at .....

Under pressure
        Example: (Name) performs best under pressure. He/She has the
              incredible ability to .....

Underscore(d) importance
        Example: (Name) recently underscored his/her importance to
              (organization) by personally .....

Undertaking

      Example: (Name's) undertaking of the tremendous job/task of .....
            led to him/her being selected to/for .....

Unexpected obstacle(s)

      Example: (Name) overcame many unexpected obstacles on
            his/her way to .....

Unexpected turn to/for

      Example: Despite an unexpected turn for the worse, (Name)
      Was able to take ..... and ..... with unparalleled success.

Unexplored avenues

      Example: (Name) discovered previously unexplored avenues on
            ways to improve .....

Unforeseen events

      Example: The unforeseen events of ..... failed to put a damper on
            (Name's) performance. He/She proved extremely
            proficient in/at .....

Unglamorous task(s)

      Example: (Name) was faced with the unglamorous task of .....
            His/Her unique ability to attain quality results, remains .....

Unique achievement(s)

      Example: The unique achievements made by (Name) have led to
            the achievement of ..... by .....

Uniquely suited

      Example: (Name) is uniquely suited to ..... with his/her remarkable
            ability to .....

Unmistakable

      Example: (Name's) unmistakable performance in/as ..... led to
            him/her being selected for/to.....

Unprecedented

      Example: The unprecedented success of (Name) in/as .....
            demonstrated his/her personal talent for/to .....

Unreachable goal(s)

      Example: (Name) sets high standards for ..... and does not
            consider even the most difficult goals to be unreachable.

Unrelenting

      Example: (Name's) unrelenting endeavor to ..... resulted in the
            most successful ..... in/since ....

Up and coming

      Example: (Name) is an up and coming superstar. He/She works
            zealously to ..... while achieving .....

Up hill

      Example: (Name's) up hill battle for/to ..... paid off when he/she
            ....

Up to the task

Example: (Name) was up to the demanding task of .....
He/She always adds more to ..... than expected.

Ushered in new era

Example: (Name) ushered in a new era in ..... with his/her
totally successful ability to .....

Valuable insight

Example: (Name) contributed valuable insight into .....
Without his/her knowledge of .... the ..... would have .....

Vastly different

Example: The (organization) is vastly different for the better since
(Name) .....

Versed in

Example: (Name) is well versed in the intricate details of .....
His/Her energetic work habits and ..... have .....

Very impressive

Example: Very impressive indeed was (Name's) performance
in/as .....

Vigorous effort(s)

Example: (Name's) successful vigorous efforts to ..... resulted in
a substantial gain in .....

Virtually eliminated

Example: (Name) virtually eliminated all ..... while at the same
time successfully .....

Virtue of hard work

Example: By the virtue of sheer hard work, (Name) was able to
complete .....

Vital (first) step

Example: (Name) took the vital first step in combating .....
The standards he/she set .....

Vital importance

Example: The vital importance of the work (Name) contributed to
(organization) cannot be understated.

Vital role

Example: (Name) played a vital role in the successful .....

Vitality

Example: (Name's) vitality and energy are ..... and have .....

Waged relentless

Example: (Name) waged a relentless battle for/against .....
The outcome succeeded in .....

Way it should be

Example: (Name) knows the way things should be done. He/She
was instrumental in .....

Welcomed addition

    Example: (Name) has proved himself/herself a welcomed addition to (organization) by .....

Well received

    Example: (Name) and his/her assistance was well received by .....

Well suited for

    Example: (Name) is well suited for difficult jobs consisting of .....

Well versed

    Example: (Name) is well versed in all aspects of ..... He/She provides daily valuable solutions to .....

Went all out

    Example: (Name) went all out to complete ..... The success he/she achieved is a direct result of his/her .....

Went far beyond

    Example: (Name's) performance in/as ..... went far beyond what is normally expected of .....

Whatever it takes

    Example: (Name) contributes to the job whatever it takes to be successful.

Whole-hearted

    Example: (Name's) whole-hearted support of ..... was instrumental in the successful completion of .....

Wide range of

    Example: (Name) has a wide range of talents. One of special note is .....

Willing to sacrifice

    Example: (Name) is willing to sacrifice personal ..... for the betterment of .....

Winning ways

    Example: (Name's) winning ways have continued. He/She set the standards for/in .....

Within reach

    Example: (Name) considers even the most difficult jobs within his/her reach. He/She always/never .....

Without difficulty

    Example: (Name) accomplishes the most demanding tasks without difficulty.

Without reservation

    Example: Without reservation, (Name) has my highest recommendation for .....

Won respect of

    Example: (Name) won the respect and admiration of ..... with his/her .....

Words cannot express

Example: Words cannot adequately express the value (Name) brought to (organization.)

Work under adversity

Example: (Name's) ability to work under adversity without a complaint is praiseworthy.

Example: (Name) worked frantically to complete ..... ahead of schedule. The result(s) was/were .....

Worthwhile goals

Example: (Name) has accomplished many worthwhile goals. Not the lest of which is/was .....

Worthy of mention

Example: (Name's) ..... is certainly worthy of mention. He/She personally .....

ADDITIONAL SENTENCE SUBJECTS

Acted swiftly
Addressed the question
Ambitious campaign

At risk
Beneficial to
Brought forces to bear

Captured mood
Clear vision
Commitment to course of action

Concrete form
Covered all bases
Crucial to success

Desired effect
Dynamic force
Embodies qualities of

Feel the energy
Filled vacuum
Focused determination

Frank observation(s)
Full cooperation
Full speed ahead

Gravity of situation
Healthy source of
In the works

Indifferent to
Infused with spirit
Inner strength

Instinctive feel
Intense personality
Intriguing concept/idea

Acute sense of
Aggressively enforced
Any number of

Beacon of hope
Best kept secret
Came full circle

Changed course of
Close knit group
Commitment to future

Consummate craftsman
Creative genius
Deeply rooted

Door always open
Eased burden
Entirely new perspective

Fiercely loyal
Firmly committed
Formidable tool

Fueled creative spirit
Full-court press
Fully committed to

Glorious effort(s)
Host of challenges
Indescribably

Inescapable reality
Inherently risky
Inspire shared vision

Integrity
Internal fire
Intrinsic values

Intrinsically superior
Irreplaceable service
Just in time

Keystone
Landmark decision
Lavished praise

Legacy of service
Lift(s) people's spirit(s)
Lit fire under

Made good on
Main ingredient(s)
Maintained composure

Marked coming
Masterwork
Mobilizes others

Moment of truth
Mounted major challenge
Nail down

Never forgot
Nip in the bud
Nourishes spirits

On business end of
Once and for all
Open-handed

Outpouring of
Outward calm
Passed the torch

Passionate defender of
Peacemaker Persona
Personal crusade

Planted the seed
Phenomenal change
Popular belief

Intuitive
Judicious effort
Keyed up

Kindled spirit(s)
Larger than life
Leader's vision

Level playing field
Light at end of tunnel
Lively spirit

Made point of
Mainstream
Make over

Marvelous
Mind-set
Moderating effect

Moral involvement
Move(d) forward
Nerves of steel

New way of thinking
Not to be forgotten
Nurtured

On hot seat
Open and above board
Open arms

Pass(ed) muster
Overall strategy
Passionate advocate

Peace of mind
Personal agenda
Personal test of courage

Pleasantly surprised
Played out on giant scale
Physical courage

Poised on edge of
Powder keg ready to explode
Power of presence

Pressed forward
Process of discovery
Profoundly affected

Provided chemistry necessary
Proving ground
Put an end to

Raised the question(s)
Rarefied atmosphere
Reap consequences

Re-energized efforts
Reform oriented
Rekindled flame/spirit

Revered for
Rich in vitality/spirit
Right thing to do

Risk factor
Rock hard
Rooted in history

Rush of adrenaline
Saw future/light
Seized the moment

Selective field
Sensitive to
Serious crisis

Set world on fire
Sheer willpower/force of
Sight set on

Sign of the times
Singular purpose
Smooth process

Potentially significant
Power base
Pragmatic

Prevail upon
Productive pursuit
Promise of things to come

Provided outlet for
Pushed envelope
Raised spirit(s) of

Rare privilege
Real powder keg
Rebuilt confidence

Reflected changes
Reinvigorated sagging
Relish with zest

Revolutionary method(s)
Right set of values
Rigorous schedule

Road to recovery
Rocky road
Run the gauntlet

Safeguard
Second nature
Seized upon idea of

Sensitive issue(s)
Sent clear message/signal
Served the purpose

Shaping the future
Short and sweet
Sign of hope

Significant inroads
Situation of extreme(s)
Social architect

Social fabric
Sophisticated role
Spawned rise of

Split-second
Springboard of/for
Square-shooter

Stand on own two feet
Stands alone
Stay(ed) in background

Straight as an arrow
Straightforward response
Strength through unity

Strict conformance/standards
Strident support
Strong advocate

Strong voice for
Struggled successfully to
Successes mounted

Summon(ed) up the courage
Supporting cast
Sustained effort

Sweet victory
Sympathetic ear
Take by storm

Taste of
Tenacious
Tenuous position

Test willpower/water(s)
Thought-provoking
Throw down the gauntlet

Timeless
Took fresh look
Took special interest in

Solid resolve
Soul of organization
Spelled success

Spotlight
Squared away
Squeaky clean

Stand up and be counted
Status symbol
Steered course of

Straight shooter
Strategy aimed at
Strengthens others

Strict control
Strike a blow
Strong influence

Structural change/reform
Studied works of
Successfully challenged

Sunny disposition
Surge of
Sweep out/aside

Symbol of
Systematic approach
Take hold of

Temperamentally suited
Tense time(s)
Test of will/character

Tested to limit(s)
Thoughtful analysis
Tight knit group

Took a stand
Took inventory of facilities
Tore down barrier(s)

Total dimension of	Total focus
Totally clear	Tough nut to crack
Tower of strength	Traditional concept/values
Transcends	Treat with courtesy
Triggered response	Triumph
True to form	True transformation
True visionary	Trusted advisor
Turn inside out	Turn over new leaf
Turn(ed) the tide	Turned the corner
Unassailable performance	Uncluttered thought
Uncompromising principles	Undaunted
Undeniable appeal	Under best of circumstances
Underlines importance	Underwent process of
Unencumbered	Unenviable position
Unfolding event(s)	Unification of
Unifying force	Uninhabited
United behind	Unlocked door of opportunity
Unshakable character	Unstoppable momentum
Up-beat/scale	Upgraded
Uplifting experience	Urgent business
Valiant gesture	Valid option
Vast numbers	Verbal support
Verge of	Very special
Viable option(s)	Vigilant
Vigorous response	Vintage
Virtually unchecked	Virtuoso
Vision of future	Vision of substance
Visionary	Vital interest/aspect
Voyage of discovery	Walk a tightrope
Warmly received	Weather(ed) the storm
Weed out	Weigh the options
Weight of responsibility	Well-founded
Went head-long into	Wholehearted endorsement

Wide-spread support
Will power
Window of opportunity

Window of opportunity
With (a) passion
With particular clarity

Withstand test of time
Won hearts and minds
Work ethic strong

Workaholic
Worked perfectly
Workhorse

World of good
Zest for challenge

Widely accepted/embraced
Win laurels
Winning game plan

Winning game plan
With honor(s)
Without second thought

Withstood onslaught
Wonder work
Workable solution

Worked closely with
Worked to end
World class

Zero in on

PROFESSIONAL MANAGEMENT SPECTRUM, INC.
PO Box 30330
Pensacola, Florida 32503
(800) 346-6114

PROFESSIONAL LIBRARY

Writing Guide for Air Force Efficiency Reports

The Definitive Performance Writing Guide

Successful Leadership Today

Other books:

Writing Guide for Army Efficiency Reports

Navy Eval & Fitrep Writing Guide

Navy & Marine Corps Performance Writing Guide

Fitness Report Writing Guide for Marines

Navy Officers Manual

Chief Petty Officers Manual

Navy Petty Officers Manual

More

Visit our web site for more information:

www.servicebooks.com